# A note from the author

This is a book about online misogyny that often reflects my personal perspective as a straight, white, middle-class, cis woman. Intersectionality plays a substantial role in how women and marginalised genders experience online harms, and while I've done my best to represent the experience of all women and marginalised genders, there are some aspects of online misogyny that I do not have the room to explore. A heads up: I talk about men *a lot*. When doing so I am inevitably generalising to an extent to reference straight, cis men, although I believe all men have a responsibility to engage in the conversation on gender-based violence, alter their own behaviours and beliefs and play a role to help end the pandemic of misogyny women are experiencing.

For the protection of people's privacy, some names included in this book have been changed. These are marked with an asterix (*).

**Trigger warning:** this book discusses topics like sexual assault, sexual harassment, misogyny, racism, transphobia and other types of violence and discrimination.

# NO ONE
# WANTS TO SEE
# YOUR D*CK

**Jess Davies** is a presenter, social media influencer and women's rights campaigner. She presents current affairs documentaries investigating the manosphere and the sexual exploitation of women both on and offline. Her documentary *Deepfake Porn: Could You Be Next?* was used to lobby the UK government to criminalise sexually explicit deepfakes in The Online Safety Act. Jess is a sociology graduate and uses her social media accounts to call out misogynistic attitudes, raise awareness of inequalities and campaign against image-based sexual abuse.

# JESS DAVIES

# NO ONE WANTS TO SEE YOUR D*CK

A Handbook for Survival in the Digital World

First published in 2025 by Headline Press
An imprint of Headline Publishing Group Limited

1

Cataloguing in Publication Data is available from the British Library.

Hardback ISBN: 978 1 0354 1657 8
Trade Paperback ISBN: 978 1 0354 1658 5

Designed and typeset by EM&EN
Printed and bound in Great Britain by Clays Ltd, Elcograf S.p.A.

Headline's policy is to use papers that are natural, renewable and recyclable
products and made from wood grown in well-managed forests and other
controlled sources. The logging and manufacturing processes are expected
to conform to the environmental regulations of the country of origin.

Headline Publishing Group Limited
An Hachette UK Company
Carmelite House
50 Victoria Embankment
London EC4Y 0DZ

The authorised representative in the EEA is Hachette Ireland,
8 Castlecourt Centre, Dublin 15, D15 XTP3, Ireland (email: info@hbgi.ie)

www.headline.co.uk
www.hachette.co.uk

*For the women in my life*
*who showed me what real love is.*
*Especially my mum.*

# Contents

*A note from the author* ix

Introduction *xi*

1: Consent *1*

2: Sexual Harassment *22*

3: Leaked *62*

4: Leaked 2.0 *96*

5: Cyberflashing *125*

6: Catfish *156*

7: Deepfake Image Abuse *186*

8: The Game Of Misogyny *228*

9: Masculinity In Crisis *257*

10: Influencers *277*

11: The Solution *303*

*Acknowledgements 323*

*Resources 326*

*References 331*

# Introduction

I have always been acutely aware of my female identity and the vulnerability that is handcuffed to it. One of my earliest memories is being seven years old and watching the news unfold on the television of the abduction and murder of Sarah Payne. The image of her red school jumper and blunt fringe that reflected mine is etched into my childhood. There followed years of rolling news reports of young girls just like me, whose lives were brutally cut short by male violence – Holly and Jessica in their Manchester United football kits; Milly Dowler standing behind an ironing board – their faces were printed in newspapers and stored away neatly in my mind's filing cabinet, shaping the way I learnt to exist in a world where I was told my life was in danger, simply because I was a girl. I sprinted home from my friends' houses fleeing the cloak of darkness that fell on my street as the lights went out. I grew a fear of white transit vans. I discovered my key doubled up as a weapon. The threat of misogyny is knitted into the threads of girlhood; it's danger ever present in our adolescence.

This danger has mutated over the years from the pavement to pixels, with the invention of the internet creating a weapon of mass exploitation for men to harm women. As a girl who grew up alongside the social media revolution, I was heckled by the boys in my school about my developing body and called jailbait by the older men in my community, while also facing sexual harassment on Habbo Hotel and being flashed by grown men on Chat Roulette. The smart phone opened my eyes to sexting, and the public spread of my intimate, private photos made me want to sew them shut.

# NO ONE WANTS TO SEE YOUR D*CK

We are a generation that lives our lives permanently online with almost 7 billion smart phones worldwide. From ordering taxis and finding dates, to keeping up with friends and buying our groceries, there is no escaping the digital realm and the connections that come with it. But the development of this digitised world has created new avenues of abuse, exposing women and girls to unprecedented levels of online misogyny that is leaving lasting, real-life harm. Hundreds of thousands of women are falling victim to deepfake AI technology that strips their clothes and inserts them into porn scenes without their consent. Each day, there are millions of intimate images changing hands in online forums uploaded by men who do not have permission to post them. Schoolgirls' inboxes are filled with unsolicited dick pics and the comments section of women's posts sharing their pain are overrun by men who boast '**Your** body, **my** choice.' Misogyny not only exists in every corner and cross-section of women's lives online, but it is being actively encouraged and rewarded by some of the web's most influential characters. When women can't post about their successes on X without receiving rape threats or upload a fun YouTube video without facing sexual harassment, it infringes on our human rights to freely partake in the digital world that modern society is built upon.

As too many women and girls will know, this dangerous behaviour does not remain exclusively online, with the entitlement over women's bodies stretching outwards into our physical worlds. We've reached a crossroads where things desperately need to change to enable a safe and equal digital existence for women and girls. At the same time, we must prevent generations of men and boys from being radicalised by internet algorithms and bad characters to despise half the population.

This book calls out the extreme misogyny that is playing out online in a variety of forms, mutating with the rapid development of technology and a shift in the social acceptance of sexism in modern times, where a desire to rewind gender equality thrives. Each chapter provides an insight into a different strand of online misogyny and concludes with a handy toolkit that you can use to better protect yourself from the dangers that exist in the digital world.

## MISOGYNY

*Definition:* Hatred, contempt for or prejudice against women and girls. Typically, but not exclusively, exhibited by men.

I have been investigating online misogyny and the manosphere (a collection of online men's communities that promote sexism, misogyny and anti-feminist beliefs) since 2020. It was during an investigation for BBC Three that year that I discovered the true scale of image-based sexual abuse I had been subjected to. I found my intimate images advertised on escorting sites, learnt that my identity was being used to extort money from men on dating apps and saw my nudes promoted under the banner of 'rape fantasies'. The discovery of the manosphere radicalised me. For so many years, I had carried the shame of sexualisation and objectification like a weighted cross on my back, while thousands of men exploited my body without any consequences. And I wasn't the only one: in these forums, *millions* of other women had their bodily autonomy taken from them by anonymous usernames who relished their pain. I needed answers. Who are these men? Why do they think it's okay to act like this towards women? And why are they being allowed to get away with this extreme misogyny online?

In the UK, police chiefs and the government have declared violence against women and girls an epidemic, and are facing calls to treat extreme misogyny as terrorism. Seventy-seven per cent of 11–21-year-old girls and young women experienced online harm in 2024, with a rise in the number of girls and young women seeing unwanted sexual images and facing cyber-stalking. Girls as young as seven report seeing more harmful 'rude and mean' content than three years ago, and 59 per cent fear artificial intelligence being used to create fake images of them or impersonate them online. Black women are more likely to experience online abuse and be a victim of cyberflashing than white women, with Glitch's Digital Misogynoir Report finding 20 per cent of social media posts were highly toxic towards Black women. The threat of harms, such as image-based abuse, doxing, cyberflashing, catfishing and physical threat, is felt strongly and disproportionately by women. The online sphere has become a cesspit of sexism for women and marginalised genders, where misogyny and white supremacy is intricately intertwined.

With the rise in popularity of male content creators whose business plan is centred around misogyny and racism, we are facing the total erasure of women's rights to a digital citizenship. Young men are being radicalised by 'masculinity influencers' and social media algorithms that push the idea that the answer to the 'masculinity crisis', which questions the blueprint of manhood, is to restrict women's rights, time-travelling back to a conservative ideal of 'trad-wives' and 'alpha-males'. Ah, the good old days, where marital rape was legal and women whose sexuality was considered 'deviant' or 'abnormal' were lobotomised.

We cannot underestimate the tyranny that can be caused in a world governed by new-age media and digital agencies that have the ability to broadcast live into the bedrooms of young men and boys across the globe. A handful of far-right mouthpieces take the helm (or a podcast microphone) and the information they spout goes unchecked, unregulated and regurgitated by boys in classrooms up and down the UK.

As women, we are truly up against it. Every single mainstream and fringe social media platform was founded by a man:

# INTRODUCTION

Facebook, Instagram, X, TikTok, Telegram, Snapchat, YouTube, WhatsApp, Discord, 4Chan and Reddit. All but one still has a man at the helm. Perhaps surprisingly, out of those listed it is X which has a female CEO in Linda Yaccarino, but with owner Elon Musk serving as chairman and chief technology officer it's difficult to see how much influence she will have over the richest man in the world.

Hateful content like misogyny, sexism and racism creates division and outrage, which then sparks engagement. The more controversy, the more clicks, the more cash for digital platforms. How do we convince tech bros who hold the keys to the cyber kingdom to put women's rights before their wallets? Their role in combatting digital harms is substantial, but stamping out online misogyny will be a collective effort.

When misogyny plays out online, we're supposed to accept it's all part of the digital experience – like it or lump it, with reports of police telling women to stay offline and delete their social media accounts if they don't want to be sexually harassed. Our physical and digital lives are seen as two separate entities and identities. This provides an excuse to quickly forgive, or ignore altogether, the harmful, toxic behaviours that women experience 'only online'. But what if I proposed to you the radical notion that we are not independent of our online behaviours, and that a perpetrator displaying dangerous attitudes and beliefs online is likely to be acting on these traits in the physical world too?

If you thought feminism has 'gone too far', trust me – you've only just seen the warm-up lap. It is more important than ever for women to stand up for our basic human rights to access the streets and surf the web without fear. We are up against computer-generated algorithms designed to outsmart humans and 24-hour live streams that are brainwashing young men to hate women. But it's not too late to save humanity. It is time to strap in, swot up and secure your social media accounts.

I hope this book can be a wake-up call to educate both women and men on the extreme misogyny and vitriol that is playing out online and arm you with a practical toolkit to help combat the challenges of sexism you may face in your online and offline world. I should tell you now that it is a heavy read; it includes my deeply personal experiences of having my consent taken away from me more times than I have been taken on dates. I dive deep into the black waters of the manosphere to expose the monsters that lie beneath and bring their depravities to the surface. I unpack masculinity and misogyny with the experts and sit down with brave victim-survivors to share their stories in the hope of inspiring you to join the fight against online misogyny and reclaim ownership of your digital footprint.

Women are not the sole victims of the patriarchy and we can't fix these problems alone. Men must join the conversation on gender-based violence and learn of the things they need to unlearn, to create a safer, healthier and more equal reality – online and offline – for all.

With men being radicalised in online spaces, it's time for women to be radicalised too. Radicalised into action, galvanised to demand better from the men who have gotten away with hateful, sexist behaviour for far too long. As the old saying goes, knowledge is power, and we have to know our enemy if we're going to stand a chance at defeating them.

# 1

# CONSENT

## Leave no room for blurred lines

'Sexual autonomy is the foundation of sexual freedom
and empowerment'
**Jaclyn Friedman and Jessica Valenti**

The six of us claimed our seats around the wooden table, our cheeks flushed with prosecco and the heat from the brick barbecue we had taken turns to tend outside our cabin. We exchanged pleasantries and potato salad before the casual conversation turned to a girl we knew from our hometown who had recently reported a historic sex crime to the police. The coal-kissed sausages made their way down the table amongst the breezy comments of how the accused *'wasn't the only one'* and how *'they were all at it back then'*. We could've been mistaken for a group of elders at a W.I. meeting, reminiscing on how we'd cheekily pinch penny sweets from the corner shop. In reality, we were a group of young women whose frontal lobes were only just fully developed, grappling with the unnerving realisation of all the wrong-doings we now recognised from the men in our past.

I took another swig from my glass and felt the bubbles climb up my throat, awakening the word vomit that had been curdling inside all evening: 'I remember waking up and he was on top of me.'

My ears tuned in to the gristle of the burnt meat between my friends' teeth in the silent seconds that hung over us before Katy* timidly offered her comfort. 'I remember you telling me about it in school the next day and I didn't say anything. It was just normalised back then.'

Her words wet my eyes, turning the plate of food in front of me blurry while my fork tried to find something to scoop into my mouth and form a physical barrier that would stop any more secrets from spilling out.

I hadn't spoken with anyone about that incident since my school days and over the next 15 years, I brushed off jokes made at my expense, each time battling internally with the lack of consent on that cheap cider-fuelled night as a young teenager and the alternative story that had somehow circulated amongst my peers. And yet hearing Katy say how she remembered the uncertainty I felt following that night granted me a sense of validation I had never realised I was searching for. It healed a loose thread inside that I'd been silently concealing for so long, tying a knot that ended the doubts and blame I'd placed on myself for all these years – I wasn't going crazy, I did not consent. Katy and I comforted each other with the acknowledgement that we were just children back then and weren't mature enough to understand how society had conditioned us to brush-off non-consensual behaviour.

My friend Soph* raised her glass, pressing it against her lips as she inhaled a large gulp of wine. 'Well, you remember what happened to me that time at uni . . .'

One by one, we took our turn to trauma-dump through mouthfuls of crisps and dip, awkward laughter and tears, recalling all the times we'd had our consent taken away from us by men in our lives. Some of them strangers, others, friends. Sometimes physically, other times through our phones and the online world. These experiences that were forced upon us lingered in the basement of our minds like thick dust on a kitchen skirting board, waiting to be blown away by the freeing words exchanged between best friends.

'It's fucked up, really,' I shrugged. The girls nodded in agreement and stuffed more garlic bread into their cheeks. Nothing else needed to be said.

'I'll grab another bottle.'

∎

There is a saying that every woman has a story of sexual harassment, abuse or assault, while no man seems to know the men who carry out these attacks. I have spoken with women who I love and exchanged stories with women that I have just met, collectively bonding over the one thing that tied us all together: male violence. Each day, women across the globe have their consent stripped from them through physical assaults, verbal abuse, coercive control and digital acts that reflect the deep-rooted sexism and misogyny that continues to thrive in our society.

It's getting home with him and feeling your whole body clam up, the alcohol hitting you as you look on through glassy eyes at the generic New York taxi poster on the wall and decide to 'go along with it' because changing your mind seemed too risky. It's rolling over in bed after repeatedly telling your boyfriend you're not in the mood only to feel an uncomfortable poke in your back before eventually giving in because you don't want to argue, again. It's having to lie to the man at the bar that you've got a boyfriend because men respect the boundaries of a fictitious man more than the physical woman standing in front of them. It's finding out that the nude photo you sent to the guy you're dating has made its way to the lads' group chat. Or how his dick pic has landed in your Instagram DMs when you don't even know his name.

I have to start this book on the subject of consent because it exists at the very heart of women's rights and our bodily autonomy. The question of consent encompasses all of my experiences with men; its necessity, its absence and in too many cases its total disregard to the outcome of my answer.

In the UK, 94 per cent of survivors of rape or attempted rape are women, while 98 per cent of adults arrested for sexual offences are men. From 1 July 2023 to 30 June 2024, 69,184 rapes were reported to police with charges being brought in just 2.7 per cent of cases; the conviction rate is even lower than this. Even if you've been sucked into manosphere conspiracy theories that will argue that women often falsely accuse men of rape,* I truly doubt anyone seriously believes that 97 per cent of rape allegations are lies.

I find it deeply troubling that false allegations have become the leading concern for many men in the conversation about rape, and not the startling reality that tens of thousands of rapists are walking free. If less than 3 per cent of murder cases ever saw a charge, I'm sure there would be an outcry about a criminal justice system that was failing to keep the public safe, with the threat of thousands of serial killers potentially roaming the streets forcing people into lockdown. Well, that is the reality now for the victims of rape who are shamefully failed by a system that, for many complex reasons, does not seem to work for cases of sexual abuse.

### Women are 27 times more likely to experience harassment online

Meanwhile, in cyberspace, a large-scale review by the European Women's Lobby on the state of online violence and harms

---

* Research from the Home Office suggests only 2–4 per cent of sexual violence cases reported to police are found or suspected to be false or listed as no crime. While Channel 4 Fact Check found that men were more likely to be raped themselves than be falsely accused.

against women and girls found women are 27 times more likely to experience harassment online, with 9 million girls having experienced some form of online harm before they are 15 years old. A report by the University of Exeter discovered three out of four victims of intimate image abuse are women, with their private images being shared without their consent.

Our understanding of the boundaries of consent and the need for them – or *lack of* them – in our physical world translates to our digital lives. If we are living in a world where an absence of sexual consent is widely overlooked offline then it should be no surprise when these behaviours begin to play out online too, with women and girls being forced to face the disastrous consequences. The online space is not only a mirror to our offline beliefs, but a demonstration of the capabilities of human behaviour when it is allowed to exist under the cloak of anonymity and go widely unchecked and underregulated. So it's hardly surprising that opportunities for abuse abound. To put it frankly, what we are witnessing is misogyny in a whole new dimension.

The rapid development of the online world means that it's easier than ever to rob a woman of her consent and thousands of men are logged on, ready and willing to do so. From the creation of sexually explicit deepfakes and the sharing of private nudes to stealing images of adult content creators to extort other men for cash and the distribution of women's private information in dodgy forums for the thrills – the deeply troubling reality is that a woman's consent is not seen as necessary in the digital world.

Are men overlooking the need for consent in the digital sphere due to a genuine failure to understand what it means at its most basic? Or are we seeing centuries of male entitlement over women's bodies mutate into pixel form?

# Back to basics: what do we understand about consent?

Often, when we hear the word consent, we might think only of physical, sexual consent, but the need to explicitly give someone our permission to do something exists in all areas of our lives and is something that most of us do daily.

## CONSENT

*Definition:* Explicit agreement or permission given to someone, or for something to happen.

When I was an assistant producer working in TV production, one of my tedious but most important tasks was to ensure all contributors signed consent forms that confirmed they were happy to be featured on screen. I've lost count how many times while researching for this book I've had to click the 'consent' button on website pop-ups about cookies, caches and data. If you're admitted to hospital, you have to give consent for the treatment you are going to receive. If you have a child, you have to give their school consent for them to include their photo in any social media posts. We get our videos swiftly muted on TikTok for using an artist's song against copyright laws – i.e., rules to stop you using someone's art without them allowing you to do so. As a society, we understand consent across so many different areas and circumstances, but when it comes to bodies – especially female bodies – confusion seems to reign.

## SEXUAL CONSENT

*Definition:* When someone agrees by choice to sexual activity, and has the **freedom** and **capacity** to make that choice. It can be given for one activity but not another, and can be withdrawn at any time.

# CONSENT

A 2024 report by the Crown Prosecution Service highlighted young people's worrying misconceptions of sexual consent and a stark regression of attitudes. The study found that 72 per cent did not know that they could withdraw consent after initially agreeing to sex online, while half did not believe it was rape if a victim did not fight back. Research also found a further 58 per cent did not believe rape could be committed in a relationship or marriage. The End Violence Against Women Coalition responded to the report blaming 'the blurring of our online and offline lives' for the concerning attitudes and beliefs, with the charity's director Andrea Simon saying how the internet has 'not only created new forms of sexual violence, but new ways to blame victims based on our behaviours online', and pointed to the widespread and unregulated misogyny perpetrated in online spaces for 'driving sympathy for perpetrators and misconceptions about sexual violence among young people'.

Issy Warren is the programmes lead and a facilitator for Our Schools Now, a grassroots project that offers workshops for secondary school pupils and colleges which explore public sexual harassment and society's understanding of consent. Pupils are given examples of scenarios and are asked to distinguish what counts as sexual harassment and what doesn't. Warren told me how they first encourage pupils to think of consent through the legal definition as an active choice: 'So have they actively said yes to what is happening? And not just in terms of having sex, but if someone's giving them a compliment on their body is it obvious that that person wants to be commented on that way? Or maybe they've chosen to chat to someone at a house party, but they haven't chosen for that person to kiss them. So that's not an active choice.'

Every incident of public sexual harassment is non-consensual, but the need for consent is often only discussed under the banner of sexual intercourse and not in terms of everyday sexual contact. Asking the pupils to do so is a positive enforcement of their bodily autonomy and their freedom to choose.

You might have seen the 'cup of tea' analogy of consent on YouTube, or been shown it as part of your relationships and sex education classes at school. The idea is that you ask someone if they fancy a cuppa and if they say yes, then you make it and they drink it. If you ask them and they're not sure if they want one, then you might make a cuppa for them but not pressure them to drink it. And if you ask them and they say no, then you don't bother making one at all. It's a pretty simple explanation that does a good job of teaching the absolute base line of consent, but when it comes to sex or sexual communications it's a little more complex than popping the kettle on.

Firstly, just because someone is dressed for a tea party, it doesn't mean they want to drink the tea. Then you have people who only have oat milk in their tea, or maybe someone starts to drink their cuppa but it goes cold and they don't want it any more. It is in these subtleties that Warren says the conversations around consent in their workshops can become interesting.

'The law mentions the freedom to consent, so I always like to ask them questions like "are there consequences if you say no?" and not just consequences in an obvious way of being beaten up for example, but social consequences. Like, is it easier to laugh it off if someone grabs your bum in the school corridor? Because the social consequences of making a fuss are worse than being groped in the first place?'

Warren also discusses the importance of digital consent with young people and the different factors that need to be considered: 'A lot of young people will bring up the pressure to send explicit images and feeling that the other person won't like them if they say no, or if they make a fuss, or if they tell someone, so it's important to think about that freedom and about those consequences.'

# CONSENT

As our offline lives continue to naturally unfold more frequently into online spaces, the need to understand digital consent and why it is required is vital if we're to build a safer internet.

■

As defined in UK law, consent can only be given when someone has the freedom and capacity to make that choice. But this is often not as cut and dried as the law makes out – for example, there are many reasons why someone may have more or less 'freedom' in their daily life than someone else.

It's important to recognise the role intersectionality can play in how people experience or give consent. The concept of intersectionality was coined in 1989 by Kimberlé Crenshaw, an American civil rights advocate and leading scholar of critical race theory. Crenshaw introduced the concept as a way to address unique experiences of oppression, explaining how she faced oppression at the intersection of her identity both as a Black woman and as a woman. For example, I experience sexism as a white, straight woman, but I do not face the same oppression as a Black, queer woman.

## INTERSECTIONALITY
*Definition:* The acknowledgement that everyone has their own experiences of discrimination and oppression through a combination of their individual characteristics, such as race, gender, sexuality, ability and class.

In an online opinion piece, Victoria Brooks, a law lecturer at the University of Westminster, explained why intersectionality means that consent is far more nuanced than the law implies. She argues that factors such as the hyper-sexualisation of queer women meaning they are often assumed to be consenting, and

9

Black women being more likely to suffer sexual offences but less likely to report them, are not recognised in the notion of 'freedom' and 'choice' in 'what is a white idea of consent'. Underlying racial biases can have devastating real-world effects, with a 2021 report from the Crime Survey for England and Wales* into the characteristics of victims of sexual violence showing those in the Black or Black British and Mixed ethnic groups were significantly more likely than those in White, Asian or other ethnic groups to experience sexual assault. Cultural and religious beliefs can also affect a person's capacity to consent freely and without fear of consequences. Intersectionality plays a role in all areas of online harms and misogyny that we're going to be diving into in this book, so it's good to get familiar with it.

If we're going to stand a chance of wiping out the potent virus of misogyny that is infecting generations of men, then it is vital that we teach young people (and the old blokes in my DMs who seem to think I want to see their flaccid dicks) to understand consent and why it is necessary in all areas of our online and offline lives. Misconceptions around it allow for rape myths and victim-blaming to flourish both in our physical and digital worlds. The internet has no borders or boundaries and with the development of social media platforms and smartphones, the digital space has become a lawless land where many log on and leave human ethics and empathy behind.

■

* The Office for National Statistics (ONS) are responsible for planning and running the UK census across England and Wales, which is why ONS statistics exclude Scotland and Northern Ireland, who run their own censuses. England and Wales also share a legal system, meaning crime, police and court statistics for both countries are gathered together.

# CONSENT

Lying alone in a single bed in Tom's* student flat I instinctively knew something was off. I had split up with my long-term boyfriend a few months earlier and after sacrificing a year at university to a failed relationship, I was in desperate need of some male validation to heal my wounded heart. But going for Tom, a friend of a friend, as my first rebound was a recipe for disaster. I wanted someone to fall head over heels in love with me and worship the ground I walked on, but all I got was low self-esteem and cystitis. I should have known he wasn't going to be my knight in shining armour when he would openly tell me how he'd brag to his friends about sleeping with 'Jess Davies from *Nuts* magazine'.

That morning, when Tom got up to shower, I had a strange feeling about the whole situation – call it the spidey-senses of a woman scorned, but I knew something had happened and I had to check his phone.* I opened up his messages and saw that he had sent a photo of me to a group chat. I was fully naked, asleep. The pungent smell of boy musk in the room heightened, its heaviness suffocating me as the panic crept in. I quickly deleted the image from his phone and put it back where I found it before he could return to the room. I wanted to scream and ask him why he had done this to me; why he had seen me asleep, naked and at my most vulnerable in his bed, and instead of wrapping me in his arms and pulling me in close, he took a photo and shared it with a group of men I had never met. But instead, when he came back into the room I just sat there and said nothing. I never asked him about it, I never let him know I knew. Truthfully, I was embarrassed. Embarrassed at how I had given myself to a man who failed to see my humanity and ashamed that I willingly accepted his disrespect.

---

* Rule number one, if you have the feeling you need to check their phone, then you already know what you're looking for.

# NO ONE WANTS TO SEE YOUR D*CK

When people tell you who you are for long enough, you eventually believe them. When I hit puberty at ten years old, I was no longer allowed to be the promising young girl with big dreams; now I was jailbait with big boobs. I had become so used to people seeing my body before they saw me, *the real me*, that I eventually only saw that too. I have given my body more than I have been given flowers, and the path to healing my internalised shame that rooted itself in my identity has been a journey over many years. Today, I buy my own flowers and know the shame belongs to the men who physically and digitally removed my consent.

I recently shared this story of how I was photographed naked without my consent and the image posted in a lads' group chat in a video on my Instagram account. I was highlighting the case of Michael Emery, a semi-professional footballer who took images of a naked sleeping woman and sent them in a WhatsApp group to his teammates alongside the words 'Anyone want a go?'.* I made the point of how, as someone who had personally experienced this, reading about the case and the sense that justice wasn't served had really upset me. One of my followers commented on the post 'Happened to you? Didn't you used to get your tits out in *Nuts*?'. This man was suggesting that because I had once consented to a photoshoot as a professional model, then it was okay for a man to take a naked photo of me asleep and distribute it to others, something I had not even had the capacity to consent to as I was sleeping.

This failure to understand how consent is not blanket given has allowed men to exploit women while blaming them for their own trauma. I can consent to having my image professionally taken without giving consent for my own private images

---

* Emery was found not guilty of intending to cause distress or harm by sending the naked photos to his teammates. The need to prove intent has now been removed in the Online Harm Safety Act 2023.

to be shared online. I can consent to posting my photos on a subscription site like OnlyFans without giving permission for it to be sold in e-whoring packs. I can consent to engaging in oral sex without consenting to being penetrated. You get where I'm going with this. The belief that if a woman is sexually active or engages in sexual communications – whether physically or online – then she is consenting to the limitless access to her body is a dangerous and predatory attitude that removes all human emotion and bodily autonomy from the woman, seeing her as nothing more than an object of desire.

## Digital consent: you don't have permission to post that

Every minute, 66,000 photos and videos are shared on Instagram from across the world with users posting in the belief that they have consented to their image being uploaded on Instagram, and only Instagram.* Now imagine the horror when you walk into a train station one morning on your way to work and see your deeply personal engagement photo has been repurposed into a billboard advertising a swingers dating app plastered all over the station walls. *Well, you posted it online so what did you expect?* Luckily, you would be within your rights to go after the brand for a hefty fee under intellectual property right laws because posting an image on Instagram isn't blanket consent for anyone on the internet to do what they want with your photo. *Thank God.* So why is this understanding of image ownership and permission eradicated when it comes to content that features women's bodies?

---

* Instagram's terms and conditions state that although they don't own any of the content you post on their platform, by posting you grant them a licence to use it.

13

# NO ONE WANTS TO SEE YOUR D*CK

There is a whole ecosystem online that thrives off of the absence of women's consent. In 2010, Hunter Moore, an aspiring DJ from Sacramento, California, gained notoriety for launching the forum website IsAnyoneUp.com, which saw him share intimate images of people without their consent. Users, typically men, submitted nudes of their ex-partners along with information like their name, hometown, social media username and place of work. Moore also hired hackers to access the email accounts of victims and steal their private nude photos, which he then shared on his website. At its height, Moore claimed IsAnyoneUp.com was being accessed by over 350,000 people a day and allegedly earnt him up to $30,000 a month in advertising revenue. While IsAnyoneUp.com was eventually shut down,* it started the genre for leaked 'revenge porn' content, which is the unauthorized release of someone's intimate images or videos, that spawned dozens of copycat sites and a network of forums that still exist today, hosting millions of members.

In these forums, a lack of consent is lucrative to its users who hunt down intimate images and videos of women they know they are not entitled to see. There is an attitude of entitlement over women's bodies, where the men believe they can do whatever they want with their images and videos, regardless of their original purpose or non-consensual nature.

While trawling the forums for my own pictures, I came across a desperate quest of men searching for 'pussy slip' images of me and many of my friends from my modelling days. Pussy slip is used to describe a photo where unintentionally and unknown to the woman, her vulva or labia is on display due to the awkward placement of underwear, see-through fabric or a risqué pose captured by the photographer. Unless the model

---

* Moore was eventually charged with aggravated identity theft and aiding and abetting in the unauthorised access of a computer (hacking – in other words), which saw him sentenced to two and a half years in prison.

has specified that she is happy to shoot full frontal nude then all of these images are non-consensual and have been uploaded through a lack of due diligence by the photographer, who has not thoroughly checked the image before posting it. Mistakes of course happen, but when working with models who have specifically set boundaries that they do not shoot fully nude then it is a photographer's responsibility to ensure that those boundaries are respected. On photoshoots, when holding a pose, I have had to put my full trust in photographers when they promised me nothing intimate could be seen – it is their job to follow through with that promise.

In one of these forums, I discovered several posts that included 'pussy slip' photos and video screenshots of models that I knew – their vulva on display through mesh underwear, in poses where their hand wasn't fully covering their genital area and in screenshots from videos where they were captured mid-changing pose. The forum users described how a female photographer who had worked for a newspaper had been selling the images on her own subscription site. It was clear from the men's comments that they were aware of the non-consensual nature of the images, but this did not seem to raise concern.

I decided to check out the photographer's subscription site myself. Signing up for free access, I was greeted by a welcome video which featured a short, behind-the-scenes clip of a model moving her hand to change pose, her vulva coming into view. I knew that the model would be absolutely mortified if she knew this was available online. My eyebrows folded inward with the wrinkles of disgust as I clicked through the photo albums, uncovering unforgiveable betrayals at the hands and lens of another woman. If this was just the free shit I could see, I dreaded to think what was being sold privately.

Most of the images on the page were years old and had originally been taken for a newspaper, with only a chosen few going to print. It seemed that the outtakes and unused images had been stored in a vault unbeknownst to the girls and had now been repurposed and sold online without their consent. By now, some of the models were mothers and/or had changed careers and left the industry completely. Almost all, if not all of them, had never posed full-frontal nude and now, years later, a woman that they had trusted and respected had set up a subscription page to sell their nude images to strange men on the internet. I don't know how she sleeps at night.

I let the women know about the images and the account I had found, and they were understandably livid. Apparently, the female photographer denied ever posting the images, even though I had provided screenshots, but the account was swiftly shut down once the girls confronted her. Maybe that was a coincidence.

There will be people out there who think the women have no right to be upset over their nude photos being shared online because of their job as models, but 'pussy slip' photos are non-consensual and feed off of voyeurism fantasies. I mean, even just the word 'slip' reflects acknowledgement that they are an accident and unintentional. The men on the forum were aware that they should never have seen those photos, yet they relished the leaks and did their best to keep them a secret. That is terrifying to me, because what else are they doing to women when they think they'll get away with it?

∎

In March 2024, the non-profit organisation Right to Equality, alongside activists including Dr Charlotte Proudman and actor Emily Atack, launched a campaign calling on the UK government to enshrine affirmative consent into law. This would see people require a clear, enthusiastic 'yes' before engaging in sexual activity rather than just the absence of a 'no'. Speaking to the *Evening Standard*, Dr Proudman explained, 'Affirmative consent is actually making clear that the question needs to have been asked. Did she want to have sex? Was it wanted sex rather than assuming it was consensual or because she was there and present and wasn't too drunk?'

Current UK law requires all participants to consent to sexual activity, but victims of sexual violence often report feeling blamed by the courts system for what happened to them, with defendants citing an absence of a clear no, instead of requiring the presence of a yes. Dr Proudman told the *Evening Standard* she believes a change to the law would put the onus on defendants to show how the victim consented: 'That's because all of the questions are about what they allowed to happen to them instead of: 'How did he make sure she enthusiastically wanted to have sex?'

The Coalition for Consent is a group of intersectional activists campaigning for consent education and accountability who believe agreement is the bare minimum. The group calls for further dimensions to be considered when giving and receiving consent, including that it needs to be informed, freely given, ongoing and enthusiastic.

Although the UK government has announced it has no plans to amend the law on consent, I personally believe that reshaping consent as something that needs to be engaged, enthusiastic and ongoing instead of seeking out the absolute minimum can only be a positive in solidifying clear boundaries around sex and women's bodies both offline and in online spaces. I can still remember the first time a man asked me if I was okay and still happy during sex, and it genuinely took me by surprise that he was checking in and considering my active participation throughout. *I mean, the bar is literally in hell.*

The internet was set alight in 2020 when BBC Three's adaption of the novel *Normal People* included a sex scene which saw the character Connell reassure his lover Marianne, 'If you want me to stop or anything, we can obviously stop,' and, 'If it hurts or anything, we can stop. It won't be awkward.' People rushed to social media to share their delight and how they were turned on to see consent depicted in such a mature way on screen. The series was busting the myth that asking for consent is a buzz-kill during sex, showing how it can be sexy, as well as necessary. Regardless of whether any laws will change, encouraging young people to seek out enthusiastic consent should be a key component of relationships, sex and health education, and any campaigns which aim to engage men and boys in violence against women and girls.

On a positive note, the introduction of consent workshops in schools is clearly having an impact. During a mixed-gender workshop at a secondary school which I was facilitating, the year 10 boys largely understood the concept of consent and need to have permission to touch someone's body, take an intimate picture of them or send them an explicit photo. One testimonial we put to the students to discuss and decide whether it should be classed as sexual harassment was of a girl sharing that her boyfriend constantly commented on her body.

'Is that sexual harassment?' I asked.

'Well, it depends,' one of the boys shouted out.

'On what?'

'On whether she'd given consent.'

I felt the tiny shoots of hope sprout inside my heart. They're getting it. The boys are getting it.

■

A recurring theme throughout this book is the lack of consent present in all areas where misogyny thrives online. Men are sharing women's intimate images, hacking their Snapchat accounts, sending them unsolicited dick pictures, writing rape fantasies about them and creating sexually explicit deepfakes because they do not believe or consider that a woman's consent is required. While male entitlement over a woman's body reigns in the offline world it will only continue to thrive in digital communities. If we are going to tackle misogynistic attitudes towards women online, then we must also ensure they are dealt with in our physical world. That can begin at the very basics of believing women should have the right to choose what happens to their body and be an active participant in any sexual communications.

A video of a farmer spraying manure on a cyclist who was found camping beside the hedgerow of his field went viral in June 2024, with hundreds of X users applauding the farmer for his heavy-handed actions because the cyclist was trespassing, asking, 'Why couldn't this guy get permission beforehand?' If only the response was this supportive to online posts of women sharing their experience of sexual assault or their private images being leaked. Here, however, men trespassing on our bodies seems to come with its own conditions. In these cases, we are asked about our clothes, our jobs, our sexual history, why we took the photo in the first place and if we don't like it, why we don't just come off social media all together?

But seriously, what did the farmer expect having a big field out in the open like that? I mean, he was practically asking for it.

## TIPS: How to understand and seek out consent

Okay, so I'm probably showing my age here, but do you remember the THINK! advert back in the nineties, in which two hedgehogs taught us how to cross a road? Well, I'm bringing that back . . .

- Before you engage in any sexual activity, I want you to **Stop** what you're doing, **Look** at the situation in front of you, **Listen** to the other person and **Think** before you act on anything. Sometimes it's literally that simple.

- This pausing to analyse, think about what you're doing and engage the other person in active consent can also be applied to online spaces. **Stop** with the scrolling and put the mouse down. **Look** at the nude pic you just took on your phone screen – do you really need to send it to them? **Listen** to the terms and conditions of a subscription website that doesn't allow resharing. And **Think** before you use artificial intelligence to strip her clothes off her body.

- Remember that consent is ongoing and can be removed at any time. You should check in with the other person each time you hook up or exchange sexy texts to make sure they're still happy with what's happening. Look out for that freedom of choice and capacity to consent that we spoke about earlier.

- If you can't confirm with absolute certainty that someone wants to engage in sexual activity or whether they'd be okay with you showing their nude photos to your friends, then take it as a no. It's better to assume a no and leave it than risk ruining both of your lives with a prison sentence and long-lasting trauma.

- It's okay to say no. If you're uncomfortable in a situation, have changed your mind or are just not feeling it, know you are within your right to say no and to not feel pressured into engaging in any in-person or online sexual acts or communications.

- Parents, please have conversations with your kids about active consent! They'll probably be taught the very basics in school through some sort of cup of tea analogy, but the likelihood is they won't have had discussions on the nuances that are also at play. Teenagers are a lot more switched on than we give them credit for, so let's treat them with respect and have that discussion. I promise it doesn't need to be super awkward.

# CONSENT

If you need any support or guidance there are helplines and websites for organisations and support services that provide help and advice on sexual assault, domestic violence and online harms at the end of this book.

# 2

# SEXUAL HARASSMENT

## Feminism has gone too far, we can't even harass women anymore

'Online abuse works against the freedom of expression
for women because it gets them to withdraw, it gets them
to limit their conversations and sometimes to leave
the platform altogether'
**Milena Marin**

I laid out the ingredients on the kitchen side, giving it one last wipe over and making sure the space was camera ready. Like many bored Brits during lockdown, I had signed up to a subscription recipe box in the search of something to do and had become half decent at cooking a meal while rambling away on a livestream. It was Covid times, I lived alone and the livestreams were something different for me. I'd only done a handful of them before, but my followers seemed to enjoy them and so did I. They provided some light escapism during a time that could feel overwhelmingly lonely. However, when I'd excitedly pulled my ingredients out of the fridge that afternoon, I couldn't have predicted that my new pastime would end with me crouched down in my kitchen, alone and in tears.

Shortly after I had gone live, the comments section was flooded with sexual comments, nasty quips about my body and the way I looked, along with jokes made at my expense and endless laughing emojis. Embodying the dark energy of a public shaming they threw virtual tomatoes at my body and basked in my humiliation. I had come across these types of men in online forums before and knew that they wanted a reaction out of me: my shame was a game to them, my tears the prize. So I continued to talk through the steps of the recipe trying to mask the quiver in my voice box – *slowly add in your stock and stir* – even though I could feel the deep vibrations in my head as the adrenaline pumped through my veins, and was fighting the urge to cry while every fibre in my body wanted to run and hide. I was determined not to let them win, not to be bullied off of my own Instagram feed. *If I can't cook a fucking risotto on the internet without being run offline, then what can I do?*

'These comments are savage,' some viewers posted, while others quietly slid into my DMs: 'That was a difficult watch, I'm sorry.'

The relentless harassment continued for the entire 40 minutes. *Why does a risotto take so bloody long to cook?* Once I'd finished my meal, I dished it up with a forced smile and tried desperately to hold back the cracked fear in my voice, thanking people for watching before shutting down the live feed. *What the fuck just happened?* The anger and fear that I'd been pushing down surged to the surface all at once and I burst into a fit of hysterical tears on my kitchen floor, struggling to catch my breath while collapsed in a heap against the cold tiles.

I had experienced negative comments and sexual advances online before but this time it felt different – it felt like an organised, planned attack. The level of harassment had caught me off guard. When I searched for the usernames of the men who had left the most hurtful comments I saw that none of them followed me. Panicked thoughts raced through my mind as I tried to make sense of why this had happened. Why me? Had my username been posted in a forum for these men to premeditate their plan of attack? Or did they just happen to stumble upon my page that day and all decide in that moment to use my pain for their entertainment? I'm not sure which answer is more chilling. My food sat cold; I'd lost my appetite.

## The normalisation of sexual harassment

If you are a woman, then you have probably experienced sexual harassment at least once in your lifetime. A builder whistling as you walked by, a boy in school pinging your bra strap, some guy in the pub groping your bum or a work colleague making an inappropriate joke at the Christmas party. A report by the Women and Equalities Committee states how relentless and routine sexual harassment 'pervades the lives of women and girls and is deeply ingrained in our culture'.

### SEXUAL HARASSMENT

*Definition:* Unwelcomed and unwanted attention, sexual advances and intimidating behaviours that happen in public spaces both online and offline.

Sexual harassment and the patriarchy go hand-in-hand, existing to keep women in their place and denying them access to spaces while also objectifying them through a sexual lens. Although sexual harassment is often directed towards women, it can be experienced by all genders. Patriarchal ideals of what masculinity 'should' look like encourages men and boys to downplay their experiences and creates a barrier that prevents male victims of sexual harassment from speaking out – just one way in which living under the patriarchy is damaging to us all.

Sexual harassment occurs so regularly that these behaviours have become normalised in our daily lives, leading us to shrug off the lewd comments about the size of our ass from the man who passed us in the street or swiftly scroll past the

'Things I would do to you :p' message in our requests folder. But recent times have seen women speak up against uninvited sexual advances and harassment, emboldened by the #MeToo movement, which broke the silence and challenged the feelings of shame that being a victim can bring. Women's desire to be treated as equals has caused an outcry from some men, who complain women need to 'give it a rest', as apparently they can't even open a door for a woman anymore without it being called sexual harassment.* Although those men will have you believe equality has 'gone too far', research consistently shows that, unfortunately, a lot of men did not got the memo that sexual harassment is supposed to be a thing of the past.

### 97 per cent of young women have experienced some type of sexual harassment

A 2021 report by the All Party Parliamentary Group for UN women found that 71 per cent of women of all ages in the UK had experienced some form of sexual harassment, with just 3 per cent of young women aged 18–24 years old reporting never having experienced sexually harassing behaviour. Following the report, Claire Barnett, the executive director of UN Women UK, called it a human rights crisis. She said, 'It's just not enough for us to keep saying "this is too difficult a problem for us to solve" – it needs addressing now.'

### 93 per cent of young women do not feel completely safe in public spaces

We raise little girls to alter their behaviours, become less than, to cover up, to wear more, to not be too bossy or confident,

---

* Now, I'm going to hold your hand when I say this, but if you don't know the difference between basic manners and sexually harassing a woman then you're probably part of the problem.

to smile politely and say less – all in the hope that they will shrink themselves small enough to escape the leering eyes and the harsh tongue of a man, and keep themselves safe. Meanwhile, we say 'boys will be boys' and excuse their potentially harmful behaviour on account of their cavemen genetics/raging hormones during puberty/lads' locker room talk/*insert another generic excuse which voids men of responsibility for their actions*. But however much we try to avoid it, sexual harassment has become part of everyday life for women and girls, the dark cloud of worry and a potential downpour following them around with no sign of clear skies ahead. Plan International UK's 2024 report 'The State of Girls' Rights in the UK' discovered 93 per cent of young women do not feel completely safe in public spaces, with two thirds of young women experiencing unwanted sexual attention in public. When women and girls don't feel comfortable or safe enough to leave their home or go online without the fear of harassment, they are being robbed of their right to design the life that *they* want to live.

The question 'What would you do if there were no men on earth for 24 hours?' regularly circulates on social media platforms and the replies from women are always devastating. Some examples that I've seen are:

'Have a massive picnic with my girls and sleep under the stars'

'Go for a walk at night'

'Go live on Xbox'

'Walk to my car alone without having to ask people to come with me'

'Post more pics on socials'

'Go to the gym and enjoy the using the weights section'

And the heartbreakingly simple:

'Live how I wanna live'

# SEXUAL HARASSMENT

In July 2024, a group of young women who worked at an Australian skincare company called TBH Skincare recreated their version of the viral TikTok trend 'boots and a slicked back bun',* which saw them chant silly comments about their outfits and their personality. The video went viral on TikTok, racking up over 4 million views, and was shared widely on the platform 'X', catching the attention of self-proclaimed misogynist Andrew Tate.† Tate shared his views on the post with his followers, saying, 'If you do not escape The Matrix women like this will be your boss' and 'Zog Corp loves emasculating men by forcing them to listen to semi-sentient females. If that doesn't motivate you to get rich. Nothing will.' The women's innocent office video had found itself on the wrong side of the internet, with men quote-tweeting the post, saying things like 'every time this video comes up on my timeline I get a little more amenable to the Saudi Arabian approach to women's rights'; bombarding the brand's comments section with sexist remarks like 'just get back in the kitchen' and rating the women on their looks and whether the men would have sex with them. In an interview with Yahoo Finance, Rachael Wilde, the co-founder of the company, said that the video had led to female staff members receiving disturbing comments and even threats to their safety. 'It was pretty surprising to see how much an innocent trend-based video quickly racked up a huge amount of hatred and trolling in the comments,' she added.

---

* The trend was originally created by three friends from London while discussing what to wear on their night out. Thank you for your duty, ladies.

† Buckle up, we're going to be hearing a lot more of this name throughout the book.

# NO ONE WANTS TO SEE YOUR D*CK

*Only 9 per cent of girls and young women feel safe online*

A 2024 report by Plan International UK found that only 9 per cent of girls and young women feel completely safe online, while a study by Plan International found 75 per cent of 13–24-year-old women and girls had experienced harmful experiences online. A separate report by Girl Guiding UK found 81 per cent of girls and young women aged 11–21 experienced some form of threatening or upsetting online behaviour in 2023, an increase from 65 per cent in 2018. These findings reflect the research of Professor Olga Jurasz in her 2023 study of online violence towards women and girls in the UK, the largest of its kind, which confirmed 'young women and girls (16–25 years old) bear the brunt of online violence against women.'

I interviewed Jurasz about her research into VAWG (violence against women and girls) that spans over a decade and she shared her concerns around the recurrent trends: 'What is really scary and really concerning is that it has become normalised; normalised within society as well as normalised particularly by younger women.' Her research uncovered that young women are the most likely to experience online violence and harassment, but also the least likely to report their experience to a platform or the police. 'I think it speaks to the point of normalisation and that this is something that just happens: "Oh, doesn't everyone receive dick pics?" And also a feeling like no fuss needs to be made about it and I think that's really, really concerning.'

These figures should send a shiver down the spine of any social media platform owner who repeatedly fails to keep women and girls safe on their site. Instead, billionaire social media mogul Elon Musk, who bought the platform Twitter, now known as 'X' in 2022, has used his site to give power to his misogynistic, transphobic and racist views. Musk reinstated Andrew Tate to the platform after he was previously banned in

2017 due to harmful tweets including a now-deleted post where he said: 'Next point, if you put yourself in a position to be raped, you must bare some responsibility. I'm not saying it's OK you got raped.' Tate's account reached 1 million followers within the first 48 hours of the end of his ban and he has repeatedly violated X's rules of hateful conduct with his extreme misogyny. One tweet he posted after President Trump's re-election read: 'I saw a woman crossing the road today but I just kept my foot down. Right of way? You no longer have rights.' The post had 27k likes, and over 1.2m views. Musk did nothing, and Tate's account now sits on 10.5 million followers.

■

In my 17 years online, I have experienced sexual harassment through several different forms, seeing misogyny shape itself around new technologies and perpetrators find their online communities. I have lost count of the sexual comments and advances I've received from men on all of the mainstream social media platforms, from the old men who love to tell me what they would do to me if they were 20 years younger, to the teenage boys who hijack my comments section with offensive remarks. Once, a man came to my flat to collect a TV stand that I was selling on Facebook. After he'd been in my home, he messaged me later that evening via Marketplace Messenger to ask me out on a date. Another time, I was greeted by a poem in my Instagram DMs: 'Roses are Red, Violets are blue. I have 6.3 inches girth circumference. That I'd love to put in you.' Then there are the messages like 'you have perfect blowjob lips' and 'go back to getting your saggers out'. I've received endless hateful remarks from men on my body or sexuality if I dare to have a political opinion online. One dad with a profile picture of him holding his young child commented, 'Feminism must be high in calories' under a picture of my size 10 body, while other men neg me for a reaction: 'Blame men for everything but you'll take their money at the drop of a hat . . . or your knickers.'*

On one image forum, underneath a post of my leaked images that had been shared without my consent, a man commented that he was from my hometown, Aberystwyth, and had apparently gone to school with me, claiming to have 'shagged her up the castle ruins one night when she came back to work behind the bar. Pretty good at sucking dick but no bum fun'. Another user replied to his post 'What was she like at school? Did she like to fuck?'

If you're from a small town, you'll know how they all have a train station, a park or some kind of disused building that has become notorious for drunk people and teenagers to sneak off to for a cheeky fumble. For my hometown, the castle ruins are that place. But I have never had sex or given blow jobs here, which means someone who knows me personally, knows where I worked, knows where I went to school and knows my hometown enough to know the shagging spots has sought out my leaked nudes online and made up a sex rumour which he shared with the internet. I think of who that man could be every time I go back to visit my parents and walk the streets of the town that I grew up in. Is he someone I say hello to when I bump into him in a coffee shop? Or a taxi driver who gives me a lift home when I'm drunk and vulnerable? Perhaps he scans my food shop at Tesco when I'm with my mum? This man hides behind a cloak of anonymity, getting his sexual kicks from my photos and making up explicit rumours online, while l live with the fear of what he might do if he ever got the chance to live out his sick fantasy.

---

* Why is it always the men who can't get out of their overdraft who accuse women of using them for money? My guy, what money?

# The internet is a gendered experience

Research shows that men and women experience the digital world differently, with a 2024 report by The Alan Turing Institute UK and the University of Oxford finding women are more at risk than men of being targeted by online harms, including misogyny, cyberstalking and cyberflashing. The report also found how fear of online harms directly cause women to retreat from online life and hold back on sharing their opinions, images and personal information, with women 117 per cent more likely than men to fear receiving hate speech online and 215 per cent more likely to fear receiving sexually violent threats. These findings are echoed in Girl Guiding UK's survey, where 54 per cent of girls and young women aged 11–21 said the fear of abuse makes them feel less free to share their views online.

*Women are 117 per cent more likely than men to fear receiving hate speech online*

In their report 'Cyber-trolling as Symbolic Violence', academics Karen Lumsden and Heather Morgan highlight how online trolling of women often includes violent rape and death threats which are used as silencing strategies and work to further isolate women from online spaces, putting women in their place on the misogynistic hierarchy of life. Mirroring how women learn to alter their everyday behaviours in the physical world in an attempt to minimise the risk of harm – *'don't drink too much'*, *'take the well-lit route home'* – we are seeing women being forced to alter their online behaviours due to the same fear.

Seyi Akiwowo is the founder of Glitch, a UK charity working to make digital spaces safer for all with a particular focus on Black women and marginalised people. Akiwowo champions positive digital citizenship, which is the responsible use of technology and the internet to engage in society. As with our offline citizenship, with that right comes rules, etiquette, security and responsibilities. Our rights to digital citizenship can also come under attack, with women having their access to an online life robbed by online harms, silencing strategies and sexual harassment. Akiwowo told me how championing digital citizenship includes 'encouraging people to help make online spaces safer by challenging digital misogynoir and holding tech companies accountable. This looks like being an active bystander and taking on the responsibility of blocking and reporting abusive posts to social media platforms. It also looks like prioritising self-care by setting boundaries about the content you follow and how much time you spend on social media, to ensure your digital experience sparks joy.'

It's important to note here the role intersectionality plays in how we all experience online harms and sexual harassment differently. Glitch's Digital Misogynoir Report 2023 discusses the ways in which misogynoir shows up in online spaces and its dangerous ability to incite offline violence. The report highlights the horrific case of white supremacist Dylan Roof who murdered nine Black church members during a Bible study class after spending time on far-right social media platforms. Seven of Roof's victims were women.

## MISOGYNOIR

*Definition:* Coined by Moya Bailey, a Black feminist writer, this describes how racism and misogyny intersect as a specific hatred towards Black women.

The report shows how Black women receive a disproportionate amount of abuse across the five social media platforms Glitch looked at, finding over 9,000 more highly toxic posts about Black women than white women. Research also showed how

Black women are more likely to be marginalised through dehumanising language and stereotypes, with the most prevalent trope being that of the 'angry Black woman'.

This is a narrative that shows up often in online discourse around ITV's dating show *Love Island*, which sees a bunch of hot, young singletons thrown together in a villa in Mallorca. The Black female contestants often face harsher online critique for their behaviour than the white female contestants on the show. When season five contestant Yewande Biala was dumped from the show, she received backlash from some X users who called her 'spiteful' and 'nasty' for her frustrated reaction towards her partner Danny, who had put her spot on the show at risk by showing interest in another woman. On the same night, Maura Higgins, a white female contestant, was celebrated for her angry outburst at her partner Tom who suggested she was an easy shag. After Yewande's exit, she was trending on X for a week as people discussed her behaviour and whether they found her attractive as a dark-skinned woman. *Love Island UK* contestant Indiyah Polack, from season eight, spoke out on her experiences of racism in an interview with BBC1 XTRA host Nadia Jae, sharing how she altered her behaviour on the show to avoid being labelled the 'angry Black girl'. She said, 'I definitely had to think first before I said certain things because I knew if I reacted in a certain way . . . angry Black girl, the aggressor, the bully.'

Digital misogynoir can also be seen in the targeted harassment of Black and marginalised female members of Parliament. Diane Abbott is the current Labour MP for Hackney North and Stoke Newington and the UK's first Black female MP. A study by Amnesty International investigating online abuse of female MPs found that of the 177 women MPs sampled, Abbott was the target of almost a third (31.6 per cent) of all abusive tweets analysed; this rose to 45.14 per cent in the six weeks leading up to the 2017 general election. An analysis by Sofia Collignon et al into 'The Gendered Harassment of Parliamentary Candidates in the UK' discussed the role of intersectionality in the abuse faced by candidates, with 63 per cent of Black, Asian and minority ethnic women reporting experiencing abuse, compared to 45 per cent of white women. Researchers at the University of Sheffield looked into the online abuse of politicians during the 2024 election, with four out of the five most targeted politicians* being of Black or Asian descent; the list included Diane Abbott and Suella Braverman. The report showed almost 20 per cent of the abuse towards the politicians were 'explicitly sexist, misogynistic or sexually explicit'.

Another prominent example of digital misogynoir is the targeted harassment of the Duchess of Sussex, Meghan Markle, who repeatedly faces much harsher judgement on social media for her relationship and her behaviour than white members of the Royal family. UK tabloids famously printed headlines criticising Markle for things like cradling her baby bump and eating avocados, while praising Catherine Middleton for doing the same thing. Researchers at the University of Sunderland analysed tweets made towards Markle after she and Prince Harry announced they were taking a step back from royal life. Their findings showed Markle was the target of overtly sexist and racist tweets that saw her described as 'royal bimbo Meghan' and 'self-loathing race traitor'. Around 400 tweets analysed were in the most severe category of abuse. Following their retreat from royal duties, Markle told Oprah Winfrey during an interview how she had thoughts of taking her own life due to the misogynoir she experienced both offline and online.

Glitch is calling on tech companies to commit to including clear definitions of misogyny, racism and white supremacy for use in content moderation, so they can implement policies

---

* The other three politicans were Keir Starmer, Rishi Sunak and Sadiq Khan, showing how the role of intersectionality plays out across both sexes.

banning misogynoir and prevent gender-based violence on their platforms. Akiwowo shared Glitch's proposals from the Digital Misogynoir Report: 'The proposals include the government investing in research to understand the links between online and offline hate and educating people about extremisms like white supremacy and incel ideologies so we can prevent harm.' Outside of the responsibilities and obligations of tech companies and the government, Akiwowo told of the role individuals and communities must play in working to understand and challenge digital misogynoir: 'We also need communities and digital citizens to understand the harmful effects of misogynoir, including racist and sexist tropes in all forms of media, so they can challenge their biases and see Black women as real and multi-faceted people. We need to implement holistic changes to the way we treat the abuse Black women face if we want to see meaningful change.'

Social categories such as class, sexuality and ability can also influence the way some women experience sexual harassment and online harms. A 2021 Plan UK report 'What Works for Ending Public Sexual Harassment' found that 92 per cent of young women and girls who consider themselves to have a disability have experienced some form of public sexual harassment. While scrolling on Instagram recently, I saw a reel that had gone viral from a content creator who is disabled. The creator has TAR syndrome, which is a rare genetic disorder characterised by the absence of the radius bone in both forearms. The video was of her dancing on holiday with the sun setting behind her and included text that read 'confidence is a decision that comes when you decide to have it'. The post was uplifting, inspiring and evidently skewed towards a female audience, but when I clicked to open the comments section, nearly all of the top-rated comments were from men leaving ableist, sexist and derogatory messages. The top comment had 17,200 likes and read, 'Bend it over and call the position raptor style', while another said, 'Real convenient. Bet she always says she can't reach the check'. Another, left by a creator with 260k followers, simply read, 'I'm still hittin it idc'.

Reading the comments left me – as us Welsh like to say – tamping, fuming, raging. This was a post from someone who was normalising and shining the light on her disability in a way that had the potential to help other people with disabilities feel seen and more comfortable in their bodies, but that had been snatched from underneath them by the men who felt it appropriate to refer to a disabled woman as 'it' and comment on how fuckable they found her. Full of rage, I left a comment underneath the creators' video that said: 'Men are fucking weird commenting misogynistic and ableist comments to try get a few likes from random guys on the internet.' Almost immediately, Instagram flagged my comment as hate speech towards a group of people, informing me it had been removed and warning me that my account was at risk of further restrictions. I was spouting hate speech by saying men were weird, but a comment with 17,200 likes sexualising a disabled woman and calling her 'it' was totally acceptable and within the platform's guidelines? Sure, my comment was a little on the crass side, but the hypocrisy on display from Instagram in telling me the ableist and sexist comments mentioned above did not break their guidelines after I reported them is a perfect example of how automated AI technology used to police social media often fails to keep users safe from actual harm. Its implementation serves as a plaster to make it seem platforms are doing the work to challenge hate on their sites, but instead, the computer-facilitated support system often fails to respond to actual trolling and online harms on the platform. And for the record, men *are* fucking weird for abusing a disabled woman online, and so are the other 17,200 people who agreed with them.

Transgender people, and especially transgender women, face a disproportionate number of online harms. In 2019, anti-bullying charity Ditch the Label and consumer intelligence company Brandwatch came together to analyse 10 million social media posts from the US and the UK. The report found over 1.5 million transphobic posts, highlighting the disproportionate scale of online abuse transgender people face.

Fae Johnson is a trans woman and activist from Ontario. In 2023, she featured in a Hershey's Canada advert as part of their International Women's Day Campaign. In response, Johnstone received a barrage of online hate that included encouraging her to take her own life, and calls to boycott the chocolate company for their decision to include a trans woman in their advert trended on X. In an interview with PinkNews, Johnstone spoke of the 'tsunami of hate' and targeted cancel campaign which saw right-wing journalists deadname and misgender her. Her inbox filled with transphobic hate, which she described as 'the latest example of the far-right dehumanising trans people, mobbing us with hate in the hopes of pushing us out of public life'.

At the Paris 2024 Olympics, social media platforms were set alight with transphobic abuse targeted at Algerian female boxer Imane Khelif after she beat her rival Angela Carini, going on to win the gold medal. Vicious attacks spread across social media with high-profile celebrities such as J. K. Rowling and Logan Paul racking up millions of views on their posts claiming Khelif was a 'man beating a woman in public for entertainment'. After the Olympics, Khelif announced she had filed an official complaint to the anti-online hatred centre of the Paris prosecutor's office, naming J. K. Rowling and Elon Musk in the cyber-bullying lawsuit. Khelif is a cisgender woman, but the online harassment and abuse experienced both by her and Johnstone shows how transphobia is a tactic used in online spaces to silence and shame both trans women and non-conforming, cisgender women.

In January 2025, CEO of Meta Mark Zuckerburg announced a change in Facebook and Instagram's hateful conduct policy, rolling back any progression towards positive digital citizenship and opening up the floodgates of online abuse. The new rules allow insults based on race, ethnicity, disability, sexual orientation and gender identity. Non-profit news organisation *The Intercept* claimed to have obtained internal Meta training materials for the new guidelines that provided examples of comments that are now permissible on their platforms. These included '*Immigrants are grubby, filthy pieces of shit*' and '*Get these trannies out of my school* (beneath a photo of high school students)'. Zuckerburg pointed to the recent US election and a 'cultural tipping point towards, once again, prioritising speech' as the reason for Meta's depressing stride back in time.

Sexual harassment is almost always about power. It isn't a compliment; it is a way of making women and marginalised people feel uncomfortable, ashamed or humiliated. Non-white, disabled and trans-women are experiencing sexual harassment at a higher rate because it is a weapon that goes hand-in-hand with racism, ableism and transphobia. Intersectionality has to be at the core of all policies and law-making to ensure we can create a safer online and offline community for the most marginalised and vulnerable in our society.

## The digitalization of sexual harassment

A rise in modern feminism and a growing lack of intolerance towards sexist behaviours has seen perpetrators of everyday sexism retreat behind closed doors, pulling their curtains tightly shut and opening their laptops to access an online world where their harassment has turned digital. We know through research (and just by merely existing as a woman) that women still experience public sexual harassment at an alarming rate, but I'd like to think that most men would nowadays think twice about whistling or heckling a woman in the street – *I did say most.* But men's newfound awareness of why public sexual harassment is now frowned upon hasn't stopped them from performing these behaviours; instead, many have simply switched up their stomping ground, masking behind anonymous usernames and finding strength in numbers through digital communities as they continue their terror of women in cyberspace. The internet has empowered these men to carry out their sexist behaviours with little-to-no fear of consequence, arming them with a sense of impunity that has seen them fall deeper into dark fantasies and their dangerous entitlement towards women. A man who once may have piped up in the queue for a drink at the club with a 'cheeky' (but still totally unacceptable) 'Nice arse, love!' can now unlock his phone and access message boards where thousands of men are exchanging rape fantasies about their work colleagues.

When we think of the term 'sexual harassment', we often assume more traditional examples such as street harassment, sexual comments and groping, which are all behaviours that cause significant harm to its victims, but the expansion of the internet has seen this harassment escalate into new-age displays of violence that are normalised in online manosphere communities.

The internet has not only created new forms of sexual harassment, it has also provided fresh platforms for perpetrators to carry out their harmful behaviours. From food delivery apps to auction websites, men are continuously finding new ways to contact women with their unwanted sexual advances. In 2018, Michelle Midwinter shared screenshots on X of unwanted messages she received from a Just Eat driver after he delivered a food order to her home. They included him asking whether she had a boyfriend and one that read 'Good night bby see you next time when i get your meal' alongside a lips emoji. Midwinter's post about the inappropriate messages went viral and she told Buzzfeed News how more than a thousand women had got in touch with her, all sharing eerily familiar stories: 'The scary thing is the sheer number of females who have had similar experiences – we trust companies with our personal details and for them to be used in this way is unacceptable.'

A 2024 ITV news investigation reported on a number of women who had told them they had been sexually harassed by food delivery drivers, with allegations ranging from flirty messages, indecent exposure and rape. The article highlighted a 2023 poll by the Information Commissioner's Office, which found that one in three 18 to 34-year-olds have fallen victim to 'predatory' text messages or calls from delivery drivers. An investigation by iNews found thousands of delivery driver accounts on Deliveroo, Just Eat and Uber were being traded on the black market for use by illegal workers, raising concerns from women's safety campaigners who warned that women are being put at risk with many drivers being unvetted and untraceable to the delivery firms. Female drivers are also being put at risk – an article by Maya Oppenheim in the *Independent* exposed how they often experience sexual harassment from male customers. One woman told how a man had opened the door to collect his delivery in his underwear and insisted she came inside to help feed him his food. Another woman said it was 'very common' for men to make sexual advances at her when she dropped their food off.

In an episode of Channel 4's *Dispatches*, journalist Ellie Flynn uncovered the dark side of the second-hand marketplace Vinted* when she found innocent images of women trying to sell their clothes on the site were being posted in an online forum titled 'Vinted Sluts', along with the tag line 'when you sell your clothes but you want the attention'. In an interview

---

* Vinted responded to the findings in the Channel 4 film, stating 'We are taking the allegations seriously. We act as swiftly we can against anything that violates our terms and conditions.'

with PoliticsJOE, Flynn told how users in the forum were sexualising women, zooming in on body parts in images, commenting on their bodies and often including personal information like the women's locations and usernames: 'It felt to me like it was encouraging people who found this website to get in touch with these women. It felt like it was opening the door to sexual harassment on the app, which is something some women have experienced.'

I've come across many posts of women sharing their experiences of sexual harassment through unconventional websites and apps. There's a joke that does the rounds on social media about blocking your ex on every social media platform, so he sends you 1p on PayPal to contact you. I'm unsure if men are getting more creative with their avenues of abuse or are simply opportunists who jump at any chance to harass women.* Is any platform safe from the DM sliding of the aubergine emoji? I asked my Instagram and TikTok followers what the weirdest platform they had experienced sexual harassment on was . . .

*QuizUp. I used to do* The Office *quiz religiously and ppl could message you after you played each other. One guy nicely messaged about one of the quiz answers, so I replied, then he went on to ask me if I like massages, does my boyfriend pleasure me. Things like that. Like come on, I just want to play a quiz.*

*I had a Dominos driver flirty text me after he dropped my food off. Contacted Dominos and they said they sacked him.*

*When I was younger, men my age and older would message me on SongPop trying to start some form of relationship.*

---

* If I were to add in an option of giving them the benefit of the doubt, I would suggest some simply lack the social awareness to realise how creepy it is to ask a girl out via Facebook Marketplace. Just some, though.

*Vinted. I bought a pair of shoes for my brother and the man I bought them from decided it was appropriate to hit on me. I was 19 at the time, he must have been about 40 based off his picture.*

*Spareroom.com. I had just broken up with my ex-gf and was living back with my mam. There was this flat really central, but it was registered really cheap. It seemed too good to be true, but I messaged him anyway. He messaged back saying we'd be sharing a bathroom with a winky face, and 'it would be great to share a room with you, why do you think the price is so cheap?' With loads of pervy emojis.*

*Generally speaking, I receive quite a lot of sleazy messages via dating apps that are very forward in nature. This has sadly become the norm because men feel it's an acceptable way to speak to women. It's not!*

*I was selling a Topshop nude-coloured cotton bodysuit on eBay and some creep messaged me asking for pics of me in it and for me to wear it before he bought it. GRIM! I blocked him and took the listing down. I was defo in sixth form too when this happened.*

Some platforms have introduced safeguarding measures to prevent online abuse and sexual harassment on their sites, with Instagram adding a feature that lets users restrict certain words and choose who they can receive comments and messages from. They have also enlisted the help of AI technology to detect potentially harmful language, with the user being asked, 'Are you sure you want to post this?' before they hit send. Stephanie Otway, a spokesperson for Instagram, told Wired.com that the feature 'gives users a moment to pause, take a breath, and decide if they really want to send that message'. The platform also introduced 'teen accounts' in September 2024, with built-in protections for under 16s* that are turned on automatically and need a linked parent account to switch off. These include a default private account, only being able to receive and send messages to people they follow and sensitive content restrictions that filter out any potential harmful content. However, these safeguarding measures often put all the onus on the person who is receiving abuse to protect themselves from harm, and with Meta's new guidelines allowing more hateful conduct on their platforms, the effectiveness of their safety measures moving forward are questionable.

Tinder, one of the world's leading dating apps, has adopted similar safety strategies, becoming the first in the dating space to use AI technology to detect offensive messages on their platform. Their tool 'Are you sure?' sends a real-time warning to the sender about their inappropriate comments, while their 'Does this bother you?' tool asks recipients if they're uncomfortable with the harmful language that has been found in screening. If the answer is yes, then they are encouraged to report the sender to the platform via a report form.

■

It was forum browsing day, time to check out the murky world of the manosphere that exists one step behind your mainstream social media platforms. When I first started learning about the communities of men who spend their days objectifying and abusing women online, I naively thought it was a world that would exist in the corners of the dark web, accessible only to those who were invited in by a Pied Piper of misogynists. Instead, these men can easily be found operating on fringe social media platforms such as Reddit, Discord and 4Chan – sites

---

* You can also manage the accounts of older teens who already have accounts by turning on 'parental supervision' in your settings. Scroll down to 'Family Centre' and send an invite to your teen's account.

that have hundreds of millions of users. *Not so niche after all.* I don't know why I was surprised, considering some of the most violent harassment I've received has been on mainstream platforms,* but the accessibility of it all makes me feel unnerved. While us girls are learning TikTok dances to Charli XCX and posting GRWM YouTube videos, there are guys discussing how fuckable a woman is in the comments underneath her stolen intimate images.

Clicking through the message boards, my eyes rapidly scanned the posts: a 'nudify' request here, the hunt for leaked nudes there, men offering to trade their girlfriend's pics further down (we'll be diving deeper into these topics further in the book, btw, but I want to ease you in first). I've seen image-based forms of abuse like this before and have become familiar with how men exchange, create and search for non-consensual explicit images of women. It sounds wrong to say I have become used to this level of hatred and abuse, but it is true.

I flicked through the hundreds of replies, and a post titled 'CAPTIONS' pulled my gaze. As a social media girly, I believe captions are a key part of creating the perfect post and often spend way too long trying to find an alternative to 'Live, Laugh, Love <3'. *Are these men asking each other for help to create the perfect Instagram caption?* I clicked to expand the post and recoiled in shock, wishing I could go back to being the woman I was before viewing what I had uncovered.

H.'s Midweek Captions > Anonymous

2024 has been a crazy year and these next weeks are awful at work, hoping to get some captions in for funsies in between the horrors of modern life. Same rules as always

---

* After Piers Morgan once quote-tweeted me, I received death and rape threats from his followers. Ironically, my tweet to him was asking him why he felt the need to encourage hate and division.

i. Drop names
ii. Include plot and/or kinks/limits
iii. No celebs unless you had fun ideas
iv. No furry shit
v. Milfs preffered
vi. Let's have fun

The men responded with glee, grateful that 'H' was back for another round of scripting captions, and posted their plot requests alongside an image for inspiration, following his rules. It quickly became clear that these men were not looking for cute IG captions to accompany their holiday photo dump; they were exchanging detailed captions that involved violent rape and humiliation fantasies of women that they knew, posted alongside their personal photos.

One user posted an image of a heavily pregnant woman caressing her baby bump alongside his request: '*Becca gets kidnapped and taken to a farm to be repeatedly bred and milked as a hu-cow.*'

Another request saw an image of a pretty, brunette woman reclining on a sun lounger on the beach. His request read: '*Grace gets drugged by a granny at the beach and wakes up tied down in a dark room in her tight bikini. Kinks: kidnapping, lesbian, rape. Dislike: gore, scat, death.*'

As my index finger cautiously moved on my track pad to continue scrolling through the stream of requests under the post, I was repulsed by the blasé tone of the men who conjured up their twisted kinks and posted women's images alongside such horrific words. For a moment, I tried to imagine what it would be like to be them, punishing myself with the thoughts of trauma that it would inflict if I were to find hundreds of men engaging in conversation about my violent attack, hijacking a photo I'd once proudly posted on my Instagram grid to feed their sick desires. The hairs on my arms shot up as an involuntary shiver took over my body at the thought, desperately trying to shake off the men's depravity.

The next post I scrolled across included a photo of a woman with short hair flexing her bicep: '*Becca, raped and knocked up by her soccer students. I don't really have any limits so go wild really!*'

The user's caption request was fulfilled by 'H' with a lengthy paragraph of some of the darkest shit I've ever read that left me terrified at the thought of these men existing alongside women in real life. I'll spare you all the gory details, but it started with Becca being tied up and gang raped by teenage boys and ended with her being kicked in the head, left for dead and the boys raping her stiff body. And, yes, that *is* sparing the gory details. 'H' followed up with another post, 'Glad you liked it!' with the user replying, 'Hehe I did and I'm glad you went all out!'

I couldn't help but wonder if it was a real student who had made this request with a photo of his teacher? And how adult men were seemingly getting off at the idea of teenage boys murdering their coach. It's difficult not to feel a total sense of hopelessness in these moments.

I thought back to 'H's original post: '*Hoping to get some captions in for funsies in between the horrors of modern life.*'

Their 'funsies' *are* the horrors of women's lives.

■

Ellie Wilson is a rape survivor, campaigner and social justice reformer. In 2022, her ex-boyfriend Daniel McFarlane was found guilty of two counts of rape and attempting to defeat the ends of justice (also known as perverting the course of justice). After sentencing, Ellie waived her anonymity to share her experience and raise awareness around the unfair and unjust treatment of victims of rape in court, and to reclaim her identity in a wave of positive media reports of her abuser: 'I kept seeing all of the reporting on him, about how he was a talented athlete and how he was a medical student and I was just nameless. I was voiceless.' Ellie told me, 'I wanted to have a voice, I wanted to have a name, and I didn't want to just be a body that he raped, I wanted to be a person.'

After Ellie sent out a tweet in January 2023 reflecting on New Year's Eve of 2018 – the night she was first raped by McFarlane – and how this time he had spent New Year's behind bars, her following on 'X' grew quickly. But as her content and story gained traction, she began to receive heinous abuse online. Ellie told me that when she first spoke out, the comments were 'not that bad', but soon after, they became more extreme. 'They started with ones that were like, "Oh she wants her fame and attention", "You're lying", "Show me proof" – all of that.'

They then escalated to the point where some men would tag and share posts of other women alongside her own and would rank their 'rape-ability'. Ellie explained, 'Some people are like, "Oh, I can see why he did it" and some people would be like, "No, I wouldn't even rape you." Honestly, I couldn't have imagined anything like that could have happened.'

The abuse carried over onto different platforms, including TikTok, where Ellie received threatening comments underneath a video she posted of a TikTok trend based on Taylor Swift's song 'Who's afraid of little old me?'

'The first photo I put was just of me smiling and the second photo includes the headlines like "Sent him to prison" and "Took action against the lawyer" alongside text that says, "Well, you should be." And then this guy commented, saying "How could I be afraid of someone I could kill with one punch?" Why would you comment that? I really don't understand it.'

Another comment Ellie received used what had happened against her in an incredibly sinister way: 'I had one comment that was like, "She seems like an easy person to rape I might find out where she lives", which is clearly quite threatening.'

Most of the online abuse and harassment Ellie has faced has come from men, but she has been surprised to see women join in on the victim blaming. 'I have had some comments from women that are a lot less on the extreme end than what I get from men. It's more speculating as to things like, "Should survivors act this way?", "She's too loud", "She talks too often about this", "She's narcissistic", "She's self-obsessed." It's all of this internalised misogyny.' Ellie's experience shows how rape myths can be perpetrated by all genders with societal tropes upholding the idea that there is a 'perfect' victim. This is the belief that victims of sexual violence look a certain way, behave a certain way and display certain characteristics. This is often where intersectionality plays a hand, and why it is extremely difficult for victims of sexual violence to see their perpetrator convicted in a court of law, with rape myths around the 'perfect' victim contributing to jury bias.

Though I've seen misogyny play out online a zillion times before, I still felt shocked that there were people out there who choose to troll rape survivors. It felt exceptionally cruel for them to use Ellie's pain as their entertainment, and I am sure she was targeted because of her advocacy. How dare a woman speak up about violent male behaviour? Their trolling was her punishment for giving survivors a voice.

I asked Ellie how she manages the online harassment, and she told me her master's degree in global security has helped her understand the behaviours more. 'I did a thesis on this, and I know it's all about radicalisation, so you can mentally tell yourself that these are people that are clearly not well. They're doing it to get a rise out of people, they're attention starved, they're radicalised. But physically, you just feel threatened, you feel unwell and it's really hard to see sometimes.'

Ellie is still worried about the attitudes which enable someone to comment such hateful abuse. 'I thought that there were some things that would be off limits to troll people about, with rape being one of them, but apparently that's not the case. I don't understand what possesses people to post that sort of thing and it is worrying. It is so worrying.'

During her trial, Ellie was unhappy with the behaviour and line of questioning of McFarlane's lawyer Lorenzo Alonzi, including his remarks to the court after his client had been found guilty that he 'fell in love with the wrong person'. When she went to make a complaint about Alonzi, she realised she needed her court transcripts to do so, which would cost £3,000, a fee she ended up crowdfunding for. After accessing her transcripts and teaching herself all the intricacies of the court complaint process, Ellie successfully lodged six complaints against defence lawyer Alonzi for his behaviour during the trial, with a Faculty of Advocates committee finding his behaviour amounted to unsatisfactory professional conduct, setting a new precedent for rape trials and the treatment of victim-survivors. It is a truly remarkable story of bravery in the face of adversity, and Ellie's courage has helped many other women. For example, she has heard from a journalist covering stories like hers how survivors have credited her campaign work for deciding to speak out themselves: 'It's amazing that women are no longer feeling ashamed and that they feel like there is this space and they feel comfortable in telling their own stories.'

After I interviewed Ellie on Zoom, I closed the call and cried. I cried tears of sadness because of what multiple men had put Ellie through – the assault, the court case, the online abuse she faced after. But mostly I cried tears of hope because speaking to Ellie reminded me of the bravery and resilience of womanhood. Ellie shouldn't have had to announce her trauma publicly for the justice system to change, or for people to think twice before harassing rape victims online, but she does so selflessly to give a voice to other survivors.

## Education and calling it out

My boobs came in early which meant by year 4, I was already wearing bralettes from Tammy Girl. My mum took me on a girls' shopping trip to buy my first ones and I felt so grown up. One of my earliest memories of sexual harassment is of a group of boys who were in years five and six cornering me in the playground and demanding I show them my bralette that they could see a glimpse of under my school top. It was soft pink and featured Little Miss characters from the Mr Men franchise. I remember a teacher came charging over, yelling at me to pull my top down, my face scarlet with the embarrassment.

### 75 per cent of girls in the UK have experienced some form of sexual harassment

A survey by Crimestoppers found that the majority of those who experience sexual harassment encounter it for the first time during childhood or adolescence, with some reporting they were just five years old when it first took place. A 2021 report by Plan International UK found 75 per cent of girls in the UK have experienced some form of sexual harassment, some of them as young as 12. Their 2018 report 'Street Harassment: It's Not Okay' found more than a third of girls in the UK have received 'unwanted sexual attention such as being groped, stared at, catcalled and wolf-whistled while wearing their school uniform in public'.

Her Voice Wales is a youth project facilitated by the Vale of Glamorgan's youth service for girls aged 13–17. In 2023, they launched their #wedontfeelsafecampaign, raising awareness of sexual harassment towards women and girls and to encourage young people to report incidents of harassment. I sat in on one of their monthly evening sessions, which left me both horrified at their early experiences of sexual harassment and inspired by their determination to demand change. The girls told me how receiving unsolicited dick pics, sexual comments about their bodies and being pressured to send nudes had all been normalised as 'just what happens'. One girl shared how she believed in-person sexual harassment had been normalised in schools, with the addition of phones having escalated the issue: 'When you get that phone you get the freedom to do it online and people don't see the problem with it because it's what they've been taught.' Another said of young boys their age: 'Online, they say whatever they want compared to real life, they don't think there's someone real behind who's going to read their messages.'

All of the girls in the session had experienced online sexual harassment across different social media platforms and messaging services. They highlighted how Snapchat was one of the worst for them due to messages disappearing shortly after sending, which they reported as having 'no consequences' for the sender. A member of staff informed the girls that you can request your chat history from Snapchat to report any unwanted or predatory behaviour, but the girls all agreed it felt 'embarrassing and mortifying to report it'.

I asked the girls when they remember first experiencing sexual harassment. Most recalled being in primary school; one was as young as year two (aged 6 or 7). Incidents included boys lifting up their skirts, which led to them wearing shorts underneath out of fear of being exposed. One girl told me that the first experience of sexual harassment she can remember was when she was just 11 years old, by a male teacher. 'I had one teacher who was particularly bad, and I brought it up to a higher teacher from safeguarding and they did absolutely nothing. Because I was 11, I wasn't going to do anything about it because I was so scared.' The girl said she was told by the teacher who she reported the incident to that the male had 'been told to stop' but his behaviour continued. 'How was talking to him going to stop it? It didn't stop it at all, and I had to go back and complain. I was so mortified. He would say, "I'm just being nice" but he didn't do it to anyone else.'

Issy Warren, who we met in the previous chapter, is the schools and programmes lead at Our Streets Now. They facilitate workshops that aim to ignite critical thinking amongst students and question the culture around sexual harassment and consent through the unpacking of real-life testimonials. Warren told me that empathy and critical thinking are the two main values they take into their workshops: 'When we share an example of sexual harassment, the young people will say, "Well, she could have done this" or "They should have just punched him" or "They should have said no." And so I ask, "OK, can you give me all of the reasons why that person didn't do that, please?" And actually, when you ask them that, they usually find it quite easy to tell you why.' They went on to say, 'If all that we've left them with is the ability to question things, I think that's the most powerful thing we can give them.'

Warren emphasised the importance of understanding cumulative impact, and how something that may seem minor or a one-off could be the tip of the iceberg for the person who is being targeted. 'It's how that effect builds up. So maybe it seems okay to you that you're going up to a girl and telling her that she's beautiful. But what if you're the seventeenth person that day to tell her that? And what if the person before was shouting it at her from behind? So, it's thinking about how this all builds up and trying to get young people to put themselves in other people's shoes.'

Our Schools Now also hosts workshops on sexual harassment for teachers and educators. Warren has experienced challenges from teachers who have misplaced good intentions that lead to female pupils being blamed for the harassment they've experienced. 'Teachers want to keep young people safe, but they can't do that because they don't have a lot of control over what happens outside of the school gates. Their response to harassment is to say things like, "Okay, you need to wear a longer skirt", "Don't go to house parties", "Don't send explicit pictures." That comes from a really good place but I worry about the consequences of all that advice, considering that actually we know that sexual harassment can happen in broad daylight whatever you're wearing.' Warren explained how a sense of blame can prevent young people from disclosing and reporting to trusted adults out of fear of getting into trouble.

In 2023, I joined Our Schools Now as an assistant facilitator for their pilot programme funded by the Welsh Government, and the juxtaposition between what some female students would tell me about their experience of sexual harassment and the attitudes and beliefs of some teachers was alarming.

In one school, I spent the afternoon with a group of roughly 20 teenage girls who all disclosed how they had experienced some form of sexual harassment, often while wearing their school uniform or via social media. They felt as if these behaviours had been normalised and shrugged it off as part of existing as a girl. That afternoon, we held a workshop for teachers where we shared statistics from Plan International UK's report about girls' experiences, along with real-life testimonials that we'd collected. I was taken aback by the frosty response of some of the male teachers, who accused the statistics of being false, complained that we were going into schools and 'telling girls anything is sexual harassment these days' and then questioned why none of their pupils had come to them about this before. *I can't possibly imagine why, Sir.* One teacher ended his rant with how he 'felt sorry for teenage boys these days'. Bear in mind, this was after we'd just spent an hour showing him statistics and a video which highlighted the endemic level of sexual harassment teenage girls face. For once, I was speechless. There was no sign of empathy towards teenage girls – in fact, they seemed irate that we were having to talk about them. When I offered to send over the report to one of the male teachers who questioned the validity of the research I'd been quoting, he scoffed that he 'won't be reading that'.

It's extremely difficult to be a teacher nowadays and I genuinely believe that most teachers are trying their best with the resources they have – the little time and funds they are given to tackle heavy topics like sexual harassment – but this is where the problem lies. Many teachers simply aren't equipped to hold these life-shaping conversations with their students, and that's okay. Just because you are a good geography teacher, doesn't mean you are naturally equipped with the skills to communicate on issues around sex and consent. As Issy Warren put it: 'This is hard stuff to talk about and there should be funding available. There should be space made for it. It needs to be a priority in the education system because that's where the change is going to happen, and I don't think it's fair to put that expectation on schools in their current working state system.' Warren and their colleagues would like to see these topics prioritised in the education system, in the same way maths and English are – something that may seem radical, but it doesn't have to be.

I asked Warren if they thought sexual harassment has been normalised in schools and wider in society. They responded that they believed it went further than that, with societal pressure on men and boys playing a huge role in upholding the culture – 'I think it's glamorised actually. Not to excuse them, but we put so much pressure on men and boys to be sexually confident, to be charismatic, to be dating and having sex by a certain age, and I think sometimes those pressures can become so strong that they become stronger than the ability for boys to care and take into account other people's comfort, which is really sad and also really telling about how strong some of those pressures are.' Warren noted it's important to hold empathy for boys while also calling them out on their behaviour.

Our Streets Now is leading the way in the fight to eradicate public sexual harassment. It was born out of a conversation between two sisters – Maya and Gemma Tutton, who were just 15 and 21 at the time. They shared the same frustrations regarding how they experienced the world as young women and decided they had to try to change things. They launched a petition to make public sexual harassment a stand-alone crime, which gained a mammoth half-a-million signatures, making its way into the hands of policymakers in government. Our Streets Now was launched off the back of the petition and in 2021, they teamed up with Plan International UK to push forward their #CrimeNotCompliment campaign to introduce specific legislation on public sexual harassment.

Finally, after many long years of campaigning by activists, the 'Protection from Sex-based Harassment in Public' bill passed in November 2023. I've been on the ground with the everyday heroes who are the backbone of the Our Streets Now campaign, I've taken part in their training, facilitated workshops alongside them and vented together over a glass of wine about the huge mountain we need to climb to eradicate gender-based violence. The Our Streets Now team run changemaker workshops, but they are truly changemakers themselves.

By calling sexual harassment out when we see it and reclassifying predatory behaviour from 'just banter' to 'unacceptable', we will slowly shift the dial, where men and boys will not feel emboldened to act out these behaviours *or* to 'perform' them in front of their friends in a display of hyper-masculinity. Olga Jurasz's study 'Online Violence Against Women: A Four Nation Study' found that while young men and boys (16 to 25) were more likely than other age groups to witness online violence against women and girls, they were the least likely to report it. Young men were also the least likely age group to support law reform and the criminalisation of violence against women and girls online. In our interview, Jurasz pointed out the contrast of experiences of the young women, who face 'fairly extreme' violence online, and the young men, who are 'least likely to see that it's their obligation to do something', adding how the juxtaposition creates 'quite an explosive mix of reactions and attitudes'.

I have facilitated workshops on sexual harassment with year 10 pupils in mixed gender classes, and almost all of them said they wouldn't know what to do if they witnessed sexual harassment online or offline. A few unsure hands went up from teenage boys, with one offering up a weary answer of how they'd 'just tell them to stop'. The boys there had a pretty good understanding of what counted as sexual harassment, and they were empathetic and thoughtful with their answers during the session. I don't think it's the case that all men and boys are purposely ignoring the harmful behaviours they see happening towards women and girls – they often just don't know how to speak up.

Jurasz told me about what she sees as a lack of guidance for young men and boys on how to be an active bystander: 'How do I appear in the spaces? What is my agency here? What do I do as a bystander? What do I do as a man when I see another man attacking a woman online? Do I turn away? Do I report? Do I react? Do I actively challenge this behaviour?'

It is vital we take a two-pronged approach to educating on sexual harassment, not only to prevent it but to enable others to feel comfortable enough to call out harmful behaviour when they see it. In 2023, the Welsh Government launched the 'SOUND' project to engage young people in the conversation of gender-based violence with the aim of creating a 'sound Welsh society in which we all can thrive'. The campaign uses social media and male ambassadors to raise awareness of violence against women and girls and educate men on potentially harmful behaviours in the hope of empowering them to call it out when they see it and check their own actions and beliefs.

Gav Murphy, a gamer and video and podcast host, fronted the podcast strand of the SOUND campaign, interviewing a host of female guests on what it's like for women to work and exist in male-dominated online spaces. In one episode, Murphy spoke to video game presenter Shay Thompson, who opened up about her experience of being a Black woman working in the gaming world and the slurs she receives online. In another episode, Murphy interviewed Twitch streamer Hollie Bennett, who described how she has to take precautions around what clothes she wears while filming videos – for example, making sure to avoid low-cut tops as the content would often be overshadowed by comments on her body.

Murphy says that sitting down with the women who work in his industry and hearing of their contrasting experiences in the gaming world, compared to his as 'a straight, white man working in a world largely inhabited by people exactly like me', opened his eyes to the online harms and sexual harassment women face daily.

'I was also shocked by just how much terrible stuff happens that women don't bother to report or speak about because if they reported/mentioned everything, they'd never get anything done!' he added. 'I was also shocked by the silence of men my age when it comes to things like this or the amount of times men haven't taken the opportunity to speak up or step in. I feel like I do the bare minimum when it comes to speaking out against misogyny or the treatment of women, but it turns out that the bar is so fucking low that even the bare minimum is absolutely loads!'

For Murphy, the experience has left him more fired up 'to work harder as an ally', and he believes that begins with avoiding 'ripping into young men for acting inappropriately' but instead speaking to young men 'in a non-judgemental, non-confrontational way about the correct way of behaving around and treating women'.

Gav Murphy has built a large male audience in a world more often dominated by men, and hearing his eagerness to learn and embrace allyship leaves me with a sense of hope. 'I think anyone with a platform – no matter the size – needs to use it to speak out and make things better and more inclusive for anyone.'

Don't let anyone tell you male empathy doesn't exist: it's there, they just have to want to do the work to find it.

It isn't enough to push harmful behaviours off the streets and turn a blind eye to them in the digital world; if it's not okay to shout sexual comments or abuse at someone in the street then it shouldn't be overlooked when it happens online. Girls shouldn't grow up expecting and accepting that sexual harassment is part of the package deal of womanhood. We know most girls will experience sexual harassment for the first time as children, so the effort to stamp it out has to start young too.

## TIPS: How to be an active bystander

Okay, so you're bored of women going *on and on* about sexual harassment. You're one of the good guys, right? Why does this have anything to do with you?

Everyone can be part of the solution to create a safer digital and physical world for women and girls. And the faster we achieve equality, the faster women will stop *going on* about it – if that's what's bothering you. It's a win all around.

Here are a few ways you can begin your journey to be an ally to women:

- **Call it out.** If you see a woman being sexually harassed or made to feel uncomfortable, be an active bystander and call it out. If it's safe to do so, tell the perpetrator (your mate?) to leave her alone. If you don't feel comfortable doing that, try interrupting them by asking the woman if she is okay or sparking up a conversation about the next tube/bus. This can work by creating a barrier between the perpetrator and the woman or distracting the perpetrator who will hopefully move on.

- **Allyship online.** Calling out sexual harassment if you see it online is also really important. A lot of men feel brave to act out harmful behaviours online because they get away with it. Having another man pipe up in the comments with a simple 'that's not cool' or kick them out of the Xbox Live Stream for harassing the only woman in the game can make them think twice about their behaviours. Also, help the woman out by reporting the behaviour to the platform. The burden shouldn't always be on the victim to act.

- **Why are you saying that?** Intention can be a big part of recognising inappropriate behaviour. Before you slide into their DMs with the 'monkey covering the eyes' emoji alongside a suggestive comment about their body, take a pause and think of what your intention behind sending it is. Likelihood is you're not sending it because you think it will make them feel good, also known as a compliment. You're probably sending it because you're horny and want to try your luck. If the intention is in your best interests and not theirs, it's best to leave it behind.

- **Do the work.** Commit to being an active ally and do the work. There are lots of free bystander courses available online that can help you understand how to step in and call out sexual harassment. White Ribbon is the UK's leading charity in engaging men and boys in ending violence against women and girls and they are always looking for male ambassadors to take their message into workplaces and communities. If this sounds too big and scary, why not start a conversation with your mates about this book and promise to pass it on to them when you're finished with it. We can all start somewhere.

## TIPS: What can I do to minimise online harms?

Of course, it shouldn't be on us as women to protect ourselves from male violence but on the perpetrators to change their behaviour. Unfortunately, we still live in a world where misogyny is rife in both our online and offline worlds. While we wait for societal attitudes to change and legislation to catch up, there are a few steps we can take to help protect ourselves from online abuse.

- **Put on the rose tinted glasses.** Utilise the hidden words feature on social media platforms to block out any words, people or conversations you may find triggering. Instagram, TikTok and X all offer the option for you to filter and hide certain words, so you can limit the type of content you are shown. TikTok offers a 'comment care mode' which will automatically filter potentially harmful comments and prevent them from being published. Head into the TikTok privacy setting to activate. I muted the words 'slut', 'slag' and 'whore' a long time ago, alongside the name 'Piers Morgan'.

- **Take control of your audience.** Although the call can sometimes be coming from inside the house, restricting your audience is a way to minimise the risk of online abuse. This could include making your social media accounts private or, if that's not possible, limit who can send you direct messages or leave comments on your posts. I've turned on the setting in Instagram that only allows people who have been following me for at least a week to comment on my posts. Because if you're going out of your way to follow me for a week just to leave hate, then that's fan behaviour. You can access this feature in the Instagram app by going to your settings and privacy tab and scrolling down to 'limit interactions'.

- **Report the account** to the social media platform. To the police. To their mum, who you've managed to track down on Facebook. Sexual coercion, threats and intimidation online is a criminal offence under the Protection from Harassment Act 1997 and perpetrators need to be held accountable. Even if just by getting a stern talking to by their mum (none of us are ever too old to have the 'I'm disappointed in you' talk).

- **Blocking out the haters.** It might be petty but my tolerance for any kind of negativity on my social media profiles has run out. If someone comments something negative or sends me unwanted sexual messages, I just block them. It's not worth your peace of mind.

# 3

# LEAKED

## Not yours to see, not yours to share

'It was like being electronically raped'
**Paris Hilton**

The classroom was alive with an orchestra of zestful sounds that ricocheted off the brightly painted walls: the dripping patter of old taps and paint brushes scraping the bottom of yoghurt pots weaved together effortlessly in a live-action ASMR YouTube video, designed to calm the nervous system. My friends and I sat around the large table gossiping about our weekend plans while I sketched away on my final project – a modern fairytale book where a princess falls in love with a postman – inspired by my awkward teenage phase of having a crush on our local postie. Ten minutes before the lesson was due to end, my creative flow was disrupted by the harsh vibrations coming from my Nokia phone, shaking me from my fairytale bliss. Reaching down into my Jane Norman shoulder bag (the must-have accessory of every teenage girl in the early 2000s), I grabbed my phone and tried to avoid the teacher's attention, punching the rubber keys to open a text message I had received from a boy I knew who was in year 13:

'Nice pictures ;)'

I held my phone under the table and re-read the message several times. *Nice pictures?* I'd had a couple of casual MSN conversations with this boy but I'd never sent him any photos.

My phone pinged again as another text came through, this time from a different year 13 boy who also referred to photos, adding how he didn't think I was 'that type of girl'. *What type of girl?* I could feel the panic begin to creep in, my fingertips throbbing with anxiety that crawled through the network of my veins. I gripped the edges of my plastic phone case and steadied my shaky hands, replying to their texts with a number of question marks in an attempt to seek some clarity. Lifting my pencil back up, I tried to distract myself from the cramped churning in my stomach, but the placid sketch strokes failed to settle my nerves, and my mind raced to the worst possible thought – *He wouldn't, would he?*

Eventually, one of the boys replied with a text that had two words: the first and last name of a boy from year 12 to whom I'd sent semi-naked pictures. *He had.* The soothing tones of the art room slipped into the background while my ears adjusted their frequency to the wave of nausea that crashed over my entire being, tuning in to the harsh buzz of the bright strip lights that hung above. My nervous system, previously calmed by the gentle classroom ambience, had fired into survival mode, circulating stress hormones throughout my body that made the prickly hair on my legs stand up.

*Everyone has seen my nudes.*

I was 15 years old, a child trapped in a womanly body that made me feel so grown up at times, and yet, I mourned the childhood innocence that my 28F boobs had taken away from me. I might have looked older in those photos, but I was still a child grappling with the premature sexualisation of my existence and how that shaped my relationship with my body and with myself.

Balancing my phone on the handles of my wardrobe and setting up the self-timer that day had felt a normal thing to do. I had experienced others passing comments on my pubescent body for years and it felt comforting to look at it through a third-person lens. The photo captured what they wanted me to be: a mature young woman who was eager to step into adult life and have sex with older boys. It was a stark contrast to the girl I knew through my own internal lens: a teenager who would retreat to my bedroom after school and sing every word to the *High School Musical* album before binge-watching episodes of *Hannah Montana*. I had been forced to mature far beyond my years by a body that signalled to the outside world that I was a woman, when inside, I was still just a girl.

*Why would he show them my intimate photos?*

*How many other people have seen me in my underwear?*

*And WTF are my mum and dad going to say?*

The bell for end of class rang out and I carried my daze into the corridor, pushing against the swarm of students who were elbowing their way through the crowd to the canteen. Their eyes darted towards me and landed on my itchy school jumper, their judgements wetting my palms with sweat. What were they all staring at? I could feel the redness creep up my neck as their whispers stripped me from my uniform, their sniggers redressing me in a cloak of shame. The clinical blue walls began to close in and for a period, I wished they'd squash me whole so I would disappear.

I soon discovered that the private photos of me in my underwear, covering my breasts, had been Bluetoothed around the entire sixth form block, transporting me to another world that re-imagined people's opinions of me. I was an alien, a spectacle, a thing for them to stare at. I was *that girl.*

My photos being leaked that day changed the trajectory of my life path. At 15 years old, I had to sink or swim, and I decided that I would take ownership of the slut-shaming and objectification that followed. As the months went on and the pictures spread throughout the entire school, I had year seven pupils run up to me in the corridor to tell me that they'd seen my photos and ask for a hug, like I was some kind of celebrity.

I would laugh and oblige, while secretly wanting to die. My parents found out about the pictures because my nan told them. My nan found out because someone told her how my photos had been circulated amongst the local men's football team, with grown adult men passing around my underage photos in the changing room. *Kill me now.* The final kick in the teeth was learning that if I went to the police about the leak, I could have gotten in trouble for distributing indecent images of children. If you are under 18, it is a criminal offence in the UK to take, have or distribute a sexual image, including selfies. This is called child self-generated imagery or video. The boy I sent the image to was also breaking the law by saving and sharing my images.

It all felt so unfair. I was embarrassed and exhausted. So, I decided to suck it up, laugh it off and eventually try to build a career out of the shame. Perhaps if everyone in my hometown hadn't seen me half-naked at 15 years old then I wouldn't have felt so emboldened to step into the world of glamour modelling when I turned 18. Making money out of my objectification was my way of trying to take back some type of power: *you've all seen my boobs, you all think I'm a slut, I might as well capitalise on it.* I couldn't be made to feel shame over something I chose to do. On reflection, it wasn't my wisest choice, but it was what I felt I needed at the time and a tough life lesson on the path towards my healing journey.

Five years after the photos were leaked, I was working behind a bar in a local pub when a group of men, including some who'd been at my school, started cracking loud jokes about my part-time job as a model, gleefully passing a phone between them. A short while later, they stumbled towards the bar, flashing the phone screen at me with a drunken smile – 'Jess, this is you, isn't it?!' It was the photo of me cupping my boobs aged 15 years old that had circulated through my school. I don't know why they had kept it all those years and I don't know if anyone still has it now. That's the harsh reality of the internet – once your image is out there, you can't control where it goes or what happens to it. I had trusted one boy with my private photo when I was a teenager and it was still in circulation amongst grown men half a decade on. It wasn't their body to see, and it wasn't their body to share.

## What is image-based sexual abuse?

Sending nudes might feel like a modern phenomenon, but the human race has been communicating erotically long before Apple's iPhone ever came about. The technologies may have changed over time, but our ancestors' eagerness to engage in sexual communications as a show of appreciation of the human form dates back thousands of years – the first example we have being *A Love Song for Shu-Suen*, thought to date back to around 2000 BCE (and to have been written by a woman). Fast forward through the centuries and almost every medium you can imagine has been used to create erotic art and represent bodies. Humankind's history of sexual communications is so extensively rich, I could argue it's practically in our DNA to get a little bit freaky through creative forms. Exchanging nude pics can be an exciting and fun way of building connection, satisfying the horn or getting an ego boost from a grateful recipient. But the unprecedented expansion of the internet and adoption of social media as a way of life saw a black hole open up, where legislation and the ethics around internet use fell short.

### IMAGE-BASED SEXUAL ABUSE (AKA 'REVENGE PORN')

*Definition:* When someone takes and shares, or threatens to share, sexually explicit photos or videos of someone without their consent.

Image-based sexual abuse is a stubborn stain on the internet that we just can't seem to clean up. In recent years, campaigners have rejected the phrase 'revenge porn' for its validation of non-consensual content as 'porn' and the victim-blaming element of the word 'revenge', that suggests the victim has done something to deserve punishment. Instead, campaigners and experts have adopted the term 'image-based sexual abuse' (shortened to IBSA), coined by Professor Clare McGlynn and Professor Erika Rackley. This term can also be used to describe other acts of intimate image abuse, like upskirting, downblousing and the creation of explicit deep fakes. Although the phrase 'revenge porn' is somewhat controversial, it is still widely used in legislation, by organisations and in media reporting, so please don't be alarmed – or cancel me – if you see it pop up again throughout this book.

The scale of non-consensual content being shared online is monumental. While researching for this book, I have logged on to messaging boards daily, each time being met with hundreds of new uploads featuring naked women from across the world. For all the research and statistics that exist, it is impossible to get a handle on the *millions* of victims, mostly women, who have lost total control over their private images and videos. The stats that are out there are terrifying, and yet experts suggest they are widely undercounted due to the nature of IBSA that means most victims don't even know that their images or videos have been taken or shared.

*48 per cent of people have experienced or know someone who's experienced image-based sexual abuse.*

In 2024, cyber security firm Kasper Sky conducted one of the largest global polls on IBSA, using a sample of 9,033 people aged 16 and over. 'The Naked Truth' report found almost half of all respondents had either experienced IBSA themselves or knew someone who had. That number jumped significantly in younger generations, with 69 per cent of 16–24-year-olds having experienced or knowing someone who has experienced IBSA, along with 64 per cent of 25–34-year-olds. Research by Professor Nicola Henry, Professor Clare McGlynn et al on the causes and consequences of non-consensual imagery found LGBTQ+ people and those from Black and minority communities were disproportionately victimised. This highlights that all-important word that keeps on popping up – intersectionality – showing how hate crimes, discrimination and abuse are inherently linked with online misogyny.

The Revenge Porn Helpline is a free UK service that supports adults who have experienced IBSA. Since their launch in 2015, they have successfully removed over 305,000 intimate images that were shared online without consent. In their 2023 Annual Report, their findings showed a 106 per cent increase in reports to their services from 2022. Horrifyingly, a 2024 report by Internet Matters found one in seven young people, some as young as 11, had experienced abuse relating to the online sharing of their nude images.

*71 per cent of images being shared without consent were of women. Where the perpetrator was known, 81 per cent were male*

IBSA is a gendered harm that overwhelmingly targets women and girls. A 2022 report on UK victims of IBSA by the Victim's Commissioner for England and Wales found women are consistently more likely to be victims of this harm across all age groups. Their findings showed the highest proportion of victims – 27 per cent – were women between the ages of 30–39, with 15 per cent being women aged 21–29 and 10 per cent girls aged 16 years and under. The Revenge Porn Helpline's 2023 report showed 71 per cent of cases they received of intimate images being shared without consent were of women. Where the perpetrator was known, 81 per cent were male. There is now a market for these images, which has resulted in communities being formed where men trade women's images with each other.

This doesn't mean men and boys don't experience IBSA – all genders can have their images and videos taken and distributed without their consent. But the way men and boys experience IBSA is significantly different. The Revenge Porn Helpline reports that men are most likely to contact them for help with sextortion cases, which is a form of blackmail that usually involves a case of fake identity (also known as catfishing). Ninety per cent of perpetrators involved in male cases were criminal gangs who are often behind romance scams. We'll be taking a closer look at the worrying rise in sextortion and its danger for teenage boys a little later on in the book.

Sophie Mortimer is the manager at the Revenge Porn Helpline and has seen the devastating effect being a victim of IBSA can have on all areas of someone's life: nearly 60 per cent of individuals who contact the helpline require signposting to mental health services. She told me how some women feel they can't go to work after their private content has been shared at their workplace, with many victims choosing to hide themselves away indoors: 'People might go to the local shop and think that *the man in the shop is looking at me funny, I'm sure he's seen my pictures.* The chances of that happening are absolutely minuscule, but that's not how it feels to that person and that feeling can be so debilitating that they end up not leaving their home and just searching the internet constantly for their images. Which is really, really damaging.'

I've been in that spiral of googling myself relentlessly, reporting photos that I had taken for my members' website when I was 19 years old that had since been uploaded onto porn sites that I'd never consented for them to be on. Each time I clicked on a photo of myself that appeared in the image search results, four more suggestions would pop up underneath, each one hosted on different sites or forums. The way they'd spread across the internet was paralysing. It highlighted that I had lost any control or understanding of where they now existed.

*92 per cent of IBSA cases included ex-partners as perpetrators*

Sharing and threatening to share sexual images and videos is often about power and control, and a continuation of other forms of gender-based violence. The engrained societal stigma of shame around women's bodies and their sexuality allows perpetrators to weaponise naked photos and videos to cause maximum harm, or to silence women into obedience. Crown Prosecution data in 2022 revealed 92 per cent of the IBSA cases sampled included ex-partners as perpetrators, while the other 8 per cent included current partners and one case where the victim was the partner of the suspect's friend. The victims were all women and girls except for one, while all the suspects were men, except for one case involving a woman. The data showed a concerning trend: suspects were often charged with additional offences, with 20 per cent of cases involving stalking charges and 18 per cent involving charges of assault.

Sophie Mortimer told me how the Revenge Porn Helpline has dealt with cases that have seen men submitting intimate images of ex-partners to family court proceedings – such as custody hearings – in an evidence bundle as an attempt to bring into question the woman's character: 'Now, what does that show other than the fact that she has a body that is doing a normal thing? She has kids; that didn't happen by magic. But they're playing into those deeply misogynistic attitudes towards women, women's bodies and female sexuality.' It's an uncomfortable reality that highlights how women's bodies and our sexuality are used to judge our humanity. Does a woman's ability to parent her child change because she took a photo of herself naked?

Sharing anyone's personal photos or videos without their consent is messed up, *period*. But there is a certain twisted betrayal in distributing intimate images or videos of your current or ex-partner. We give so much of ourselves to another under the assumption of unwavering trust – for them to go on to break that by sharing us at our most vulnerable and hand over the reins of mass distribution to strangers online is an unforgivable act. To put it frankly, what type of sick bastard does that? Well, a lot of them actually.

Kaspersky's 'The Naked Truth' report told the story of Alice*, whose partner of ten years passed away after a long-term illness, which saw her take on the role of his carer. After her partner's passing, Alice received several messages from strangers on Instagram that informed her that her nude pictures were circulating online. She initially dismissed them as spam, knowing she'd never taken any naked photos so it couldn't possibly be true. However, a month later, Alice received another DM which featured a screenshot from a porn site that included her full name alongside a derogatory message. Distressed and confused, Alice turned to the Revenge Porn Helpline, who found several intimate images of Alice that had been shared across a number of websites. The photos were voyeuristic in their nature and seemed to have been taken while Alice was asleep or intoxicated. The only person who could have taken images of her in those vulnerable situations was her late partner. What a sucker punch to the soul for someone who is grieving the loss of their life-partner, only to find out they've been betrayed by a person they never really knew.

In my conversation with Sophie Mortimer, we questioned the thought processes of the many men who felt entitled to share women's intimate content, even if it was originally taken and sent to them consensually. 'I always say my husband's got access to my bank account, but that doesn't mean I would think it's okay for him to plunder it if we had a row or split up, so why would sharing images or videos be any different?' Sophie asked. 'Do you know what couples do? They trust each other and they share things that they don't share with other people. If some people go on and abuse that trust, that's where the issue is for me.'

The issue and blame should lie solely with the perpetrator who is taking or sharing them without consent and not with the person whose trust has been broken. Unfortunately, women know all too well that this often isn't the case. And it can make them scared to share their experience as a victim of IBSA due to the blame society shifts onto them which can have long-lasting effects on their personal and public relationships. Cultural factors also play a huge role in the shame women feel around IBSA and their choice not to disclose, which is reflected in the lack of representation of Black and minority communities amongst survivors who've publicly shared their stories.

When my mum found out about my intimate photos and how they'd been shared at school, she was angry and asked why I'd sent them. I didn't really have an answer to why – I just sent them because he had asked me to. I never thought they'd end up in the hands of 20-something-year-old men or that my nan would see them. I know her reaction came from a place of worry and wanting to protect me, and both my parents were furious that my images had been shared without my consent, but I couldn't shift the feeling that people thought what had happened to me was my stupid fault.

This sense of blame is something Mortimer sees a lot at the helpline. 'So often, the first thing that somebody says to you is "Why did you do that? Why did you send that picture? If you didn't send that picture in the first place, then this wouldn't have happened." That's the wrong thing to say because that then goes around the person's head and that's the bit that they can't cope with.'

As someone who's experienced the all-encompassing feeling of wanting the ground to give way underneath you due to the embarrassment of having your private photos shared amongst those who were never meant to see them, I can promise you that I have been asking myself why I sent them ever since. Trust me, you do not need to ask someone that question too. Mortimer reiterated the importance of avoiding victim-blaming when dealing with cases of IBSA: 'We're always trying to come back to this idea that you're not on your own, there is help, we can do something about this, and you haven't done anything wrong. That's always an important thing to focus on – this isn't your fault.'

The Revenge Porn Helpline truly do God's work and are a vital organisation to have in your back pocket, if you ever find you need them. Do you remember how as kids we would memorise the Childline phone number off by heart and use it to threaten our parents with if they dared 'parent' us a little too hard?* That's what I think every woman should do with the Revenge Porn Helpline's number. I've spoken with women who've used the helpline in their hour of need who have said it quite literally saved their life.

*Call the helpline on 0345 6000 459*

∎

Ellesha was 22 years old when her life was turned upside down with a single text that started 'I don't want to worry

---

* And by parent us a little too hard, I mean being grounded for using the F word and missing out on a trip to the cinema to see *Shrek the Third*. OMG, Mum, you're SO unfair!

you but . . .' – a phrase sure to send anyone into an immediate spiral. The message was from a woman called Kelly*, who was the most recent ex-partner of Ellesha's ex-boyfriend with whom she had split up a few months prior. Kelly had reached out to Ellesha previously, recognising that they both must've experienced the same toxic relationship and wanting to check in on her mental health.

Ellesha described the relationship with her ex as being 'as bad as it could essentially get without being physical', telling me she had been mentally and emotionally abused by a man with a history of violence towards women. 'I found out whilst I was with him that he'd been to prison previously for harassment. Both he and his parents really played it down; they completely manipulated the situation and made it out to be some sort of retaliation to him being domestically abused and how he'd lost control of who he was and what he was doing.'

When Ellesha informed Kelly during one of their chats that their mutual ex had a murky past, Kelly turned to the internet in an attempt to uncover the truth of what else he had been hiding from them. The two women expected to find evidence that their ex had been cheating but instead they discovered a more sinister betrayal.

When the text came through, Ellesha was out shopping with her parents. 'We were on holiday – just me, my mum and my dad. I was stood in the middle of the shopping centre, and I just got this message that said, "I don't want to worry you, but I think you need to look at this." Then she sent through these Pornhub links.' At first, Ellesha thought Kelly must've been hacked and ignored the messages, believing them to be spam, until a follow-up text came through a short while afterwards. 'She said, "I'm really scared, Ellesha, I think this might be you." It was then that I was like, okay, this is serious.'

Making her excuses to avoid an awkward conversation with her parents, Ellesha left them in the shopping centre and headed back to their accommodation. 'I walked back fretting, worrying. My heart was in my mouth the whole way, just pre-empting what might be on there, and I was racking my brain thinking, *why would I be on Pornhub?* I've never taken anything; I've never videoed anything, so what is it?'

As soon as she walked through the door, Ellesha clicked and opened the link that would change everything. 'I watched the videos and I realised that whilst we'd been having sex and I wasn't facing him, my ex had picked his phone up and videoed us. Not once but twice. At least, that's the ones he had posted.' Ellesha's ex-boyfriend had set up a public profile on Pornhub using his real name and email address where he shared multiple solo videos alongside two videos of Ellesha that she had not consented to being taken or shared, with a title that referenced 'fucking the ex'. Ellesha knew that what he'd done was illegal, remembering how she'd previously refused his offer of filming them. 'On several occasions when he asked, I'd told him no, so he knew where I stood with that and yet he took it upon himself to do it anyway.'

The day after she returned from her holiday, Ellesha headed straight to her local police station to file a report. 'It's really strange to go in and talk about you having sex to someone that you've never met before. I was always quite a private person, so I found it really difficult.' Her experience seemed promising at first, with the police officers showing empathy towards her situation and avoiding any victim-blaming, but as their conversation unfolded, it became apparent to Ellesha that the police weren't quite sure what to do next. They were unable to access Pornhub on the station computers due to the site being blocked, leaving Ellesha with the task of collecting evidence.

'It was like, we need you to go home, we need you to screenshot the site, we need you to screen record the videos, we need you to get as much information as you can from the site. Can you get the details of stuff like if it's been downloaded, how many times it's been viewed, any comments, what dates they were uploaded.' It seems a heavy task for a young woman who had just found out the life-altering news that her ex-partner was not who he said he was to have to immediately revisit her trauma on screen.

Before she left, the police disclosed to Ellesha that her ex was wanted in another city for a similar report made by someone else. 'At that point, I was like, okay, he's fucked then, surely? That made me feel a little bit more hopeful because I was like, surely he can't get away with it if he's done it to two separate people?' Ellesha collected all the information and evidence the police had asked for and returned to hand it over, hoping for an end to the nightmare that, unbeknownst to her, had only just begun.

Two months after Ellesha's initial report and with pushback from Pornhub, who did not respond to emails requesting information on the case or remove the illegal content, her ex was arrested and, on his release, he deleted any trace of his Pornhub account, taking all evidence with him. 'That was it. He never had his phone taken off him, the police never looked through his phone. They had no intention at all in taking or retaining any evidence.'

In the UK, perpetrators of non-consensual intimate image abuse are not legally required to have their devices taken away. It is also not a legal requirement for criminals who have been convicted of IBSA to delete the images or videos they have been convicted of sharing. So they can remain online, with the threat of repeat sharing and the knowledge that their abusers still have access to their intimate content retraumatising victims.

Ellesha spent the two months following the arrest chasing the Crown Prosecution Service (CPS) for an update. 'I needed to know what was going on. I was fed up of looking over my shoulder and googling myself twice, three times daily to see if I'd popped up on some other site.' Eventually, Ellesha received a response from the CPS, which said they wouldn't be charging her ex-boyfriend for taking and sharing the intimate videos due to a lack of evidence. 'It was really shit. I felt trapped because I was like, I don't know what to do now. I know he's done this to me and he's full-on gotten away with this, and I don't know how to sort that out.'

Ellesha told me how they had both played the same sport and socialised in the same circles, with the experience affecting her personal relationships after she spoke out about what had happened to her in an attempt to protect other women. 'I thought, *I'm just going to tell you all because if it's going to stop other girls from looking at him twice and that's going to protect those girls, even if it means I'm going to get slated for it, I'll do that.* And I did get slated, I got told I was unfair for pursuing legal action against him. I was unfair for calling him out. But nothing changed for him at all. No one even batted an eyelid. Nothing changed for him and yet everything changed for me.'

Ellesha's experience happened in 2018. Since then, legislation on image-based sexual abuse has been updated in the UK. Sharing or threatening to share intimate videos without consent can lead to a six-month prison sentence. If the perpetrator shared the content with the intent to cause distress, harm or humiliation, or for sexual gratification, then they face a two-year prison sentence and will be put on the Sex Offenders Register.

However, although 'revenge porn' laws have been in place in the UK since 2014, research by Refuge in 2023 found just 4 per cent of all intimate image offences recorded across the 24 police forces that responded to their FOI request saw the alleged offender charged or summonsed. Twenty-two per cent of the recorded offences resulted in no further action due to 'evidential difficulties'; examples given by Refuge include perpetrators likely being asked by police to attend a voluntary initial interview that provides a window to delete evidence, and police being unsure of what evidence they would require to proceed with an

IBSA case. Refuge report helping one woman whose own phone was taken by police as evidence, instead of the perpetrator's. The Revenge Porn Helpline are calling on the government to update IBSA laws to include 'court-ordered deletion of illegal content and the permanent confiscation and destruction of devices that contain illegally shared non-consensual intimate images'.

## Celebrity sex tapes: stolen content is not a porn genre, it's a crime

I was born in 1993, a cohort of a generation of half-bloods that got to experience a unique childhood muddled with cassette tapes, SMS texting and mass internet expansion. On a Sunday, I'd go with my parents to the local car boot sale, where I'd rummage through random, useless items that sat on worn blankets laid out on the grass looking for Barbie dolls to add to my collection, before spending the drive home caring for the digital pet that lived inside my Tamagotchi. Life was simple and yet complicated.

Pop culture's crazed obsession with celebrities reached new heights in the early noughties, with paparazzi tussling on the street to get their exclusive, journalists bugging stars' hotel rooms and MTV reality TV shows inviting us into famous people's homes for the very first time. The general public had an insatiable appetite for all the salacious details of a celebrity's life with their privacy stripped from them by new technologies. We watched on with glee, salivating at the tear-down of their carefully curated Hollywood image and relishing the exposé of our favourite actors' messy, imperfect lives, that made us feel a tiny bit better about our own. It was an era obsessed with sordid details and one which birthed the phenomenon of an infamous 1990s icon, the celebrity sex tape.

# LEAKED

The theft and leaking of Pamela Anderson and Tommy Lee's sex tape in 1995 led to a surge in demand for stolen content that saw leaked images and videos become its own 'porn' genre. Adult entertainment companies would buy the rights to leaked films, selling physical VHS copies and publishing the videos on the internet, while the front pages of newspapers were plastered in headlines reporting on their release and the inside pages hosted stills from the films. Celebrity sex tapes were marketed like blockbuster movies, designed to draw as many eyes as possible to the screen, but one conversation was always absent from their promo trail – they didn't have consent to be sharing them.

In 2003, media personality and businesswoman Paris Hilton became a victim of IBSA when her ex-boyfriend Ricky Salomon released a video of them having sex on the internet, which he then sold and distributed on DVD in 2004 with pornographic film studio Red Light District. Hilton was 19 years old in the film while Salomon was 31. When it was released, she shared a statement that said she had not consented to the tape being released publicly, but that didn't stop millions of people flocking to view a teenage Hilton engaging in sex acts, which reportedly saw Salomon rake in $10 million dollars in the first year alone. Despite Hilton speaking out about the non-consensual nature of the film's release, publications continued to report on the tape, making light of a case that nowadays would see Salomon face prison time. In an online article for *Esquire* published in April 2017, journalist Paul Schrodt reviewed celebrity sex tapes ranking them 'by cinematic value'. The piece opens with Schrodt proudly saying he'd watched dozens of celebrity sex tapes and pondering some questions that the films had left him with:

'Are they being themselves?
Are they acting?
Are they acting well?'

I wonder if the question of consent and whether the women intended for him to see their intimate tapes ever occurred to him during his viewing sprees? Schrodt ranks Hilton's tape at number eight, claiming she was 'so bored out of her mind that at one point she stops to answer her phone' and scoffing at a comment Salomon makes in the film where he claims, 'It looks like we're having a good time', with Schrodt pointing out, 'No, it doesn't, Rick. It really doesn't.' If it looks like Hilton is bored and not having a good time, it might be down to her claim that she was 'out of it' on drugs and alcohol during the filming and had been pressured by Salomon to create the tape.

Hilton had spoken publicly about the questionable ethics around the video long before Schrodt wrote his article, but that didn't stop him from including it in his piece and potentially drawing new eyes to a non-consensual video. It's hard to believe that just six months after the *Esquire* article was published, the #MeToo movement swept the internet, calling out the predatory nature of Hollywood and raising awareness of rape culture, sexual abuse, harassment and assault. In her documentary *This Is Paris*, Hilton likened the filming of the tape to being 'electronically raped', and in her memoir she told how she had called Salomon and begged him not to release it. His cold response was to insist that he had every right to sell something that belonged to him, leaving her shaken in shame and terror.

When you hear someone mention Paris Hilton's sex tape, do you think of Rick Salomon? Or is it Hilton's life that has been permanently altered and shaped by the non-consensual distribution of her sex tape as a teenager while the perpetrator who cashed in on her trauma gets to move on without shame? Pamela Anderson, Paris Hilton, Kim Kardashian – the men who feature alongside these women in their intimate videos are all second thoughts while the women are judged under the harsh public microscope for their equal role in a two-player game.

# LEAKED

The desire for leaked celebrity content reached new heights in 2014 with 'Celeb Gate'. Also known as 'The Fappening', Celeb Gate saw the private nude images and videos of hundreds of female celebrities uploaded online after their email and iCloud accounts were hacked and their content stolen. The women's private intimate images were distributed across several image boards and websites in an unthinkable invasion of privacy. We all knew that we were never supposed to see these women naked; we knew that we weren't the intended recipients of their intimate images and we knew about the violation of privacy that had to have taken place for us to be viewing them. And yet, so many people decided they did not care. Millions of individuals pushed aside the criminal aspect of the leaks to put their intrigue and sexual desire to see naked celebrities above the women's right to have a say over what happens to their bodies and who gets permission to see them. It was a display of wicked entitlement, with people holding the opinion that because the women worked in the entertainment industry then they weren't worthy of a private life.

Actor Jennifer Lawrence was one of the first celebrities to be targeted in the leak. At that time, she was riding a wave of success after fronting *The Hunger Games* franchise and winning her first Oscar for Best Actress playing the character Tiffany Maxwell in *Silver Linings Playbook*; it would be difficult to argue that the attack wasn't calculated to target a young woman who was at the peak of her career. When we rise, they try to knock us down. Lawrence's nude images had been taken for her boyfriend at the time and were now being circulated around the entire world. In a podcast for the *Hollywood Reporter* in 2017, Lawrence likened the leak to being 'gang-banged by the fucking planet' and described the experience as 'so unbelievably violating that you can't even put it into words'. Even though the years have passed, Lawrence said she is still struggling to come to terms with what happened and the fact anyone with access to the internet could pull up her intimate photos while at a barbecue with their mates or having a drink at the pub. The women whose images were involved in the leak went from movie stars to porn stars overnight.

Ryan Collins, a 36-year-old man from Pennsylvania, was found to be the ringleader of Celeb Gate; he had used a phishing scam to obtain his 600-plus victims' usernames and passwords. Collins was sentenced to 18 months in a federal prison for the violation of the Computer Fraud and Abuse Act. One and a half years behind a jail cell. That was it. Meanwhile, Lawrence has spoken of never shaking the feeling that having her privacy violated had left her with, telling *Vogue* she is on edge whenever her publicist calls, waiting to be blindsided with life-shattering news once more.

Under UK law, while taking and distributing an intimate image of someone without their consent is a crime, non-consensual intimate images are not classified as illegal content – so tech platforms are not required by law to take them down, even when it is known what they are. And of course, the longer the content stays on a website, the more likely it will be redistributed. The nature of 'revenge porn' and being a victim of IBSA means you are repeatedly violated and retraumatised every single time someone chooses to share your naked body with the world, again. It is a digital sex crime that has no expiry date.

Three other men were also charged in the 2014 hacking scandal, receiving between 9- and 18-month sentences. The Fappening website still exists and hosts thousands of hacked and stolen intimate images from hundreds of female celebrities and content creators. Including me.

## Collectors culture: we are women, not Pokémon cards

When I was a child, my dad collected stamps and coins that were neatly stashed away in large red folders that rarely made a trip down from the attic. In my early teenage years, my brother and the other boys that lived on our street would gather on the kerb outside our house to trade Pokémon cards. It's giving wholesome nostalgic vibes. But today, men have found a new hobby to turn their attentions to: collecting and trading women's stolen and leaked nude images across forums that act as filing cabinets for non-consensual content. Men forage amongst the female body parts seeking out the rarest memorabilia and their personal fan favourites to add to their collections, filling out their World Cup sticker book with breasts and vulvas of unknowing women from across the globe.

One popular forum that refers to itself as an adult social media company recently moved most of its content behind a paywall after it was temporarily shut down in 2018 by Dutch police during an investigation into the stolen intimate images hosted on the site. The forum boasts an online 'Slut database', with an archive of 3TB (terabytes) that stretches back 14 years. There is no mention on the site of any men featuring in the archive. I asked Google how many images 3TB of storage could hold. It depends on the image quality, but I'm going to assume most of the photos were taken on a smart phone – that means we could be looking at anything from 750,000 to upwards of 1 million pictures stored in this one archive.

On the forums that host leaked content, the women are often categorized geographically or by their relationship to the perpetrator, with men advertising their stocks and opening up their portfolio to trade with others.

'I'm looking to trade pics and vids of ex's for gfs and other ex's drop your snaps below and I'll add up'

'Trading my exes nudes/arab'

'I have teen leaks. Hit me up'

'Trading my gf and her friend'

The names of towns and cities from across the UK fill up the forum threads with men hunting down the explicit content of women in their local area, trading their collection of nude images that they've acquired through the years by hacking private social media accounts or having been sent them by a woman with an expectation of trust and privacy that has been cruelly broken. One image forum website dedicated to women's leaked and stolen images has 5,420,644* members, with a forum called 'Local Girls – United Kingdom' holding 81 pages and 1.6k thread topics that all list geographical locations:

'Hull' 1k replies. 478k views

'2022 Isle of Wight' 827 replies. 574k views

'Newcastle/Sunderland' 1k replies. 1 million views

'Glasgow/Scotland' 4k replies. 3 million views

'Any North Wales or Anglesey girls?' 755 replies. 279k views

It became obvious to me that no town or city is safe from the men who had decided these women, many of them known to them personally, were nothing but objects – collateral damage that they were willing to sacrifice for their obsession with sex

---

* While writing this chapter, I often revisited this forum for research. With each visit, the members tally increased, one time gaining 5,000 members in just 72 hours.

and the camaraderie of fellow men. The word 'bro' was littered throughout posts of naked women and men exchanged Telegram and Discord usernames to continue their chats in private groups in their attempt to evade being caught.

One member advertised his large haul of Welsh women's nudes:

> Have a welsh mega for sale 30gb, 340 folders,
> 5400 files
> £5 via cashapp
> dm for details if interested

Is it possible that my photos are being sold in this mega folder? My body cringed at the thought. Other men replied to the member's advert with contempt – not because they were disgusted at how he was illegally selling intimate images of hundreds of women, but because he dared to want money for them.

> 'I have it free lads we're here to trade and help each other out'

> 'Or you can get from me for free because I'm not an ass hole'.

I dunno mate, I think the women whose images you are sharing would argue differently.

## MEGA

*Definition:* a large collection of content that is stored in folders on online databases. They can be downloaded via a link.
*Example:* 'Anyone got a mega link/mega folder of Jess Davies?'

Men on this forum often post their requests for intimate images of specific women, often called 'wins' – ('Looking for any wins of XXX', 'Share your wins of XXX lads'). Some will share rumours they've heard of certain girls' images being leaked as they try to track them down ('Is there anything of Lucy? Friends with Mia and a massive slut – would be shocked if there's nothing out there of her'), while others will post their request in the hope of uncovering an exclusive ('Sussex sisters. Must be nudes on ex-bfs phones etc?'). Underneath the women's images that do get posted, the men make sure to let the others know their verdict:

> 'Manchester Milf – She'd get taken to an empty park and shagged'

> 'Louise milf 36. She'd get dragged into an alleyway and fucked up her top hole'

> 'Teasing 19yr old slut – Fucking slut keeps teasing wish someone would r4pe her good.'

It's in moments like these where I feel nothing but rage. I try my best to believe 'not all men', but here in these forums where thousands of women's bodies are swapped, rated and degraded by *millions* of men, it is extremely difficult to hold space and empathy for the 'good guys'. If this is what millions of men think is an acceptable way to treat women, then, simply put – we're fucked.

An international study of IBSA victims and perpetrators by Powell et al found one in six respondents had engaged in IBSA perpetration, with most victims being targeted by known perpetrators. If one in six people are self-disclosing their role in perpetrating IBSA, I can only imagine what the real figures are, including those who didn't feel comfortable admitting to a crime.

In 2021, a woman from my hometown contacted me on Facebook for some advice after her private images were shared on a forum without her consent under a thread seeking out nudes of Aberystwyth girls. A small coastal town in mid-Wales, Aberystwyth has a population of 14,000 that swells during term time with an additional 8,000 students. It is one of those towns where everyone knows everyone, and the woman told me that news of her leaked images had become hot gossip. She sent me a link to the site. It was one I hadn't come across before, but it looked similar to most others with endless posts made by anonymous members. The discovery made me wonder how the men from my small, coastal town that was the end-stop on a single-track train line were finding foreign message boards that hosted this illegal content. And not only that, but clearly enough of them were active on the site to be fulfilling each other's requests for local girls' images.

The woman sent me a follow up message: 'I've just seen you're also on there.' *Fucking fantastic.* I combed through the 653 search results:

'Anyone got Aberystwyth sluts?'

'Any Aberystwyth nudes?'

'Aberystwyth nudes. Anyone got trades?'

'Any Aberystwyth babes in the nude?'

Seeing so much activity around my hometown was sobering. With each click, I readied myself to see the private photos of a woman I had gone to school with, while sitting in the bitter reality that I probably knew the men who were sharing her images. If my small, liberal Welsh town that brimmed with familiar faces wasn't safe from online perpetrators and the collectors culture trend then every other town or city in the UK must be the same. These forums allowed men to have instant access to the naked bodies of women in their lives.

I discussed this uncomfortable familiarity with Sophie Mortimer. She told me about a comment posted on a forum about a woman the helpline was supporting that had always stuck with her: 'He said, "I really like talking to her boyfriend knowing that I've seen his girlfriend's nudes and he doesn't know." Why would you get a kick out of that? But clearly he did and he was very proud to say that.' Mortimer stressed how these men were moving in the same circles as the women that they were targeting. 'So who do you trust? This is your brothers, your friends, your cousins, your fathers – these are the people that you circulate with.'

■

Kate Isaacs is the founder of NotYourPorn, a UK-based movement to protect non-consenting adults, sex workers and under 18s from IBSA. She became an accidental campaigner while doing a market research job when her friend's iCloud account was hacked and private videos of her having sex with her then-boyfriend were uploaded onto multiple porn sites without her consent, including Pornhub. After doing some digging, Kate discovered it was completely legal at the time for the website to host this content, thanks to their user-upload platform which devolved them of responsibility and a now-updated loophole in the 'revenge porn law' that meant requiring consent did not apply to businesses. Recalling the discovery, Kate said, 'I just remember this bubbling fury inside of me where I was so angry. I was angry for my friend because she was falling apart and she felt so exposed and so assaulted in that process, and then on the other hand, I was also furious for every single woman out there. It became bigger than her. The campaign NotYourPorn was born out of fury and fear.'

Her anger ignited a flame in Kate that she was determined to keep alive until some sort of justice was served for her friend and all the other women who had their intimate content shared without their consent. 'I don't think anyone in their right mind would be able to stop because you can't just go back to your normal life and forget about that. So that's what I did, I kept digging.'

The campaign kicked up a notch when she collaborated with the *Sunday Times* on an investigation which turned up child sexual abuse images on the platform. Eventually, Kate's campaigning caught the attention of Pornhub. Their PR team reached out and offered to work with her, but things quickly turned south on a phone call. 'As soon as I started producing facts – like we just found this underage content on your site and my friend didn't consent to being on this website – they got very, very defensive very quickly.'

Kate told me that a representative on the call suggested they could relate to how her friend must feel. 'A woman said, "We actually get a lot of our videos stolen from us and uploaded to other websites so in a way we're victims too," and she laughed. And I just thought in that moment *this woman is so disconnected from reality.*' Kate's campaigning against Pornhub went on for almost two years, until one day she had the lightbulb moment to hit them where it really hurts, deciding to go after their payment providers, Visa and Mastercard. 'We presented them with all of the evidence that we had and testimonies from victims and survivors, and all the content that the *Sunday Times* had found which discovered children on the site. We sent everything to them, and we said you're working with this company who are actively promoting this content that is illegal and we're going to tell the world about it so you might want to rethink your relationship.'

Kate never heard back directly from Visa or Mastercard, but a short while later, the payment providers announced in the media that they were going to carry out internal investigations into Pornhub and suspend their payment services, leading to a mass panic at Pornhub, which saw them purge 80 per cent of their content, roughly 10 million videos, overnight. Kate remembers, 'I woke up and I was just like, *what's just happened?*

It was such a surreal moment, it was just wild.' Along with Kate's campaigning, an investigation by *The New York Times* had also raised concerns around non-consensual and underage content on Pornhub; the mass purge was of all videos on their site for which they couldn't verify the ages of participants, or had no record that participants had consented for the video to be on the site.

Multiple videos from my subscription website had been uploaded to Pornhub against my strict instructions to those running my site not to promote me on any porn site. Dozens of my videos had been uploaded on the platform by multiple users over the course of years, and although I'd contacted the website to get them removed, they stayed where they were, for everyone to see. I cried many tears over those videos being on that site; I'd hated filming them, I hated that millions of people could now watch them and I hated that there was nothing I could do about it. I felt powerless, until Kate came along.

I hadn't met her at the time but her campaign work directly helped me, and millions of other women, to claim back a sense of control over our bodies. Recollecting that day when Pornhub removed millions of their videos, Kate said, 'I remember feeling incredibly proud, but it was one of those campaigns that never felt finished. When I posted that announcement on Instagram, it felt like we won a battle but not the entire war; it felt like a victory but not a celebration because we weren't done. We were never done. We're dealing with the internet – it's never going to be finished and that was incredibly daunting.'

Two years after the mass exodus, I met Kate to interview her about the fallout from her campaign – which saw her home address doxed online and her face edited into deepfake 'pornography' – for a BBC Three documentary. Sitting opposite the woman who had lifted a heavy cloud of shame off of my shoulders, watching her eyes fill with tears as she told of the abuse she had faced because of her selfless work to help women like me was deeply moving, and a poignant turning point in my life. Kate lit a fire inside me that day that I have not stopped tending to since. It is one that I hope I can pass on to you through this book because together our small embers can unite to burn down the system that is keeping women in chains and men in their man-boxes.

Look, I get it, *not all men* are perpetrators who are actively engaging in harm towards women, but *plenty* of them are voyeurs who watch on from the sidelines and profit from our pain. The scale of image-based sexual abuse is catastrophic, with women from towns across the UK having their intimate images immortalised in cyberspace for eternity, thanks to the men that they live alongside. How are women supposed to feel safe in our offline communities knowing we are being traded online like Pokémon cards by our exes and our colleagues? But then, even Pokémon cards are treated with more respect and admiration than the women whose intimate images are uploaded to the forums alongside degrading and violent commentary. I'd bet these men would never trade their precious, priceless collectors' cards for free – but women's naked bodies? They pass them around like a pack of gum. The men who've adopted the hobby of collecting and trading women's nude images are not partaking in an innocent pastime, they are ruining women's lives.

It is time for the 'good guys' to actively engage in calling out the casual behaviour of their peers who share women's intimate images in the lads' group chat or pass their phone around the table in the pub so everyone can have a look at her naked. Because each time you treat this predatory behaviour as banter – or worse, content that you get a kick from – you're validating the perpetrator and his negative attitudes towards women. A perpetrator who's called a 'legend' by his IRL mates then decides to seek out online communities to share a woman's private content with other men for a further ego boost, paying no mind to the trauma he will cause to the woman who can no longer pop out to the corner shop without coming across someone who has seen her naked body.

This nonchalant attitude towards women's bodies is all part of a dangerous pyramid of perpetrator escalation that needs to be acknowledged. The fact is that if a man feels comfortable publicly exploiting a woman's body online, then there is a high risk that his digital acts could escalate into physical harm somewhere down the line. And while correlation doesn't always equal causation, CPS findings show 18 per cent of 'revenge porn' cases also involve a charge of physical assault, which emphasises the importance of speaking out against perpetrators of IBSA, and the risk of real-world harm. In these forums, the men's anonymity allows them to feel safe expressing how they truly feel about the women in their communities, and this paints a pretty bleak picture – but these men are not anonymous in their offline worlds where their sexist and misogynistic behaviours often go unchecked. We need to cut off the desire for leaked content at source, which is why I'm calling this a rally cry for the good guys to step up and speak out when they hear of a woman's private pictures being shared without her consent.

If you are someone who has ever shared or received a nude pic then you have a duty to ensure those around you are responsibly engaging in sexual communications that keeps everyone safe – the same way you'd like your private photos to be treated. Even if you've never engaged in sexting before, any decent person should understand the role of consent in viewing and sharing someone's most intimate moments. To put it bluntly, if she wanted you to see her naked then she'd have sent you the photo herself. And if being a good person just isn't enough of a reason to treat women with a basic level of respect, perhaps knowing that by sharing someone's nudes without their consent, you are committing a crime that could land you in prison and on the Sex Offenders Register will be enough to encourage you to delete her pics and give the forums a miss.

Because no one wants to be mates with *that* guy.

## TIPS: What to do if your intimate images or videos have been leaked

Firstly, I'm sorry. It's shit. It's shit that someone would betray your trust like this – but take it from me, as someone who has seen *thousands* of folders of women's private content through my work, you're not alone in this and it doesn't need to ruin your life.

- Get a prenup for your nudes! Even if your content hasn't been leaked yet, submit your intimate photos and videos to https://stopncii.org. This is an incredible free preventative tool that uses technology to scan and create a 'hash' (digital footprint) of your photos that will be shared with participating companies including Meta, Pornhub and OnlyFans. Using the hash, they can track whether your intimate images/videos appear on their sites and have them removed. Not very romantic, but a smart move.

- As hard as it can be, screenshot any evidence you come across that someone has uploaded or shared your content as this can be used as evidence for police reports. Also, collect any information on usernames, URL links of the web pages and websites and the dates the content was shared.

- You can report the crime to the police either in person at your local police station, by calling the non-emergency number 101 or online at https://www.police.uk/pu/contact-us/.

- Reach out to the Revenge Porn Helpline who can offer free advice and support, and help you in tracing and taking down your content online. They also have a 24-hour chat bot called Reiya available on their site that can offer general support and advice. https://revengepornhelpline.org.uk

- Contact the website where your content was posted and inform them that the content has been shared illegally and request they remove it from their site. Many forums and sites have a 'contact' form or a DMCA (Digital Millennium Copyright Act) takedown section in their header or footer. When filing a DMCA takedown, you must include the link to where your content has been posted, a link to the original source or reference where it has been stolen from (mobile phone, Snapchat account, etc.) and a description of your ownership. For example: *'My intimate photo I took of myself on my iPhone and sent to an individual on WhatsApp was posted on this website without my consent and I would like it removed.'*

- You can submit a report to Google to request your photos not appear in search results, minimising the risk of the content being found. The link to file a report is: https://reportcontent.google.com/forms/rtbf

- If this all sounds too complicated, please use the Revenge Porn Helpline, as they can submit DMCA takedowns for you. Like I said before, they're doing God's work!

- If you are under 18 or know of someone who's under 18 and your/their private images or videos have been shared, you can anonymously report this to the Internet Watch Foundation who can help with removing child sex abuse content online https://report.iwf.org.uk/en or reach out to Childline UK.

- Telling someone that this has happened to you may seem difficult, but know that you don't need to feel shame or be embarrassed for someone else's bad behaviour. Sex is a normal part of everyday life and the person who shared your private content is the only one who should feel shame. Sharing what you're going through can help you feel less alone.

- For the love of God, if someone discloses to you that their nudes have been shared without their consent **do not ask them why they sent it**. Avoid victim-blaming language and reassure them that they have done nothing wrong and pop the kettle on – a cuppa makes everything better.

# 4

# LEAKED 2.0

## You've paid to view, but they're still not yours to share

'How quickly they learned that the stuff in their heads
was of less value than the shape of their bodies'
**Emily Ratajkowski**

When I was nine years old, my parents gifted me a karaoke machine for Christmas with an adult-sized microphone that would receive my screeches each evening after school. On a Sunday, I'd sit cross-legged beside the clunky machine to tape record Radio 1's Top 40 chart and play out my *Stars in Their Eyes* fantasy, dreaming of being transformed into Britney Spears within the four walls of my canary yellow bedroom. I had an unwavering belief that I was destined for the red carpet, telling anyone who would listen how I was going to be a popstar when I grew up. That dream came to a car-crash end when my teacher gave me strict instructions to mime in the school choir if I wanted to keep my place. So, at the ripe old age of 11 years old, I retired my quest to become the fourth member of Atomic Kitten and turned my attention to the next obvious career choice – I wanted to be a model. I'm not entirely sure where I pulled the confidence from at the time, sporting mousy blonde hair styled into choppy emo-layers and baby teeth that I held onto for way too long. But my star sign is an Aries and we do thrive being the centre of attention. This young, dumb confidence of mine led me to reach out to modelling agencies and at 18 years old, I signed my first contract with an agency in London.

I set firm boundaries from the get-go, telling my agent at the time that I would only shoot up to lingerie and swimwear level. Then, while on my first professional photoshoot, for *Nuts** magazine, I was made to compromise on this after a 'miscommunication' that led the booker to believe I was happy to be photographed topless. The photographer and I came to an agreement on set that saw me pose 'implied' topless, using my hands as a bra to cover my bare breasts – essentially replicating the pose in my private photo that had been circulated around my school just three years earlier and been such painful betrayal.

A few months after that first job, I was on another photoshoot where I was asked to wear a pink mesh bodysuit. I agreed, but only on the understanding with the photographer and my agent that my nipples would be edited out of the pictures, because, as we all knew, I didn't shoot topless content. Everyone agreed to my request and I trusted them to put it into practice. A month or so later, I received a message on Facebook from a fan who told me how much he loved my photos in *Nuts* magazine's summer special. *Huh? He must have it wrong. I hadn't shot for their summer special?* A quick Google search confirmed my biggest fear – there I was, printed in a magazine that had been sold in shops, scanned and shared on the internet, dressed in a fuchsia pink mesh bodysuit with my nipples proudly on display. My images had been sold to the magazine without being edited as I had asked. I remember crying in my mum's arms that day as she comforted me with the reassurance 'you look so pretty in

* For the Gen-Z babies who missed the magazine era, *Nuts* was a weekly lads' mag that featured topless women, cars and shit jokes.

the photos!' and how she 'didn't even notice' my nipples. She was lying, of course, but I appreciated that she still saw beauty in my eyes and my smile, and not just a body.

Soon enough, my boundaries had completely collapsed into a pathetic heap of lost hopes and broken promises. Encouraged by my agency at the time, I signed a contract to have my own official website which would include subscription content that members would pay a monthly fee to access. This was over ten years ago, before subscription sites such as OnlyFans and Patreon became common. The website was managed by a company and one of the clauses of my contract was that I would take 'selfie' photo sets that would be uploaded on to the site. Let me tell you, *I fucking hated taking these pictures* and I made sure everyone knew it.

For some women, their ambition is to be a glamour model and they find empowerment in taking their clothes off, and who am I to tell them that isn't empowering? But for me, taking my bra off was my least favourite part of the job. The young girl with the mousy blonde hair knew she wanted to be a model, but with my body shape and my height my options were limited, and so I compromised. I rolled my eyes and obliged each time a photographer instructed me to unclip the hooks of my bra because I enjoyed the warm, fuzzy feeling of the studio lights and the art of learning to contour my body in front of a lens. And then there was the pampering that would make my inner child squeal with joy. Taking my place in the make-up artist's chair, where they gently painted my face and curled my blonde locks, while a stylist pulled up beside us with a rail of hand-picked outfits, I felt as if I was back in my childhood bedroom again, living out my *Stars in Their Eyes* fantasy of being transformed into a superstar. In contrast, taking photos of myself on my phone in my dingy, student house share wearing my high-street pants did not have the same effect. I hold no judgement for anyone who makes their money creating amateur content, that is totally your choice and if that job makes you happy then I'm genuinely pleased for you, but it wasn't for me.

I tried my best to get out of taking the selfie sets but was told by those running my website that it was in my contract and so I had to do them. I was supposed to send a set weekly, but near enough each week I would be late uploading them or fail to send any photos at all, avoiding the dreaded task of snapping away that left me with a sinking sense of disappointment at what I'd managed to get myself into. Fed up with my lack of submissions, the website company told me that they would fine me for every day that that I was late sending over the photos, taking a cut from my monthly payments. At the time, I was a student living off of my loan, the occasional modelling job and some shifts at my local pub. The website was only paying me around £200–300 a month and I simply couldn't afford for them to take the money from me, so under pressure to get something sent over and avoid any more fines, I would often snap last-minute pictures that involved no effort, with a make-up free face or my hair shoved in a messy bun on the top of my head. I figured that as I was only making a couple hundred quid from membership fees, then there must only be 30–40 people who were signed up to my site and therefore able to view them anyway.

I wish I could step into my phone screen and slap my teenage self with a wet fucking fish for being so naive. The pictures were a mess, as were my eyebrows, and it makes me physically squirm to look back at them.

Eventually, after complaining to my agent about how much it pained me to take and share the selfie sets, she said I wasn't obliged to take them and that was that. No more fines, no contract breaches. I never sent over any selfies again. But those amateur photo sets that I despised spread across the internet like a bush fire penetrating every forum, were used to advertise escorting services and uploaded to porn sites that I had never consented to being on.

I felt so incredibly exposed watching my personal photos take on a life of their own, being viewed and commented on at an unbelievable scale that corroded my self-worth and made me question if I would ever live a normal life again. The shame I carried was overwhelming and hijacked each corner of my life. I would spend hours tracking how far they'd spread, too afraid to apply for other jobs in the fear someone would google me and resurface my trauma, too embarrassed to date because the thought of a boyfriend's parents finding out about my photos was excruciating. The reality was that they were just a pair of tits – or, as a photographer once called them, 'big balls of fat that earn us money'. Was it really *that* big of a deal? At the end of the day, I hadn't killed anyone, and I had to learn to let go of the shame that I felt society had forced upon me. I wasn't a bad person; I'd just showed a bloody nipple. Something millions of men do each day on beaches, in gyms and on Instagram posts. Except my rounded bits of flesh were tied to my humanity, while theirs were simply skin.

The men in manosphere forums perceive that because my few amateur selfies were originally uploaded somewhere else online, that gives them full permission to distribute and repurpose them however and wherever they wish. For me, those 'leaks' took on such importance that they almost ruined me.

Do these men believe that they can download and share Netflix films online that they had signed up for a subscription to view without facing any consequences from their legal team? You can't even share your Netflix subscription with your own family members anymore without an additional payment, due to the company cracking down on illegal viewing. So, why did so many men think it was okay to share my subscription content with the entire internet?

## OnlyFans: a new era of digital sex work

Unless you've been orbiting the planet in the Boeing Star-liner for the last four years, you've most probably heard of the subscription platform OnlyFans. Founded in 2016 by UK businessman Tim Stokely, who received a £10,000 loan from his dad and former banker Guy Stokely to get it off the ground, OnlyFans is one of the UK's most financially successful and fast-growing tech startups. The premise is simple: a subscription-based social media platform where fans pay a fee for exclusive access to their favourite creator's account, allowing the creator to monetize their content instead of posting it for free, like on other social media sites. These days, OnlyFans has carved a name for itself as an infamous pop culture staple, with celebrities like Cardi B and Iggy Azalea joining the platform, and Queen B herself, Beyoncé, singing lyrics about starting her own OnlyFans page on the remix of Megan Thee Stallion's 'Savage' track, which caused a huge surge in traffic to the site. Although OnlyFans doesn't market itself as a porn site, its over 18s policy and content guidelines that allow pornography to be shared on the platform made it an obvious choice for adult content creators. You can find an array of material on there, from yoga and cooking classes to fitness and comedy sketches, but the bread and butter of OnlyFans that has made Stokely and his shareholder Leonid Radvinsky multi-millionaires is the NSFW[*] content, which makes up 98 per cent of all media on the site.

The platform exploded in 2020 with the Covid pandemic forcing us all to seek shelter in our homes and turn to our

---

[*] NSFW stands for 'not safe for work'. It's basically a warning that you're about to browse a site that you probably shouldn't open while your boss or someone from HR is around.

devices. People living through their screens and losing liveli-hoods due to businesses closing down was the combination that created the perfect environment for the online subscription platform to flourish. In 2020, between March and April alone, OnlyFans saw a 75 per cent increase in new creator sign-ups. While the number of registered subscribers jumped from less than 15 million just before the pandemic to over 305 million in 2024, with an astonishing 500,000 new subscribers registering daily. In 2025, there are over 4 million creators, surpassing the entire population of Wales. Seventy per cent of creators on the platform are women, while 87 per cent of subscribers are male. OnlyFans is ranked in the top 70 most-visited websites in the United States, beating Adobe, Disneyplus.com and Outlook.

*The number of creators on OnlyFans surpasses the entire population of Wales.*

OnlyFans' website design is similar to most mainstream social media platforms, featuring a user profile, a newsfeed and direct messages. There are two different types of accounts that people can register for: a creator account for those who post and sell content, and a subscriber account for those who subscribe to view and engage with the creators' pages. Unlike with platforms such as Instagram, to view a creator's page and access their content, you pay a subscription fee which typically varies between $4.99 to $49.99.* Creators keep 80 per cent of all revenue they earn on the platform, with OnlyFans taking a 20 per cent fee. Creators monetise their content through the monthly subscription fee, which they set themselves, tips from subscribers and

---

* Creators can choose to have a 'free subscription' page but most people charge for access to their content. Those who do have free pages usually use them for cross-promotion to encourage subscribers to sign up to their main subscription page.

by selling content privately via direct messages, where subscribers can choose to pay extra to gain access to exclusive content.

As a platform, it provides a unique opportunity for women – including those from marginalised groups – to make a decent wage creating and sharing amateur pornography from the safety and convenience of their own homes. It helps to keep in-person sex workers off the streets, if that's what they want, and provides an income stream for disabled sex workers – some of whom have called the platform a lifeline after illness made it difficult for them to work in more traditional sectors. But not all women who turn to digital sex work are doing so as a last resort or just for the allure of potential riches – for many, it's the sense of reclaiming their sexuality that brings them joy. In an article for The Conversation, a disabled digital sex worker said, 'I started posting nudes on a social site and fell in love. I can remember being younger, watching porn and thinking *no one would want to see me doing that* . . . I started camming. People did want to see me, and I really did love it.'

OnlyFans has seen its revenue soar to eye-watering heights, paying out over $20 billion to its creators to date and reaching a gross revenue of $6.63 billion in 2023 from the 20 per cent it takes of all payments made on the site. There's some *serious* cash trading hands on the platform. Internet personality Bhad Bhabie, a.k.a. Danielle Bregoli, who shot to fame at 13 years old after a TV appearance on *Dr Phil* went viral,* broke records as the fastest OnlyFans creator to make $1 million, which she did in six hours when she joined the platform a week after her eighteenth birthday. She's since turned over an eye-watering $57 million net profit through her semi-nude content, all while still being only 21 years old.

Newspaper headlines are packed full of success stories of

---

* Yes, she is the 'catch me outside, how about that?' girl who terrorised her mum and stole a crew member's car during filming.

women who have fought their way out of poverty to become millionaires through sharing their spicy* content online, like Rebecca Goodwin, a single mum from Mansfield who signed up to the platform in desperation after being unable to afford baby formula. These days, she earns over £100,000 a month as an adult star on OnlyFans and has set up her own affordable housing scheme to help those that are struggling like she once was. I'd be lying if I told you that it hadn't crossed my mind once or twice to start my own account on the platform, but those thoughts usually come during the humbling moments of having nothing but cereal to eat for dinner.

From the outside, it may seem like this money-printing business model is too good to be true – which would probably be a pretty fair evaluation. Because for every rags-to-riches story that makes the papers, there are hundreds of thousands of creators who are posting their intimate content online and barely scraping minimum wage. In his investigation, titled 'The Economics of OnlyFans', researcher and data analyst Tom Hollands estimates the top 10 per cent of creators are earning 73 per cent of the platform's revenue, while the average Only-Fans creator is making $180 a month, or $2,000 a year. That would just about cover two months of my rent and a multi-pack of mini cereal boxes.

This is partly because building an audience for your content on the site is extremely challenging, whatever field you're in. In an interview for the *Financial Times*, OnlyFans CEO Keily Blair highlighted the unique business model of the social media platform which chooses not to track their customer's usage patterns: 'We're not trying to encourage people to stay online more, or suggesting things to them, or using algorithms to look

---

* Most mainstream social media platforms shadow-ban users who make posts promoting their OnlyFans page, leading to creators coining the term 'spicy content' to let their followers know they're active on *that* 'spicy' site.

at their preferences.' Unlike mainstream social media sites, OnlyFans does not have a homepage feed or use algorithms to push creators' content, which makes it incredibly difficult to become an overnight success on the platform, compared to sites like TikTok.* So, unless you already have a fanbase or an online following, you're going to have to turn to other social media platforms to promote yourself, where your exclusive content isn't so private anymore. And you're going to have to try stand out in a crowd of 4 million creators who, just like you, are trying to win over an audience. One OnlyFans adult creator told Vice how she works 12-hour days, 7 days a week, and often ends up dreaming about editing her videos: 'I always feel like I can be doing better and I always feel like, because the industry I'm in is so fast-paced, if I stopped doing something, someone will take my place.'

This saturated market of competitors can lead to women crossing their initial boundaries of what level of content they are comfortable creating, joining the thousands of others who are producing explicit images and videos in the hope of catching the eyes of male customers. Competing with others for business, many creators feel pressured to drop their prices to entice an audience, their customers haggling with them for the lowest rates while they ensure their storefront is stocked daily with new treats to keep them sweet. Being an OnlyFans creator is an exhausting and time-consuming job that entails high risk and no guarantee of reward, and can take a physical and mental toll on the women who spend their days filming themselves in various stages of undress and answering the lewd DMs from their subscribers.

---

* OnlyFans have introduced a 'Suggestions' feature that will recommend similar users who are in the same network to subscribers. For example, if I cross-promote my friend Jane* on my page often, Jane's account will be suggested to my subscribers.

In an article for Buzzfeed News, six OnlyFans creators shared their daily schedules, involving working on the platform until 2 or 3am, and messaging subscribers the minute they woke up. One creator told how her revenue drops from $300 a day to around $100 if she takes a break from the site due to most of her money coming from tips, meaning she has to be constantly active and engaged. I've lain on a sun lounger next to my friend on holiday listening to her vent her frustrations at having to take time out of her vacation to reply to her male fans on Only-Fans before they get annoyed at her absence – a gaggle of men demanding her attention in a parasocial relationship they've built in their own minds with my friend who they've never met. Meanwhile, the male subscribers who are spoilt for choice get to live out the adult equivalent of being a kid in a candy store each time they log on to the platform.

Whether you're a creator that is hitting six-figure months or someone who's using the platform as a side hustle to supplement your income, the exclusivity of your content will be one of the main drivers for your audience, meaning it's vital that it cannot be accessed and viewed for free elsewhere, if your business is going to thrive – or survive.

## The house of leaked OnlyFans content

To update Benjamin Franklin's observation, only three things in life are certain – death, taxes and your OnlyFans nudes being leaked. It almost seems ironic that OnlyFans' original logo features a padlock because there is near enough zero chance of your intimate content staying under lock and key. On the few occasions where a woman has turned to me for some advice as they're thinking of stepping into the 'spicy content' creating business, I tell them all the same thing: *please* only ever create content that you'd be happy with everyone you know finding out about, because it will get leaked. I want to make it clear that I am in no way condoning this behaviour – it's messed up and it's not fair – but it's unfortunately the reality.

OnlyFans does not allow users to download and save images or videos from their site, to be clear, with creator's content DRM-protected (a term used to describe a technology that controls and restrict access and usage of digital content) and copyrighted as laid out in their terms and conditions. Yet this doesn't stop some users continually ignoring the website's rules that they agreed to when signing up, screenshotting and screen-recording creators' content, or installing a browser extension and bots to rip the images and videos directly from their feed. This isn't an issue exclusive to OnlyFans; if you upload adult content on any other subscription site, such as AdmireMe, Patreon and ManyVids, it's unfortunately equally inevitable that a man will screenshot and post your nudes else-where online. However, due to the immense popularity of the OnlyFans platform, its adult content creators are more vulner-able to being exploited by those who feel entitled to view their bodies for free. Though it is worth pointing out that OnlyFans is turning over billions of pounds in revenue because there are a lot of people who *are* happy to pay for subscriptions and services on the site, and it is unfair for those morally good individuals if others are bypassing payment to access a service they're paying for. I know I'd be pretty pissed off if I went to a bar and found out I was the only person who had to pay for my drinks.

Elena Michaels co-founded NotYourPorn, a grassroots campaign fighting to protect non-consenting adults and sex workers from IBSA, along with Kate Isaacs, who we met in the previous chapter. She talked about how, no matter what the nature is of someone's content, whether it's sexual or not, 'Nobody is entitled to take content and post it somewhere else. You don't own that image, they do. It's still exploitative.' We spoke of other industries and careers where plagiarising or stealing someone's work would come with consequences and an avenue for the victim to claim some form of compensation: 'Arguably, when somebody's work is based on their body, the level of harm is even higher. So why do we go in the complete opposite direction of being like, well, you knew what the risks were, therefore you should just take the consequences?' Here, Michaels was putting forward the argument that plagiarising work that includes someone's vulnerable body is more harmful than stealing art such as music, recognising how upsetting that is to an artist but that 'given the political, social, and historical stigma that's related to someone's body, if anything we should protect it even more.'

When something is behind a paywall that's for a reason, and when you buy pay-per-view images and videos from creators you're doing exactly that – paying to view. Much like when you go to the cinema to watch a screening of your favourite actor's new film, you don't own the model's content indefinitely, you're just paying to consume it on a platform. But though the older, wiser version of me, who's been weathered by a decade-long storm of online misogyny, wants to pre-warn you as an act of preparation and protection that any intimate content you post on a subscription site will be leaked, this does not mean I think we should accept that this is 'just the way it is'.

The entire backbone of the OnlyFans platform is for fans to show their support to their favourite creators, which enables them to make a living from their work, the same way music fans buy concert tickets for shows and sports fans buy their team's new jersey. There are many millions of male fans who clearly admire the women who are producing adult content on the platform, showing an interest in their artistry and seeking out their exclusive nudes to add to their collection with the same enthusiasm as a baseball card collector, and yet, when it comes to the women's intimate images that show them in a vulnerable state of undress, some of these men don't only believe that the women should not be paid, but they go out of their way to harm their revenue stream by distributing their content for free. Michaels suspects a fundamental sense of entitlement over women's bodies is driving men to seek out creators' content free of charge 'It's this idea of, "I've consumed it, now it's mine." Well, it's not, it's not yours.'

One image-board site boasts of being the 'House of Leaked OnlyFans content', where thousands of free images are uploaded to the forum amongst links to mega folders that members can download, each holding huge files of women's intimate content. This site is just one of hundreds, if not thousands, that hosts women's explicit images and videos that were only ever intended to be viewed behind a paywall. The scale of these leaks is monumental, with swarms of men congregating to ensure these women who dared commit the ultimate sin of making money from their bodies would instead have to give away their content for free. One site I was browsing featured a graphic which would regularly update, keeping track of the leaks on their platform:

Statistics OnlyFans Leaks

Models: 160,134

Count of content: 6,828,465

Last update: August 18, 2024,

5:31 pm

There is a sense of camaraderie in the online forums where men scratch each other's back, sharing the content of women they've personally paid to subscribe to. Cries of 'Thank you King!' ring out on threads as fleshy photos change hands and their $12 monthly subscription fee is stretched across servers. On one forum, I witnessed men start a kitty with strangers, chipping in to buy a reality TV star's pay-per-view content that was then shared amongst the group. *And they say that women are cheap?*

Tina Skye* is a UK-based OnlyFans creator who joined the platform in 2019 after a successful career as a glamour model. She posts lingerie and topless content on her page, uploading weekly photo sets that are often leaked elsewhere on forums within a few days of posting. The forums' virtual bro-mances frustrate Skye, who calls out the men that bond over women's misery. 'The whole fucking online community of these men is barbaric, I can't get over it. They talk to each other like they're mates and it's like – you're not! You don't know each other but you think you're best buddies because you're sharing content of women against their will.'

Skye doesn't produce explicit content and has previously experienced images from her lads' mags days being distributed elsewhere, but it's still distressing for her to see the content she's produced exclusively for her subscription page shared in the forums. 'It's a great business opportunity, but I'm left with an ill-taste in my mouth with OnlyFans because I know what the men are like; I know my content has been fucking spread everywhere like the plague and how they speak about me.'

Like many creators and models, Skye's content is popular on VK, a Russian social networking site founded by brothers Nikolai and Pavel Durov, who's also the founder of the messaging app, Telegram. VK is notorious for its refusal to comply with social media regulations and content moderation, often ignoring DMCA takedowns and copyright removal requests, making it the perfect breeding ground for women's leaked images. In an attempt to keep track of her photos, Skye created a fake account using a man's name to gain access to a forum on VK that was sharing leaked OnlyFans content, including her own. 'The main guy who runs one of the forums on VK posted about me in there, saying "I'm not going to stop sharing her content until she dies."' The thought of her intimate images being immortalised in cyberspace for eternity is one that Skye struggles with. 'Even when I die, I know that those images are going to be online forever, and the men are never going to leave me alone unless one day the internet just completely stopped. That's what jars me a little bit.'

It's a depressing thought, and one I've tortured myself with before. Even in death, I will be unable to reclaim my body from the savage claws of the internet that has squeezed every last drop of humanity from my photos. My soul will be free and still my body will continue to be exploited by men on Earth.

## DMCA REMOVAL REQUEST

*Definition:* Short for digital millennium copyright act, a US law that protects copyright holders from online theft. A DMCA removal or takedown is a tool for copyright holders to get user-uploaded material that infringes their copyrights taken down from websites.

The sexualisation of her body makes Skye uncomfortable. She tells me she faces an internal battle of being disgusted by the men who trade her images and that pass sexual comments on her body, while acknowledging that on OnlyFans, she's profiting handsomely from men's desire to see her half-naked.

When I asked for her thoughts on why she believes the men feel entitled to access women's content for free, Skye puts it down to a total lack of empathy or care for women in general: 'They do it because they don't care about women. Point blank. They feel so entitled to my body, and yet they'll say, "I'm not paying for that, but I want to see it." They'll pay another man if they're leaking it and selling it for $5, but they're like, "I'm not buying it from her."'

For Skye, the positives of the platform outweigh the negatives for now. Recognising how men have often sexualised her body since she was a teenager, she feels she might as well make use of her objectification while she still can. 'We're making money, that's the winning aspect. But you don't see any other jobs that are offering that level of money for young women, nothing with clothes on, only when men are sexualising us. It's annoying because I'm in two minds. Like, if you can't beat them, join them.'

Elena Michaels believes that, from sex work to Instagram photos, we're living in a time where cis and trans-women's bodies are an innately political and capital issue that sees people exploit women's bodies for profit while also having issue with women reclaiming and owning their sexuality. 'I think that confronts a lot of our underlying ideals about how women function in capitalist societies and opens a wider conversation about essentially the commercialisation of women's bodies and also about their pain.'

OnlyFans is a male-founded, British success story, thanks to the women who sell their bodies and their time on the platform, and the men who are willing to pay to access it. For many female creators on the site whose lives have been transformed with unimaginable riches, or a subsidised income that's allowed them to feed their children, the sexualisation of their personhood has positively impacted their world and empowered them to live independently.

But can a lion ever truly live in harmony alongside the vultures eager to feed off its carcass?

∎

Milly Dixon* signed up to become a creator on OnlyFans as a first-year university student, worrying about managing her finances alongside studying for her degree. Dixon began posting non-explicit lingerie content on the platform, which helped raise much-welcome added funds to support her life as a student. But when the Covid pandemic hit and her university shut down, Dixon moved back home where, just a few weeks into lockdown, she received a DM on Instagram that would change everything. 'I got a message off this guy who's a famous gamer and YouTuber, who has made content with the Sidemen and KSI. He was like, "I've seen that you do OnlyFans, do you know how much money you could be making on there?"'

The Sidemen, a group of seven male best friends including KSI and Ethan Payne, have become well-known internet personalities with a combined following of over 146 million subscribers. The group has been called out on several occasions for making light of sexist tropes in their content, with rape jokes a regular occurrence in KSI's early videos and OnlyFans models often featuring on the channel where they are asked sensationalist questions on dating and about their body.

The YouTuber* told Dixon he was interested in managing her OnlyFans account and suggested a phone call. 'He sold it as the dream. Basically, saying all I need to do is take the photos and then they'll sort everything out for me, and I don't even need to chat to the men on there.' After exchanging messages on Instagram with the YouTuber, who fed her promises of turning her into a streaming star alongside the OnlyFans account, Dixon jumped on a call with the man. 'He seemed really lovely and genuine. He said, "I do think that you should be charging more for what you're doing and also go that extra mile. You should be doing videos where you go topless and get your down-below exposed and everything."'

Dixon was apprehensive of his suggestion – she'd never had the desire to create explicit content – but the promise of riches as a struggling student enticed her to reconsider. 'He said, "Look at this girl I'm managing; she's literally on something stupid, like £50k a month, you'd easily be able to make that,

---

* The woman has asked to keep both herself and the YouTuber anonymous out of fear of repercussions from what she calls a 'powerful man with money'.

you'd go over that!" and I thought, *I guess for £50k a month all I need is to do OnlyFans for a few years and then I could just retire myself and not worry about anything.'*

So Dixon signed up to the YouTuber's OnlyFans management company, handing over the reins to the creative direction of her content, full access to her account and 20 per cent of her earnings each month, on top of OnlyFans taking a 20 per cent fee. A young male employee was assigned to manage Dixon's account. His roles including dirty talking with her male subscribers, passing on custom video requests and scheduling her content. 'I got the major ick because the guy I was paired up with, who was running my account, was around 19, and I'm obviously sending him all this explicit stuff and I just thought there's no chance he's not there just having a wank over it himself and that really grossed me out.'

Although the YouTuber positioned himself as the head of the management company and was involved in directly recruiting models, there is no public information that ties him to the business of OnlyFans management, something Dixon finds disturbing. 'It's pretty sinister with him being the face of it as this person who's got loads of followers because it gives that legitimacy to his business that makes people believe in him, and that's so fucked. It's a really sneaky way behind the scenes to profit from girls' bodies and no one knows that he has anything to do with it.'

*Teenage boys are fed masculinist, anti-feminist content within their first 23 minutes on social media*

YouTube is the most popular social media platform for teenage boys, where misogynistic content posted by controversial influencers including Andrew Tate and Adin Ross is up-ranked on the platform. A 2024 study by Dublin City University's anti-bullying centre tracked and recorded the content recommended to accounts that were registered to teenage boys aged 16–18 on TikTok and YouTube Shorts. All of the accounts were found to have been fed masculinist, anti-feminist content within the first 23 minutes of the experiment, regardless of whether they'd engaged with or sought out any male supremacist-related content. There is something rather sardonic in a man with a large, loyal following of young men capitalising in private off of the commodification of women's bodies.

In her first few months working with the management company, Milly Dixon saw a large boost to her earnings, yet she couldn't shake the sense that her boundaries had been seriously compromised. 'I felt guilty in some way, I felt like I shouldn't be doing this, and I don't want to be so exposed online. Then, that's when the leaks came through.'

Dixon had raised her concerns around leaked content to the YouTuber in their initial chats, concerned about her younger brother who was in high school and the repercussions if her explicit content got out from behind the paywall. 'He said that nothing would get out and that it's copyrighted anyway, so if they do, you could take legal action because it's illegal.' But Dixon discovered her intimate content had been leaked from her OnlyFans page after a friend texted to let her know that a video was circulating in their hometown and soon after, her inbox was inundated with messages from individuals telling her how they'd seen her content.

'It was really daunting and I freaked out. I was like, I'm going to stop doing this now. I don't want people to see it or what if it gets back to my family?' The mass distribution of her subscription-based content had put Dixon off the platform and she felt ready to throw in the towel, until the management company persuaded her to continue by offering a lifeline in the shape of DMCA takedown support. 'They said you can pay someone to take things down online for you and just keep on top of it; that's what the other girls we manage do. So, I started doing that for a while and carried on.' With a bustling roster of successful female OnlyFans creators on their books, the management company was no doubt cashing in a sizeable profit from the women's bodies, but they failed to safeguard their creators' explicit content, instead recommending that they hire their own DMCA protection service that came at an added monthly fee to the models.

Although Dixon initially decided to continue on the site, the leaks had stripped her of any motivation to produce content, seeing her delay filming for days on end and not delivering on custom requests that the management company had accepted on her behalf. A short while after, feeling overwhelmed and grossed out by the whole experience, Dixon cut all ties from OnlyFans and the management company, ending her short-lived career as an amateur adult content creator. But while her OnlyFans page has been completely shut down and she has since tried to move on with her life as a single mum, Dixon's explicit images and videos live on through the online forums. 'I still see people on the forums asking for my content. It makes me ill to check, it makes me sick. They were like thirsty dogs on the threads, begging each other to exchange my photos. I try to blank it out because it doesn't make me feel great; it doesn't do any good to my mental health.'

Dixon has reached out to some of the forums asking that they remove her leaked content, stressing how she's now a mother and has left the industry behind, but she hasn't received a reply – or had her request fulfilled. She reached out to the YouTuber asking for more help and advice on how to deal with the leaks and the stress they were causing but felt dismissed by his reply. 'He said "Yeah, it is a bit shit. You could just get a name change." They were all big IT guys, so I'm sure they would know how to do the DMCA takedowns themselves, but they didn't care.'

After she left the company, the teenage boy who was in charge of managing her OnlyFans account reached out to Dixon to ask if he could buy one of her custom videos she had uploaded to the site, confirming her fears that he was getting sexual kicks out of watching her content.

In Dixon, I saw so much of my younger self – naive with a raw innocence of the world that led me to trust blindly and always assume the best in people. It pained me to also recognise her anger and cynicism caused by the chains of misogyny that had rusted us both from within.

Dixon is raising her son as a single mum, working a nine-to-five job, hoping one day she will have enough money to pay for a professional DMCA takedown service that will eradicate her content for good. 'I did manage to get a few things removed when I paid to get a professional takedown done before. It all disappeared for about six months and then it all just came back. You have to keep on top of it and I can't afford to be doing that every three or six months.'

Although becoming an OnlyFans creator seemed like a get-rich-quick hack that would set Dixon up for life, coming to accept her intimate images and videos have been distributed across the internet where they will remain indefinitely is a slow and painful task that often sees her triggered by misogynistic behaviours she sees online. 'I always like to start the day hoping I'm not going to come across anything that will remind me of the leaks because it's still a long road. Some days, I'm like, don't worry, it's fine, and then some days it really holds me back. It's going to be a long road to recovery just trying to get over the whole thing and put it fully behind me.'

Dixon is not alone in the betrayal and exploitation she experienced from the men who deemed themselves entitled to consume her body without charge, and those who viewed her as nothing but a cash cow. All of these men failed to see the human beyond the surface of their sexual desire or financial gain. Dixon is an academic with a sharp mind and an infectious laugh whose life did not end aged 23 years old because men on the internet tried to disintegrate her worth as a human. 'It's not anything morally wrong that I've done, I've not been mean, I've not been horrible to anyone. I was just young and vulnerable and maybe a bit silly, but I don't think I should have to pay some kind of price and be punished for it, with my leaks being shared everywhere for the rest of my life.' It is unjust that society will judge this young woman more harshly than the men whose parasitic entitlement drained the joy from her soul.

■

OnlyFans management (OFM) is a fast-growing industry made up largely of young men who have decided they want in on the lucrative world of online sex work, without having to take any of their clothes off. Skipping the societal judgement that comes with exposing yourself intimately to the internet, boys as young as 16 years old are setting up online management agencies where they recruit women via social media with promises of riches, transforming them into amateur adult content creators. Referred to as 'E-pimps', the world of Only-Fans management has made its way into the mainstream, with controversial internet personality Harrison Sullivan a.k.a. 'HS Tikky Tokky' gloating on Telegram to his 454,000 subscribers 'OFM = fucking bitches and be a pimp sickcunt'. In a Discord server with 19,000 members run by YouTuber Markus Hussle, who claims to have made $5 million through OnlyFans management, I saw several posts from teenage boys all seeking advice on how to run their own OnlyFans management company and secure their first model.

One post simply read, 'I'm 13 and I wanna know.' Another member replied, suggesting the teenager wait to set up their OFM agency – 'Once you're at least 15–16+ I'd recommend it' – alongside his reasoning, 'I don't think being this young and exposed to porn is a good idea.' Hussle suggests that the men take a 50 per cent agency fee in exchange for running the women's accounts, but I've seen men in Telegram channels discuss how they take a 60–70 per cent cut of models' OnlyFans earnings, valuing their time and effort at a higher worth than the models they encourage to strip and masturbate on camera. One user on Telegram suggested the models should only be paid a set-rate fee: '$500 salary is enough. Offer salary, she has to be miraculously beautiful to claim 50 per cent.'

Since I began my career in the entertainment industry, I've been represented by three different talent agencies, all of them taking a standard agency fee of 20–25 per cent. A rate of 50 per cent or more is absurd and extremely exploitative of young women who wouldn't know any better, but offering a mere $500 in an industry that claims to rake in tens of thousands of pounds a month is a spiteful display of intentional power play and misogyny taken straight out of a pimp's playbook.

YouTube is littered with step-by-step guides from young men advising others on how to set up their own 'OFM' agency, encouraging others not to miss out. In a Telegram channel dedicated to 'OFM Jobs', a user advertised his online 'university' by goading his potential clients: 'I've told you a million times that OFM is the BEST BUSINESS MODEL OF 2024! But have you taken action yet? You probably haven't because you're too fucking lazy to get rich selling some pussy pics online.' If the secret to success is selling pictures of your genitals online, then, my guy – *why aren't you selling yours?* Male YouTubers brag of $250,000 months and encourage others to flood their Instagram feed with images of private jets and expensive watches that hint at a luxurious life, in an attempt to convince the women they're trying to recruit of their success, even if the reality is that they have no cashflow and zero experience in the industry. A reminder here that it is *real women* these men are taking on the responsibility of 'managing'; women who are sharing sensitive content and access to their bodies. Nowhere in any 'how-to' guides or support chats on Telegram and Discord did I see safeguarding and the wellbeing of the women mentioned. The focus is on generating as much wealth for the men as possible.

## Tackling the leaks, one DMCA takedown request at a time

Male entitlement and the exploitation of women's bodies did not start on OnlyFans and it will not end on OnlyFans (I'm *literally* writing a whole bloody book on other aspects of online misogyny), but its insane reach, popularity with young people (the average OnlyFans user is 29 years old) and social media element has birthed a new era of digital sex work that has powered the demand for leaked content, elevated the risks for creators and seen misogynistic, slut-shaming attitudes resurrected by men dismayed at having to pay to view women's naked bodies. Its presence in pop culture and the participation of high-profile celebrities who strip off on the platform has arguably enticed more people into the adult industry through a glamorised lens of wealth and success that feels attainable for the everyday person – if they take their clothes off or perform sex acts on camera. Millions of women are trialling sex work, willing to sacrifice their bodily autonomy in exchange for a chance at financial freedom because, for millennia, it has been ransacked anyway for free. It feels unjust as a woman to have men vulgarly feast on your abundant, sweet nectar without ever dipping a finger into the jam jar and stealing a taste yourself. But where there are sticky fingers, pests will inevitably swarm.

The deep-rooted male entitlement that claims ownership over the female body is a mildew rotting the moral structures of society, and one that is going to take some heavy duty work to fix. Until then, there are ways of temporarily patching up the leaks that can help women take back some sort of control over their images.

# LEAKED 2.0

*'We're removing about 30 to 50 million images and videos every month'*

Brand protection agencies are launching across the globe from Ireland to Australia, a direct response to the gargantuan task of removing OnlyFans creators' stolen and leaked content. The innovative tech start-ups are using AI technology to scan the internet for unauthorised leaks and serve automated DMCA removal requests with impressive success rates. One company told me how their takedown service is removing 30 to 50 million images and videos every month, the type of numbers that would be infeasible for content creators to achieve by manually completing and submitting their own removal requests. For some adult creators, the services are a lifeline that help protect their privacy and their pay cheque,* and have helped them to reinvent themselves when they've chosen to leave the industry behind.

It seems frustrating that brand protection services are necessary, but if we look at content creation through a business lens, all companies that distribute, stream, play and broadcast media will have a copyright team hired to protect their brand. During one of my spirals of racking my brain for how to print some fast cash, I turned my hand to Canva and designed some prints to sell on Etsy. One design read 'I LICKED HER TIT OR WHATEVER' in reference to that iconic line muttered on season eight of *Love Island UK*, and immediately I was served a copyright notice by ITV. *Who knew tit licking was copyrighted?!* That was sadly the end of my graphic design career.

It is important for creators to understand that they hold the copyright to their content and are afforded similar copyright protections as large brands and corporations. Much like buying a ticket to a fine art exhibition, subscribers are paying to view

---

* When a user subscribes to a creator on OnlyFans, they are paying to access exclusive content. Each time a creator's content is leaked that exclusivity drops in value, with people able to access their intimate images for free.

what they see as beautiful pieces of art, but they don't get to take the painting home with them. While adult content creators are early adopters of these type of protections, in an age of misinformation and deepfake technology, it might only be a matter of time before we all need to take out an insurance policy on our digital footprint.

The individuals that share women's leaked and stolen content act as bottom feeders, scavenging for crumbs from the discarded body parts that lie in the dark depths of message boards. Their pathetic desperation props up an entire eco-system of websites that exist solely to host leaked content. Although brand protection services help with content removal, which can minimise social and emotional damage for creators and re-claim their lost revenue through protecting the exclusivity of their content, unfortunately they cannot stop the threat at source, which means at some stage your intimate content will most likely end up in the public domain. And even if your DMCA takedown request is fulfilled, there is nothing stopping someone from re-uploading the content to the platform, leaving the victim having to repeat the takedown application process which can take time, money and an emotional toll on the victim.

OnlyFans' website notes they have a proactive team that issue formal DMCA takedown notices on creators' behalf. In December 2024, the platform filed 1,376 DMCA notices to third party sites hosting leaked content. However, in the same month, 53,364,543 pieces of content were posted on their platform. With that gargantuan figure in mind, the platform submitting an equivalent of 44 takedown notices a day in the month of December is barely leaving a pin-pricked dimple in what seems the Sisyphean task of re-gaining control of women's stolen, intimate content. Perhaps OnlyFans could do more in their attempt to protect creators on their platform, with one suggestion being the implementation of a technology that is used by many other streaming sites which produces a black screen when a screenshot or screen-recording takes place, but the reality is that no matter what protections or terms are implemented, there will always be men who will find a way to bypass them.

OnlyFans was supposed to be a platform that put the control back in the hands of the creator, and has produced one of the few jobs where women are the majority income earners, but the platform has been savaged and hijacked by the men who saw it as an excuse to exploit women at both ends of the scale – stealing and distributing their content for free, and encroaching on the production side as 'managers' and rinsing them for as high a fee as possible. Over the last couple of years, I have spent many hours with friends dissecting collectors' culture and why leaked content is in such high demand that it's become its own 'porn' category. Each conversation has ended with the same conclusion as Elena Michaels, Tina Skye and Milly Dixon have come to: pervasive male entitlement to women's bodies.

## TIPS: How to protect your spicy content

Whether you're posting nudes for financial purposes or swapping sexy pics within a situationship, here are a few tips on how best to protect yourself against leaks:

- **Minimize identifiers for you**: Cardi B was a real one when she sang 'No face, No case'. Keeping your face and any identifiers such as tattoos out of your nude selfies will minimize the fall-out if you do find your content online. No face? Then that ain't me. Let's move on.

- **Maximize identifiers for them**: Add a small number or letter to your nudes so you can keep track of which image you sent to who, helping you quickly identify the leaker if your nude does end up somewhere else. This should be hidden somewhere the person receiving it won't notice, like a skirting board or door, so that they won't edit it out.

- **Think smarter:** Perpetrators go out of their way to ensure your images go undetected on the forums to avoid being held accountable, swapping out letters for special characters and numbers in creators' names. For example, my name could appear as J3$$ D@V!E$ in a forum dedicated to my stolen photos. Be creative when searching for your leaked content by trying out different variations.

- **Mark it:** OnlyFans offers a free digital watermark service to all creators, making it harder for the original content to be used or resold without permission. You can edit this in their privacy and settings page.

- **Invest in yourself.** If you are a content creator online who posts spicy content, I highly recommend that you subscribe to a DMCA takedown service. This investment will not only provide you with some sort of control but from a business point of view, you're losing revenue each time your photos are shared without consent. You can serve DMCA takedowns yourself, but it is a lengthy process to do on mass scale, and many of these businesses have direct contact with Google and other servers which can help get your content removed within hours. Female tech-start up Image Angel uses invisible watermark technology to protect creators from digital image misuse by linking consumers with the content.

A side note, when Google receives a lot of reports on an image, its algorithm will learn that the content is something that shouldn't be shared and will eventually downgrade it from appearing in search engines.

# 5

# CYBERFLASHING

## No one wants to see your dick

'The men out there who do this, they're looking to
shut us up, they're looking for power over us
and control'
**Emily Atack**, *Asking for It*, **BBC**

For years, my morning routine had stayed the same, consisting mostly of having to force my eyes open to the rude awakening of my alarm and reaching for the bedside table to feel around for my phone. Defying the library of self-help podcasts that warn me against it, I couldn't resist opening social media and stealing a scroll from amongst the comfort of my bed sheets. Sleep gunk still stuck to my eyelashes, I'd browse from one app to another, absorbing any breaking news I may have missed in the last eight hours and catching up on the lives of strangers across the world before I could garner up the strength to roll out of my pit for my morning pee.

Then, one morning, I opened my emails during my morning app check to see a message that had landed in my inbox over-night. As a freelancer, it isn't unusual for me to receive emails with work offers, interview requests or PR invites, so a message from an address that I didn't recognise wasn't an obvious red flag. There waiting for me were multiple images of a man's bare torso and his erect penis, taken from all different angles. An eery, unfamiliar chill washed over me as I lay there cocooned in my duvet, alone.

This wasn't the first time a stranger had sent me an unsolicited picture of his penis – it has happened to me hundreds of times before, the first being when I was only 15 years old, but this time it felt different. This time it felt invasive, it felt personal. My bed was my sanctuary, a safety blanket. It was where I dreamed of climbing into when the workday ended and where I've spent countless hours rotting away in goblin mode after a big night out. A place to recoup, recharge and recover . . . but now? This man had invited himself in. This alien and his erect penis weren't physically in my bed, but the forced invasion of my personal space made it feel like he was. Every thought started racing through my mind as I began questioning his motive, his identity and why he had chosen me.

Who is he?

How does he know me?

Why did he send me these images?

Did he think I'd like them?

Is he going to find me in 'real' life?

What has caused this man on the internet to take a photo of himself naked and find my email address to send it to?

Was it something that I'd done?

### CYBERFLASHING

*Definition:* The sending/sharing of a sexual image online without the recipient's consent. Also referred to as indecent digital exposure.

Men sharing snaps of their penises is such a common occurrence that we've given this type of image its own name – *the dick pic.* Cemented firmly in the dictionary of internet slang somewhere before 'selfie' and after 'catfish', a dick pic has become an expected consequence of being a woman online.

Sure, you may have originally signed up to Facebook to share a sweet family memory of your gran's birthday with your cousin who lives across the Atlantic, but the outcome of you opening a social media account is that you now have to accept the reality that a man is probably going to send you a photo of his penis on Messenger because, well, *the internet.* Whether it's checking your Instagram DMs for any cute sliders and seeing some old guy's penis staring back at you or logging on to Chat Roulette* during pre-drinks and being greeted by a naked man aggressively masturbating at the screen, almost every woman I know has been sent or shown a penis online that they never asked to see.

*75.8 per cent of girls aged 12–18 have been sent an unsolicited image of a man's penis.*

Studies consistently show that cyberflashing is a common occurrence, with women predominantly being targeted. Much like the physical act of 'flashing'† your genitals in public, cyber-flashing is the act of sharing a sexual image or video of yourself to someone online without their consent. Research by YouGov found that 41 per cent of women have been sent an unsolicited image of a man's penis, with that figure jumping to 75.8 per cent when we look at girls aged 12 to 18. It's important to note how

---

* Chat Roulette is a video chat website which randomly selects another user for you to webcam chat with. When I was at university in 2014, we would load up the site while pre-drinking to see what weird and wonderful people we could come across. Although their T&C's note no sexual behaviour is allowed, nine times out of ten, you would find a man masturbating on camera, which meant ultimately there were just a lot of dudes wanking to each other on that site.

† Although we know it informally as 'flashing', this term has been called out for being problematic in how it downplays the seriousness of the crime. The legal term used is indecent exposure or exposure.

intersectionality plays its part – a study by Our Communia found that a Black woman is twice as likely to be a victim of cyberflashing than a white woman.

Cyberflashing happens on social media apps such as Instagram, Facebook and Snapchat, via texts or instant messaging, as well as on online dating platforms like Bumble, and even via AirDrop.* There's no clear pattern when it comes to the type of men who are sending women photos of their dicks or what their genitalia may look like. Unfortunately, I've been forced to see them all – I've been sent images of hard ones, soft ones, shaved ones, hairy ones, small ones, old ones, different coloured ones, circumcised ones, one being next to a Coke can for scale and even one wearing a knitted hat.† Often, they're accompanied by graphic sexual comments about what the sender would like to do to me, making their presence in my inbox even more sinister.

I've received so many unsolicited penis pictures over the years that I'm now almost numb to their presence, not allowing myself to sit in the fear or the shame for too long because two days later, another strange penis would pop up to terrorise me all over again. If there was a naked guy on the corner of each street masturbating at women and shouting about all the ways he wanted to fuck them, it would make worldwide news and women would understandably be too afraid to leave their homes. Yet every time I log on to my life online, I am expected to overlook the barrage of sexual comments and unsolicited

---

* AirDrop is a Bluetooth feature on iPhones which allows users to share files with each other for free. There have been many reports of women being sent unsolicited penis pictures via AirDrop on public transport, raising safety concerns due to the need of both iPhone users to be in close proximity.

† When the PR team for Innocent smoothies came up with the campaign putting Nanna's knit tiny hats on their bottles, did they ever imagine their beanies would be used as willy cosies?

images sent my way by men demonstrating predatory behaviour because, for some bizarre reason, we've decided that the men being misogynistic online is different to men being misogynistic in person.

There is a sub-culture of cyberflashing that exists in the manosphere called 'cum tributes', where men film themselves masturbating over a woman's image or take a picture of them ejaculating on her photo, their bodily liquids proudly on display. I've found 'tributed' images of myself online vandalised by a man's sperm and the grotesque sense of violation it left me with was the total opposite of a compliment or celebration. In one forum, I saw a man share images of his girlfriend alongside a request for more contributors to share their 'cum tributes'.

> 'this is my innocent irl named Rose. shes from Montreal, and i've been spreading her to pervs, getting her tributed i've been working on a big compilation project of her taking loads, so far i have 20tribs, but the final goal is 50'

The man shared a link to a gallery of images of his partner, along with the 'tributes', her innocent smiling selfies covered in strangers' semen. Some men appear to see their 'tributes' as a display of appreciation, but for most it is a harmful display of power and has been used by some perpetrators as a racist harassment tactic. In an interview with mashable.com, political journalist Ash Sarkar told of 'hate wank' videos featuring her likeness that had been uploaded onto porn sites. Similar to 'tributes', these videos included men masturbating over a woman's image but the intent was to cause maximum distress and humiliation for the woman involved. One of the videos was titled 'racist hate wank for Ash Sakar' and included a man masturbating to images of her that had been taken from her public Instagram profiles. Mashable's report found racist 'hate wank' videos targeting high-profile women of colour including BBC presenter Naga Munchetty and the former Home Secretary Priti Patel. Professor Clarissa Smith told the publication that 'tributes' and 'hate wank' videos reflect a longstanding 'tradition of raging against women' who are seen as opinionated or outspoken, with intersections of race and class influencing the abusive behaviour. Smith explained: 'There are long histories of the use of sex, sexual innuendo, and insults to silence women and some of these videos take their place in that form of bringing women down.'

The idea of 'hate wanks' almost seems absurd – can you imagine if I filmed a video of myself masturbating and uploaded it to the internet as an act of defiance towards Elon Musk in a protest against his political endorsements? First of all, his male supporters would call me a slut for sharing the video to begin with. But the more sinister reality is that they play on women's fear of sexual assault and having their consent taken from them. Leaning in to the use of rape threats that overwhelmingly target women, 'hate wanks' are used to silence and scare women in a display of online harms that does not generally hold the same weight as it would if directed at a man.

## Indecent digital exposure begins in schools

I feel lucky to have grown up on the cusp of the social media age, relishing in Bebo and sharing the 'love' with the boy I fancied in my class, but just missing out on Snapchat and having to navigate the explosion of non-consensual dick pics at school.

*71 per cent of 18-24 year olds were sent their first dick pic below the legal age*

Research by YouGov found that 71 per cent of 18–24-year-old women were sent their first dick pic below the legal age of consent, while a study by Jessica Ringrose, Kaitlyn Reghr and Sophie Whitehead on sexual double standards and the normalisation of image-based sexual harassment argued that the bombardment of unsolicited dick pics on teenagers via apps such as Snapchat normalises harassing behaviours, highlighting the complexities girls face in trying to manage or report receiving an unsolicited dick pic from their school peers compared to being able to ignore or block random, older users. They found that the schoolgirls quickly developed coping strategies to manage the receiving of unwanted images from older men, such as ghosting them, blocking them or 'mid/half sliding' the pictures and videos to make the notification disappear without opening the chat or letting the sender know they'd viewed it, but the girls found non-consensual photos more difficult to manage when the sender was a boy they went to school with, due to the fear of repercussions. Trying to navigate teenage angst is tricky enough in itself, but the added mental workload placed on young girls to police male behaviour at such a young age forces them to mature faster in an attempt to keep themselves safe.

These findings reflect my own encounters with teenage girls when facilitating workshops on sexual harassment in secondary schools, or during filming for my documentaries with Welsh-language channel S4C, for which I've interviewed teenage girls about their experiences with social media. On a number of occasions, groups of girls have shared with me how boys in their school sent them unsolicited dick pics, and responded with hostility if they didn't get a positive response, or dismiss their behaviour as 'banter'. The girls said that if they blocked them or didn't send a nude image back, in some cases, boys would bully or harass them online. A few girls also shared how they regularly received unsolicited dick pics from older men on Snapchat or in their Instagram DMs, even when they had their pages set to private.

I reconnected with Laani, one of the teenage girls I first interviewed a few years ago, who is now in her first year of university, to reflect on her experiences of navigating dick pics while underage. Laani's school was rife with unsolicited penis pictures and she explained to me how she doesn't know of a girl at her school who hadn't been cyberflashed, experiencing it herself for the first time when she was 15 years old when she met someone at a party who added her on Snapchat. 'About two weeks later, I got about 30 images of his dick and of him playing with his dick and I was just like, *Oh my God, what the hell?* I didn't really know what to do.' The man was older than Laani and went on to request images of her in return. 'He was like, "This is what it means to grow up." That is one thing that he said to me. Like, this is what it is to be mature. Everyone's doing it.'

Laani said that at the time, she didn't know who to turn to about the images, feeling she couldn't tell her parents and worrying about being judged if she told her friends. 'If everyone was doing it, I was scared of being judged for not doing it. And then if I was the only person who was being targeted, I was scared to speak to my friends in case they would just be like, "Well, why are you friends with someone like that?"'

Laani decided to keep it to herself and blocked the man after he sent her more unsolicited dick pics, but that first experience of being cyberflashed has had a complex and lasting effect on her own feelings around sex and her body. 'When I was 15, I wasn't ready to think of myself in a sexual way. It made me feel really gross and uncomfortable because I was forced into a situation where it was like one day, I opened my phone and then there were dick pics and I was told that the mature thing to do was to send nudes back.' Laani opened up on how, when she became sexually active, she had a warped notion in her head of how normal relationships develop. 'It gave me a really unhealthy relationship with my body and with seeing other people's bodies, where I thought if you're given something, you have to receive. And also that it's the normal thing to do if you're romantically interested in someone; there is no way to go about that without sending nudes.'

My conversations with Laani and the other young girls felt depressingly familiar and I sympathised with the stripping of their innocence through their early sexualisation. The girls had been forced to adapt to and navigate male predatory behaviour, and skirt around men's egos before they had even reached the legal age to have sex. Do girls really mature faster than boys? Or are they simply expected to act as adults when they are still children themselves?

In a disturbing example of how technology abuse is continually adapting, some participants of Ringrose, Reghr and Whitehead's study described how they knew of some boys who had sent fake dick pics to girls to coerce them into sending a nude image back as part of a transactional trade without having to share their own nude photo. Carrie*, a year eight pupil, disclosed: 'I know some people go on Google Images and just find one that matches your skin tone, so don't actually send their own one, and then they get something back.' While another pupil, Sam*, said, 'People have Photoshop, they can do anything.'

It's a disturbing thought that boys may be making sexually explicit deepfakes of themselves to lure girls into a mutual exchange that could be used against them, laying bare the contrast of societal stigma around gendered bodies and the different consequences that exist for men and women. Girls might be gripped by the fear of being placed into deepfake 'porn', while it appears some boys are distributing their own deepfakes for their advantage. I crave a world where teenage girls aren't having to find and trade techniques to avoid being sent dick pics on social media and can instead enjoy the awkwardness of just being a kid online and making annoying Taylor Swift edits.

Through my own encounters, research and talking with friends, I've always assumed cyberflashing was something most women have been exposed to at some point in their lives and yet it still makes my stomach churn to hear women's stories of receiving them. I asked my Instagram followers if they'd been sent an unsolicited dick pic and many of them shared their experiences with me. Their stories varied, but all their encounters had had a lasting effect on the women. I've decided not to share their names for anonymity.

*When I started burlesque, I seemed to go through phases of having lots of dick pics in my DMs with comments like 'you know you want it'. I ignored these at first, then I decided enough was enough and that this is never gonna change if we keep ignoring it. So I'd call them out on it, tell them that it's sexual harassment, and that I'm going to report their accounts. They'd come back with things like, 'don't put yourself out there if you don't wanna receive this attention', as if I was asking for it. Which I most certainly was NOT!*

*I've actually had two occasions where it's been guys I've known. One being a bouncer in Cardiff that used to look after me when I worked his bar as a shot girl. We had a good rapport and banter, and when I finished working that job he got in touch, we just had general chat then he started complimenting me, but in a way that felt odd to me. It didn't feel comfortable so I didn't really answer properly anymore, then suddenly it was something like 'I dreamt about you last night' with a pic of his hard on! I knew that he was recently married and his wife had just given birth to twins. I called him out on this – he teaches personal safety too, which is laughable! I reported his account and blocked and deleted him. It was a horrid situation where I didn't really know what to do.*

# CYBERFLASHING

*My husband was shocked that my AirDrop is off unless I accept. He asked me why and I explained that I had on a few occasions just received a dick pic randomly.*

*I dated a guy briefly last summer. He was in his early thirties. Then just started sending me pics of his naked body and I was like, yeah that doesn't really do it for me – also we've been on one date. The message was NOT received, obviously. He then sent me a video a few days later of himself with a towel on, and then drops the towel. Honestly, I couldn't believe it. He then got really shitty with me when I politely called him out and said we were on different vibes, and I didn't really appreciate being sent shit like that. The video came at like 8am as I was on a train to London and the conversation hadn't even been REMOTELY sexy or sexual. He totally blew it off and said it was just some 'cheeky photos/vids' and totally didn't understand why I was like, ew, no. It's never welcome in my opinion, but the fact that we hadn't even kissed and we'd only been on one date – I was like . . . pardon?*

*The first time I think I was around 13. Men are disgusting.*

■

Katie Weir is a lingerie expert who managed social media accounts for multiple market leading lingerie brands; she regularly hosted live streams on Instagram and private online bra fitting sessions for customers. I interviewed Katie about her job, which entailed posting content of beautiful, semi-nude women including herself. She told me how the brands' Instagram and Snapchat accounts would be inundated with dick pics by horny men who had taken a liking to the women's fashion brands, to the point where navigating unsolicited penises became a part of her job. Katie said, 'I think sometimes you think it's because that person wants to date you, or they want to slide in your

DMs and ask for your number. But they didn't care if they were sending it to multiple pictures of women who didn't have a name, because every picture was a different model. And then obviously how brands work, there are different people working at different times. It's like, who are you even sending that to?' Katie questioned what the men were getting out of their blanket dick-sharing, and whether it was the distributing of this content that satisfied their sexual urges as opposed to any expectation of something in return. Many of the brands value themselves as a company that seeks to empower women through their lingerie, and Katie thrived in her role of educating women on finding the right bra size and being comfortable in their bodies, but the additional labour of having to manage dick pics and sexual comments about the models and the staff put a downer on the job she loved. 'It's intrusive and it starts to take a toll on your role within the industry. Personally, I was putting myself out there in my underwear and for me, I was just doing it for the women, but actually, I know that there were a lot of men that are creeping out there too.'

One experience saw Katie have a booking for an online bra fitting over a video call. The customer had booked in as a woman, with a woman's name, and spoke with a high-pitched voice during the call, but they refused to put their camera on. Katie felt instantly that something was off. 'I had a gut instinct. I felt like something wasn't right, but I didn't want to judge; working for a brand that's inclusive and diverse we do come across cross-dressers and transgender people, and sometimes voices don't sound like the voices you were expecting.' Katie was wary of upsetting a customer who may be transitioning. 'I didn't want to be weird about it, so I was like, if you don't feel confident to come on camera no problem, I'll just talk you through the bra fitting. So, I demonstrated the scoop and sweep method.' This is a genius hack that helps your boobs sit perfectly in your bra. It involves placing your hand inside your bra and under your breast like a scoop, before sweeping in an upwards motion, lifting everything up and filling out the cup. After the first demonstration, the customer asked Katie if she could do it again, which she did. They then asked Katie to demonstrate for a third time, which rang alarm bells in her head: 'In that moment I was like, *no, this isn't right*. Like, you wouldn't need it that many times. It was obvious what was going on. But as I said no, I'm not going to do it again, they turned on their camera and there was a man just wanking down the camera. It was the most horrific experience because I just felt so violated. I didn't know what was going on. I was being violated within work time. You're trying to be the better person by helping someone, but they were there just taking advantage and being gross. It took a long time for me to get back into it again because I just didn't trust who was on the other side of the camera for a while.'

A women's lingerie brand designed and created for women, that was filming and posting content with the purpose of selling products to women had been hijacked by men who were simply seeking sexual gratification out of the brand's images.

When I asked Katie for her thoughts on the disturbing behaviour demonstrated by the men who flashed their penises to her online, she said it worried her to think of what their motives may be. 'The most scary part, I think with everything, is if these people can do it online, what do they do in real life?' Men are not only often the perpetrators of this behaviour, but can also appear to play down the seriousness of cyberflashing or deny that it exists altogether. After all, what harm could a few dick pics in the DMs really do? Katie said that her male friends often seemed to shrug off her experiences of sexism: 'They're like, well, we would never do anything like that. And it's one of those where when you see it so often, it feels to me that every other person is sending me a dick pic, so someone close to me has to be doing it?'

## Why is this happening?

Why *are* so many men sending pictures of their penises to women who have never asked for them? It's a question that's been asked many times, often alongside a quip of 'Do they really think that it'll work?!'. But by what definition would these unsolicited images be deemed a 'success'? If by 'work', we mean receiving the image will make the woman want to have sex with the sender then the likelihood is no, it will not. A YouGov study found that 58 per cent of women were likely to describe dick pics as 'gross', with 56 per cent of men agreeing that women would find them gross. If over half of men believe that women would react negatively to being sent an unsolicited dick pic, what is their motive for sending them in the first place?* Like in-person flashing, cyberflashing can feel like a power play. There's a sense of 'I'm going to show you my penis and you can't stop me.' At its most basic, it's gross and invasive, but pull back the layers and you can see the levels at play that can have a damaging effect on the receiver, their sense of self-worth and their safety.

Investigative journalist and broadcaster Ellie Flynn set up a fake profile on multiple dating apps for a Channel 4 documentary investigating sexual harassment, listing her age as 18 and using images of herself as a teenager. Flynn told me she wanted to demonstrate the onslaught of harassment that women face daily online. 'I think when you try to tell people what it feels like to be flashed, or what it feels like to be harassed online, or what it feels like to be on a dating app as a woman, they don't really get it. They just kind of feel like you're going on about

---

* In the same study, 51 per cent of men thought dick pics were 'funny' with only 28 per cent of women agreeing. And they say women have shit humour? At least you can laugh at yourself, lads.

something that is not that big of a deal, so I wanted to show what it feels like and the reality of what women experience on a day-to-day basis.'

Almost immediately after setting up the profiles, Flynn was inundated with unsolicited penis pictures, videos and graphic sexual comments, with some messages coming from men in their late forties. Even though she was accessing the apps as part of an experiment, she told me how draining it was to constantly be receiving these type of messages from hordes of men, with her producer, the director and Flynn all taking it in turns to reply and manage the influx.

Explaining how she went about the experiment, Flynn told me that, for legal reasons, she had been given a few stock phrases, questions and answers that she was allowed to use. 'I could just say, I'm sorry, I'm at work; I'm busy now or I could answer basic questions about my age, my location, my job and I could ask them questions like what are you doing today? What do you do for work? It was really, really basic.' Because of the legal restrictions, Flynn's chat towards the men was dry and boring, showing a lack of interest in getting to know them on a deeper level: 'And yet, I had so many responses of people sending me dick pics. I've not even given you a glimmer of interest. I'm not even really having a conversation with you. These are just kind of nothing responses and it's still leading to that?' Flynn expressed her frustrations at the men's sexualised behaviour, coming to the conclusion that there was nothing she did to encourage it and nothing she could have done to prevent it. 'If they want to send you a dick pic, they're going to send you a dick pic, because it's about their desires and their motivations, and it's got nothing to do with you.'

The lack of control is what makes indecent digital exposure feel so invasive – the power lies solely with the sender. Like all sexual crimes, there is nothing that the victim could have or should have done to prevent this from happening to them; the perpetrator had already made their decision. The taking and sharing of a dick pic without consent is premeditated. A man would have to have taken their clothes off, got out their camera, taken some photos and chosen which image to send, before scouting out the person they were going to send it to, opening a chat, uploading the image and clicking the send button. At no point in that process is the victim involved in the decision-making, yet so often they are faced with the blame.

Each time I've spoken to the press or on social media about my experiences of cyberflashing, I've received negative responses from both men and women seeking to shift the blame onto me. The first interview I did was with BBC News in 2021, which was posted on the homepage of their website. Overnight, the article was read more than a million times, an incredible reach that raised awareness of a disturbing trend that hadn't been covered much by the press or the government at the time, but the consequence was people tracking down my social media accounts to tell me why these dick pics were my fault. One of those people was radio host Julia Hartley-Brewer, who screenshotted eight images of me in lingerie from my Instagram account and posted them to her 460,000 followers on X, asking them, 'This is just a selection of the photos posted by this "influencer". Still wonder why men are sending unsolicited dick pix?' and 'Are we really supposed to be shocked and horrified that men are sending obscene photos to a woman who posts these images of herself?'* Yes Julia, yes you are. All the images I had posted adhered to Instagram's no nudity guidelines – the dick pics, however, did not. In another interview

---

* A DMCA takedown was submitted to X for Julia's tweets stating copyright infringement and my images were removed from her posts, although she kept the original posts and text up. Seeing the pictures be taken down and replaced by a copyright notice on her feed felt like a small but satisfying F U.

for the *Daily Mail*, I spoke of receiving hundreds of dick pics over the span of 12 years, yet the top-rated comment pointed the finger at women: 'Let's start criminalising these thirst trap pictures of half-naked women while we're at it.' Other most-liked comments included: 'Hope she has learned not to open pictures from unknown sources', 'If it's bothering you so much just block the senders, or even better, get off social media altogether!', 'Put your smartphone down once in a great while and stop sharing your number with strange people', and 'Why of all people does she gets them on her email? Not once have I got any?' Lucky, lucky you, reader.

Emily Atack, an actor best known for playing Charlotte in the TV series *The Inbetweeners* explored her experiences with cyberflashing and sexual harassment in the BBC Two documentary *Emily Atack: Asking For It?*, recalling how she's often blamed herself for the unwanted attention. 'I do sit there and go maybe this is down to me and I've even had people I love say to me maybe you should change your content.' When Atack confronted one of the men who was harassing her daily through unsolicited images and texts, he blamed her for his behaviour, shockingly claiming her 'reputation of sleeping with lots of men' didn't help. Ellie Flynn faced similar victim-blaming during her investigation for Channel 4. When she asked a man why he had sent her images of his penis, he simply replied, 'Your profile told me to do so, if not I wouldn't send that.' There was nothing on her profile that asked men to send her photos of their dick.

I've noticed a trend amongst men in the comments sections on my posts that talk about cyberflashing, where many of them seek to flip the conversation around towards women, pointing out how women also send these images, questioning whether women would be prosecuted and bringing up OnlyFans creators who advertise their content on social media:

'Does this law extend to females'

'Would a girl be charged for the same haha'

'But women can wear leggings that show their camel toe and that's not flashing in public'

'I say we start reporting female flashing on OnlyFans'

'So they gonna do same for woman flashing there bits on TikTok?'

'Amazing, does this mean we can now report all the women pushing their OF to the police instead of having to block them?'

'What about OF . . . what about women getting naked on line for money !??!?!'

I don't doubt that there are women out there who have sent a man an unsolicited image of their genitals and I agree that this is wrong, regardless of gender. It is also illegal under the Online Safety Act, just as it is for men, and you could seek prosecution. When I sat down with model Ben James for a podcast episode to discuss his career and his experiences with social media, I was taken aback by the sexualisation he has faced from women in his comments section and the unsolicited nudes he has received, where he told me he was treated like 'nothing but a wank bank'. He shared his frustration whenever he speaks up about this issue: 'What's funny is I talk about it and blokes are like "Oh, it's like every bloke's dream!" and I'll tell you now it's not, it's degrading; it's radically degrading when you're trying to achieve something of worth and you make a piece of content that you really care about and you go online and all there is, is that.' He went on to tell me how many of his experiences of being objectified echoed the female experience.

In this instance, we see how a stereotypical view of masculinity – that men can't be victims of sexual harassment and should instead 'enjoy' sexualised behaviour from women – works to play down their experiences and can be harmful to the men involved. This is reflected in the lack of research on men as victims of cyberflashing and is another example of how unhealthy ideals of masculinity harm men as well as women.

However, the attempt by some men to hijack the cyberflashing conversation protects the men who do it and stops them having to take responsibility for their behaviour. We know that studies consistently show how women are overwhelmingly targeted by cyberflashing from men, with Bumble finding 48 per cent of women aged 18–24 received an unsolicited nude in the year of 2021 alone. There is often – as we see in the examples above – an element of slut-shaming towards OnlyFans creators and women who share their nudes online from men who seem unable or unwilling to understand the difference between consensual and non-consensual content.

Women who share their nudes to promote their subscription sites on platforms such as X and Reddit, which allow nudity and sexual content, are not breaking the law or cyberflashing you. When you sign up to these sites you're agreeing to their terms and conditions, which allow users to post nudity on their main feed, which subsequently could end up on your main feed. However, if a user privately messages you an image of their genitals on social media without consent, then that is cyberflashing and should be reported to the platform and the police. If you receive an explicit DM on OnlyFans, it will be from an adult content creator's account that you have subscribed to and therefore consented to receiving this content. You might not like seeing naked women on your newsfeeds on certain apps, as much as I don't like seeing videos from GB News on mine, but legally they're both allowed. If you're concerned about nudity on a platform, check out their Ts & Cs.

■

Cyberflashing may seem less harmful than being flashed in person due to the perpetrator not being physically in front of you, but Rebecca Hayes and Molly Dragiewicz have raised safety concerns on dating apps where cyberflashing is prominent, as GPS technology accessing a user's physical location to connect with others in close proximity means the sender may have access to information about the receiver's location or live nearby. Some dating apps also require real names to be used, and encourage users to link their social media accounts such as Instagram directly in the app, making it easier for the sender to find more personal information about you, like where you work, your family members or where you live. Safety is a real concern for victims of cyberflashing with the guise of anonymity under the cloak of the internet adding a dark layer to digital sex crimes, leaving victims paranoid about who the perpetrator may be and what their motive is.

Speaking to *Stylist* magazine about her BBC documentary, Emily Atack shared how receiving hundreds of graphic sexual messages and dick pictures had left her feeling unsafe in her own home, especially as a woman living alone, with every noise in the night inciting fear that the men sending the images and messages may turn up at her front door. 'If you get a dick pic you haven't asked to see but then you block and delete them straight away, that image is still there in your mind. It doesn't go away; the damage has already been done.' In the film, Atack documented receiving 37 unsolicited dick pics in one morning alone, alongside graphic sexual messages. One message read, 'I'm gonna fuck you with the telescope that I'm using to spy on you and I'm gonna rape and kill you.' Atack described how vulnerable and frightened the messages make her feel, and how she makes sure that she triple locks all her doors.

In-person flashing, known as indecent exposure, has proven to be a gateway crime to more dangerous and sometimes even fatal crimes, with perpetrators sometimes showing a pattern of predatory behaviour before going on to rape and even kill. In a speech in Parliament for International Women's Day 2023, Dame Diana Johnson spoke about how, since 2018, almost 250 men found guilty of exposing themselves went on to be found guilty of rape. A review of evidence from 2014 found that a quarter of people who had been found guilty of indecent exposure had subsequently reoffended, with up to 10 per cent escalating their behaviours to more serious sexual offences.

In 2019, Libby Squire was studying philosophy at Hull University when she was raped and murdered by Pawel Relowicz. Since 2017, he had been committing a string of non-contact sexual offences including voyeurism and sexually motivated burglaries. Three weeks prior to Libby's rape and murder, Relowicz confronted two groups of women in public at night and masturbated in front of them, following one group home and ejaculating on their front door. Lisa Squire, Libby's mum, believes that her killer exposed himself to Libby on her way home weeks before her murder, and just hours after he had killed Libby, Relowicz was out on the streets of Hull exposing himself again. Speaking to the *Guardian* Squire said, 'Not every non-contact sexual offender will go on and become a rapist, but every rapist was a non-contact sexual offender at one point. So, I think we need to take them for the red flags that they really are. We need to understand that this is not normal behaviour and it's not OK.'

Lisa Squire is right: this predatory and dangerous behaviour is not okay, and yet each day, hundreds of women are flashed online without their consent and forced to read disturbing sexual comments about what the perpetrator would do to them if they had the chance, while society gaslights them into believing that these messages and images are just harmful banter and they should simply 'get over it' because 'no one has died of a dick pic'.*

In an article for *Cosmopolitan* magazine, Professor Clare McGlynn, a Professor of Law at Durham University and an expert in image based sexual abuse, shared her safety concerns on cyberflashing: 'Women can be very fearful for their physical safety, wondering who sent them this photo and what will they do next?' She explained how 'it limits our freedom to live our lives as we choose.'

When I asked Ellie Flynn for her thoughts on the motivations of the men who sent her dick pics and sexual comments during filming, she said, 'I know the escalation of these behaviours. I know how when you find someone who is committing the most heinous of crimes against women, that's not going to be the first thing they've done. And so, there's this kind of conflict – I feel like I'm talking to an idiot 19-year-old who has done it for a joke or a laugh, but then the other part of me is like, okay, but what is he getting from this? Does he enjoy it? Does he do it again? Does he suddenly not get enough out of sending them online? Does he then want to do it in person and where does that behaviour then lead?' Lisa Squire is now campaigning for earlier intervention and tougher measures in lower-level sex crimes.

Along with the heightened fear around physical safety, indecent digital exposure can have psychological effects on the victims. I have felt the internalised shame cyberflashing can bring, questioning my actions and behaviours, and accepting the unsolicited dick pics in my DMs as an admission of guilt for daring to exist in this female form. What did I expect, being a woman who shares my life on the internet? The Cyber Helpline highlights how cyberflashing can evoke feelings of humiliation,

---

* This was a genuine comment I received after the BBC News interview. It's comforting to know that only at death will we then draw the line.

shock and violation, as boundaries are crossed and victims lose control of their digital space. The psychological damage lingers much longer than the ten-second Snapchat photo of your dick.

## What is being done about it?

Professor Clare McGlynn has been working in the violence towards women and girls arena for many years. She told me how she decided to use her expertise to lobby the government to criminalise indecent digital exposure after noticing new ways in which women and girls were being abused that weren't addressed by law, and how, broadly speaking, criminal law in the UK has not been written with women's harms in mind. 'As women, we're having to slot ourselves into the existing law and my perspective is that if we start from what women are experiencing, what should or what would the law look like?' It almost seems unfathomable to know that exposing yourself to someone without their consent online was not a crime in the UK and in multiple countries across the world until recently.

When female-first* dating app Bumble carried out research within their community on the safety and experiences of women online, they were shocked to learn how common the receiving of unsolicited sexual images was amongst their users. I interviewed Alana Saltzman, the communications director for Europe at Bumble, who talked about how the company's work on cyberflashing was a direct response to this research in 2018. 'We found that in the US, one in three women reported having received unsolicited lewd photos from someone they hadn't yet met in person. As you can imagine, an overwhelming number

---

* On Bumble, if you're straight and match with another user, the woman has 24 hours to send the first message. The guy then has 24 hours to reply. If you both fail to do so, you will be unmatched.

of these women – 96 per cent – were unhappy to have been sent these images.' The app was founded by Whitney Wolfe Herde, whose mission was to create an online space where women could experience the dating pool without the fear of misogyny or harassment, after Herde's own negative experiences online. With dating apps playing host to thousands of unsolicited dick pics being sent daily, Herde, Saltzman and the team at Bumble decided in 2021 to take a stand and put their mission into practice by campaigning for a safer online space for women through the criminalisation of cyberflashing. 'While it was a crime to pull your pants down on the street – a Class B misdemeanour, punishable by a fine or jail time – there was nothing stopping anyone from exposing themselves in your DMs, texts, or other channels. The discrepancy between the physical act of flashing and the increasing digital act of flashing was problematic,' explained Saltzman.

Their initial research into the laws in place in the US, and specifically Texas, home of Bumble HQ, served as a shocking reminder to Saltzman of the lack of support out there for women. Working closely with politicians, and with Herde testifying in the Texas State House and Senate, Bumble successfully campaigned to make the sending of unsolicited sexual images online punishable by law in Texas. As their campaign continued, other states followed, including California, New York and Washington DC. In March 2024, Bumble endorsed a US federal bill to address the issue of indecent digital exposure, known as the CONSENT Act.* If the bill is passed, it will criminalise cyberflashing at federal level and will provide victims across the US with the right to legal proceedings against anyone who

---

* The Republicans took control of the Senate in the 2024 November election leaving the fate of the CONSENT Act up in air, as it will need to be signed off by a president with a questionable history of supporting women's rights.

sends an unsolicited sexual image. With their work initially focused on the US, they soon turned their attention to the UK. Saltzman told me, 'During the pandemic, it became clear that we also needed to advocate for more action in the UK. With so much of our lockdowns spent online, there were increasing reports that cyberflashing was only getting worse.'

Bumble, alongside Professor Clare McGlynn and a coalition of experts, including the organisations Glitch, Refuge and UN Women UK, as well as campaigners who bravely spoke out about their experiences of receiving unsolicited sexual images, began lobbying the UK government in 2021 to make cyberflashing a stand-alone offence in England and Wales. In 2023, a new law was finally introduced to criminalise cyberflashing as part of the Online Safety Act. This means that anyone who sends an unwanted image or film of their genitals could face prosecution and find themselves on the Sex Offenders Register, facing a hefty fine or sent to prison for a maximum of two years.

Speaking of the response from Bumble's users to the company's activism on cyberflashing, Saltzman told me how positively their switch from dating app to campaigning platform had been received: 'We received thousands of messages of support on social media as well as personal stories about individuals' experiences. Some were familiar to many of us and others were unbelievably upsetting – like a woman who was cyberflashed through Airdrop at a family funeral. All of them, however, were a stark reminder of the experiences of women online.' I honestly thought I had heard it all when it came to the pits of dick pics, but hearing how a woman was targeted while grieving a family member ignites the female rage in me once more.

In February 2024, Nicholas Hawkes became the first person in England and Wales to be convicted and jailed for cyberflashing after he sent unsolicited photos of his erect penis to a 15-year-old girl and a woman via WhatsApp. He was jailed for 66 weeks, given a 10-year restraining order and made to sign the Sex Offenders Register. On the surface, the sentencing seems like a positive in the fight for justice and for his victims, and that it is, but in the grand scheme of things, Hawkes' case was seen as an easy win. He was a previous sex offender who had been found guilty of sexual activity with a child under 16, who had breached an order and a suspended sentence for another offence, and he pleaded guilty to two counts of sending a photograph or film of his genitals to cause distress, harm or humiliation. This clause in the law where proof of malicious intent and/or sexual gratification is needed allows wiggle room for perpetrators, who can insist their actions were innocent and just a bit of 'fun'. I can't see how sending an image of an erect penis can be viewed as anything other than for sexual gratification – you'd think the presence of a sexually aroused penis would give it away. But in criminal law, when it comes to proving the intent of the perpetrator who has sent an unwanted dick pic, unfortunately, it will not always be as straightforward as it was in Hawkes' case to get a conviction.

Campaigners including Emily Atack and Bumble are continuing their efforts to see a consent-based law passed, which would remove the need to prove the intent of a perpetrator. 'To drive societal change, we believe that cyberflashing laws must be based on non-consent,' said Saltzman. 'While motivating factors will always be relevant, requiring proof of the perpetrator's motivations puts considerable onus on the victim and creates a very high threshold for repercussions. We'll continue to advocate and support calls for a consent-based approach, recognising the violating nature of the harm and making accountability, and enforcement, more likely.'

In the UK, the Online Safety Act gives media regulator Ofcom the responsibility and power to provide guidance to social media platforms on how to manage cyberflashing on their sites and keep women safe. However, initial draft guidance published in 2023 places the responsibility on victims to report, take down, block and remove unwanted content, instead of taking a preventative approach. The guidance also suggests to platforms that it would be incredibly difficult for perpetrators to be convicted under this law, minimising the seriousness of the crime while removing the need for tech companies to act.

When I spoke with Professor McGlynn about her hopes for the future, she told me her aim isn't to see hordes of men imprisoned for cyberflashing, but instead a change of conversation around the harm these actions have on women. She's diverting her attention from criminal reform to pushing the regulators to act to put women first. 'What I want Ofcom to do is to say how harmful cyberflashing is so that the companies need to take the steps to prevent and reduce that material appearing through their sites.'

When it comes to a prevention-led approach, Bumble is leading the way as the first dating app to moderate unsolicited explicit images with the creation of their AI-powered tool 'Private Detector', that identifies, captures and blurs nude images sent on their app, before sending a warning to the recipient, giving them the power to choose whether they view the content or not.

However, Alana Saltzman emphasised the importance of addressing the wider challenges of misogyny in society. 'After years of refining Private Detector, we released an open-source version of the feature to help the wider tech community combat cyberflashing and work to make the internet a safer place.' It has taken five years for outside tech platforms to begin to implement the technology, even though they could use it for free.

Instagram has also begun using AI technology to detect and blur suspected nudity in direct messages, although when

I have reported a blurred, unsolicited dick pic in my DMs to Instagram, I received an automated response that the content was not in violation of their T&Cs and the report was closed, so I'm currently cautious of its functionality.

It's impossible to ignore the hypocrisy of men who see no real issue in sending an unsolicited dick pic while lambasting women for taking private nudes. Men have shamed me online, calling me a whore while partaking in the non-consensual distribution of my content, but willingly and intentionally distributed their dick pics in my DMs without a shred of shame or guilt. The entitlement of men and their 'human right' to show us their genitals online is upheld to such a level that men and women will speak out in their defence through infantilising shrieks of 'WHAT DO YOU EXPECT?!', while actively targeting female victims, bullying them into silence in an attempt to rid *le coq* of all responsibility. But their victim-blaming does not work, the responsibility still lies solely with the sender. If we are to believe that men are far superior at controlling their emotions compared to women, then why are so many failing to demonstrate restraint and discipline in their displays of indecent digital exposure? People like Julia Hartley-Brewer may be happy to accept and normalise this behaviour, but I don't believe that men have such an emotional response to seeing a woman's image online that they can't help but send her a photo of their penis. It is offensive to the millions of men who don't send women unsolicited pictures of their dick that this is the baseline behaviour we're accepting from men. They *know better*, so expect it from them.

## TIPS: How to deal with unsolicited nudes a.k.a. cyberflashing

Receiving an unsolicited sexual image can feel extremely invasive and ruin your day/week/month. Here are some tips on how you can protect your, or your child's, social media accounts from non-consensual images:

- Airdrop is extensively used by sexual predators to get their kicks by sending dick pics to unsuspecting iPhone users close by. Make sure your Airdrop settings are switched to Contacts Only when you're in a public space so you can't be discovered by strangers.

- Instagram is trialling a new feature that will allow you to limit the type of content that accounts you don't know can send you, blocking any images from being sent until you have marked them as safe. When available to you, I recommend switching this on so you can't be forced to see some dude's chipolata when you wake up on a Sunday morning.

- If you receive a DM on social media that includes an unsolicited nude, report this to the platform as this will be against their terms and conditions. You can also block the username to prevent them from sharing any more images with you.

- If you feel up for it, report the account to the police, as cyberflashing is a crime in England and Wales under the Online Safety Act. Make a note of the username that sent you these images and screenshot any conversations as evidence. If you don't feel comfortable phoning a police station, many local forces now have a system for you to report online crimes online or through live chat. To find your local police force head to https://www.police.uk/pu/find-a-police-force/

- If you're a parent, please have an open conversation with your kids about cyberflashing. I can promise you that they will already know about sending nudes and, as cringe as it may feel, creating an environment where they will feel comfortable telling you if they've received an unsolicited pic without being scared of being blamed will help ease their mental load of trying to navigate the unwanted attention. It will also help keep them out of trouble if they know that the sending of sexual images without consent is a crime. You can try opening up the conversation in a way they can relate to, sharing how you watched a TikTok video or read an article on unwanted penis pics and asking whether this is something they've heard of or have experienced.

- Put to use the 'Teen' account feature on Instagram for any children under the age of 16, which allows parents to manage their child's privacy settings. This will automatically make their account private and prevent anyone they don't follow from sending them messages. To activate, click the settings tab on the platform and scroll down to 'Family Centre' where you can invite your teen's account and accept.

- If you want to take matters into your own hands and get a few laughs out of this horror while watching the perv squirm, use this template as a response to their image sending and see how fast Mr Dick Pic regrets his decision:

'This is an automated response generated by [*insert social media platform here*]. Your image is found to be a violation of the UK Online Safety Act (2023) by our AI bot, which flagged your content as an unsolicited sexual image. Your account will be reported to local authorities for online sexual harassment and indecent exposure. Think we've made a mistake? Our bot is currently in testing mode. If you believe this message was in error, reply 'HELP'. Otherwise, you will be contacted by your local authorities within 24hrs.'

I can confirm the satisfaction watching the repeated 'HELP' messages roll in is simply *chef's kiss*.

# 6

# CATFISH

### 'Why have you not messaged back, baby?'

'You are a shameful citizen'
**Machine Gun Kelly, *Catfish* co-host for one iconic day**

When MTV launched *Catfish: The TV Show* in 2012, taking up hours of my life bingeing on the sofa and securing Nev Schulman a lifelong spot in the pop culture hall of fame, I could never have imagined that less than a decade later, I would be presenting a TV show of my own, investigating identity theft after falling victim to the cruel world of romance scams. But unlike Schulman, who had been tricked into an online relationship with a woman who was posing as a young family friend, it was my own identity that had been stolen. Time and time again. Over its nine seasons, MTV's infamous show exposed a network of online identity scams in its quest to uncover the truth for those who've fallen victim to scammers and to understand the motivation behind the fraudsters' deceit. And yet, one individual who is often overlooked as a casualty in all the trickery and confusion is the person who's unwillingly become the face of someone else's pain – the one being used as catfish bait.

### CATFISH

*Definition:* A slang term used to describe someone who is pretending to be someone different online, usually to attract and trick others.

156

# CATFISH

I was 19 years old when I received my first Facebook message from a stranger letting me know I had an impersonator. MTV's show was dominating the airwaves at the time and as a university student whose social media following was growing quickly, I was kind of flattered at the news. *Does this mean I'm a somebody?* Having someone steal my photos and pretend to be me made teenage Jess feel important. Plus, it gave me some good content to bring to pre-drinks in my student halls.

Over the next few months, my online presence continued to grow while my pictures spread further across the internet. But the bigger my following, the more my inbox filled with strange messages from men demanding to know why I hadn't replied to them on other social media and dating sites, or asking me to share photos with them to prove that I'm the 'real' Jess. As the years passed, I lost count of the fake profiles that had stolen my likeness and the DMs from men seeking answers from their new girlfriend. Some guys would send a simple message: 'Someone out there is pretending to be you trying to scam people!' While others would take their anger out on me: 'You've been caught, Jessica. What do you gain from lying? I'm about to expose you, I'm about to expose you hard. Your downfall is coming soon . . .'

I had learnt to deal with the hate comments by now, and appreciated the men who let me know of the fake accounts so I could report them to the platforms – although most of the time they would take no further action or claim the fake account wasn't doing anything wrong. But I was not prepared for or equipped to handle the emotional labour of having to gently break up with the men in my inbox who believed they were in a relationship with me, when I had never spoken with them before.

I felt somewhat obliged to let the men know that they had been scammed. It wasn't my fault but it felt brutal to leave their messages unanswered in my requests folder. From my past experiences, I knew some men struggle to handle rejection at the best of times, but throw in the feeling of humiliation about being duped, plus losing their hard-earned cash after being tricked into transferring the scammers money, and I was juggling with some steaming hot potatoes. One man sent me abuse about my 'little saggy breasts' followed up by an apology for holding a grudge because 'someone robbed me with an account with your profile and I still can't believe I fell for it'. He went on to tell me how he'd love to meet the real me in person, which was a common theme from the men who I'd politely informed had been speaking to someone who was using my identity. My glimmer of kindness had seemingly inspired them to shoot their shot, sending through flirty messages on how they had been 'looking forward to sharing cocktails some day in the future. Can only hope the real you is as nice as "they" were' and 'u look cute I was disappointed it wasn't u'. These interactions left me feeling frustrated and I'd often end up blocking the men while also feeling guilty, like I was somehow responsible for their emotional baggage.

Most of the men were significantly older than me and would share stories of how they'd spoken with 'me' about kids, how I was due to catch a plane to live with them across the Atlantic and how we had exchanged those sacred three words (no, not 'please send cash'). It must've felt exciting for them to fall in love online, but there was always a grimier side to their love story. These men who had decades on me had matched with a fake profile that was using semi-nude photos of me as a teenager, including some of my professional modelling photos, and they genuinely believed that they were in some sort of relationship with me. *Lord, grant me the delusion of a middle-aged, balding white man.* Some of the fake profiles using my photos had suggestive bios, easing the men in for sex chat, such as 'shy first naughty in nature lol. If you think your adventures is dangerous try me in your bed', 'I'll be the best you ever had. Bad girl' and 'Hi guys do you like me? Do you want to see my pics and videos just message me privately . . .' Knowing that some of the men who were messaging me for answers had most probably been sent my nudes and engaged in sex talk about them left me feeling dirty and ashamed. I wanted to feel sorry for the men who had been fooled by my fake profiles, and mostly I did, but I couldn't shake the bleak sense that they had also been seeking out young women to take advantage of.

For those who ended up sending money to the catfish, there would almost always be a sob story involved – a tactic often used by fraudsters when extorting victims. The stories were generic and taken straight out of a scammer's script: my mother has cancer and I'm struggling to feed my family; I've been kicked out by my parents and I'm living on the streets; I've had a baby and need money to feed my child. It was kind of the men to send them some cash . . . but the cynic in me questions why adult men were engaging with seemingly vulnerable teenagers online and were happy for them to continue sending naked photos throughout their suffering. If they really believed they were in a relationship with a teenager who was facing homelessness, or one that couldn't care for her infant child, did any of them consider reaching out to the police or social services out of concern for the young woman's welfare? Or did exchanging a couple hundred quid for some nude photos make them believe they were a good guy? These men were victims, and it was wrong and unfair for them to be deceived and taken advantage of, but perhaps some of them simply lost a game of power play they'd become so accustomed to winning. If the 'women' with the traumatic stories behind my photos were actually real people, would we view the exploitation and perception of victimhood through a whole different lens?

## Beware of the catfish

Catfish scams are embedded into internet culture. A 2023 survey by Express VPN found almost a quarter of Brits have experienced catfishing themselves, with 40 per cent knowing someone who's fallen victim to fake profiles. In 2018, Facebook reported they had removed 1.3 billion fake accounts from their platform over a six-month period, while Express VPN's report shows dating app Tinder contributes to 31 per cent of all cases of romance scams. The online catfishing business is a lucrative one, with the National Fraud Intelligence Bureau receiving 8,036 reports of romance fraud in the financial year of 2022–2023, amounting to a loss of a huge £92 million, which equates to an average loss of £11,500 per victim. While research for the UK Finance's Take Five to Stop Fraud campaign discovered 38 per cent of people who met someone online had been asked to send money, with 57 per cent of those asked lending or sending it. People of all ages and genders can fall victim to a catfish, whether you're finding a friend to talk to online or looking for a more intimate connection.

*The most effective fake profile was of a female aged between 12 and 25*

A 2024 report titled 'What Makes Fake Profiles Effective?' by Cyabra, an AI tech company that shields brands and companies from disinformation and bad actors, analysed 42,037 fake accounts across X, Facebook, Instagram, and TikTok. Their findings showed that fake profiles impersonating women, and more specifically young girls, received more engagement, influence and click-throughs than fake profiles posing as men, with accounts claiming to be female and between the ages of 12–25 receiving more views than any other age group. Their research found these accounts were three times more likely to receive views than their male counterparts.

I asked my Instagram followers whether they'd had any experiences with fake accounts and received responses from both men who'd been victims to fake profiles and women whose images had been stolen and used to trick others. Some of the men said they felt foolish that they had sent money after the scammers had claimed they needed help to pay their rent or bills. These men had met their catfish on dating apps and told me how the experience had 'made my trust issues even worse than they already were' and that 'it caused a lot of anxiety as a single man, trying to meet girls again and in relationships in general'.

One man told me how he'd built an online relationship over the course of two months after meeting a woman on a dating app who claimed to be from his area in South Wales. They spoke on the phone regularly and exchanged sexual chat and images, but the man became suspicious of unanswered follow requests and after doing some digging, he found a Facebook profile that looked like the woman he'd been talking to, showing she was in a relationship. The man discovered he had been catfished by someone using the real woman's photos, including her hacked intimate images, to exchange nudes with the man. He never found out who was behind the fake account – who now held a copy of his naked photos.

A female follower told me of the 'insane' number of times people have used her images to catfish people, including one experience of a man from Scotland who had set up an elaborate network of fake profiles using her photos over a five-year period, telling his work colleagues of his new girlfriend and creating fake accounts to pose as her family members. Another scammer used her photos for a number of years to trick people into sending money, which involved sending leaked nudes of her on Snapchat. She said that the men who fell victims to the scams and contacted her were 'a total mess'. I recognised the woman's description of the awkwardness of having to manage the men's feelings after they'd been scammed by those using her photos from my experience: 'I always found the people who have been catfished find it really hard to comprehend that they don't actually know ME when I end up talking to them because they have known my image for so long. It's honestly the weirdest experience and feeling.'

### 1 in 10 profiles on dating apps are fake

With online reports suggesting one in ten profiles on dating apps are fake, and a 2023 YouGov survey discovering 71 per cent of male and 47 per cent of female dating app users in the UK have come into contact with a fake profile, it's important to be clued up on the risks of online dating before you download the apps to ensure you can spot the bogus amongst the babes.

Currently, 'catfishing', also known as online impersonation, is not a specific crime in the UK, but the act of catfishing may still be illegal if the person running the fake account is partaking in criminal activity. For example, someone using a fake account or false identity to make money could be committing fraud under the Fraud Act 2006. If a catfish account is used to harass someone else, this could be seen as breaking the law under the Protection from Harassment Act 1997 or prosecuted as malicious communications if the catfish sent their victim threats, or a message that is indecent or grossly offensive. The global reach of catfishing makes prosecuting these crimes a difficult task: it is difficult – but not impossible – for local police to seek justice for romance scams that are carried out by perpetrators abroad, where laws and regulations may be different. This is similar to many digital crimes, including deepfake sexual abuse and the distribution of intimate images without consent, which is why campaigners are calling for a comprehensive law on image-based sexual abuse to be introduced and recognised worldwide that will help victims pursue justice, wherever their perpetrator may reside.

## We've matched, now what?
## Tips on how to spot a fake profile

So you've swiped right on a dating app and hit the jackpot with a match. But do you know what signs to look out for to protect yourself from scammers?

- **They're giving too much away**: like *wayyy* too much. Sorry to say, but a woman you meet on a dating app who is real and interested in you isn't going to be sending you a pic of her tits, sexting with you and asking for cash to save her dying nan all in the space of 24 hours.

- **Their followers and following list don't look real:** This is an easy giveaway on platforms like Instagram and TikTok, where you can look through people's follow lists. If they only have a handful of followers that all happen to be other attractive women, or they only follow men, then steer clear because they're probably a catfish.

- **Check them out, but properly this time:** On Instagram, you can find out when an account was first created and if they've changed their username before by clicking the three dots next to an account's username and selecting 'About this account'. Both of these are pretty clear pointers of fake profiles.

- **Their content isn't consistent:** Most catfish will be repurposing someone else's content and won't pay close attention to timeline of images, so look for inconsistencies in the quality of their images (e.g. they could've been taken years ago on an older iPhone) or things like hairstyles (if someone's hair keeps growing and losing a few inches, then that's a little suss).

- **Keep an eye out for spelling mistakes**: If you're allegedly talking to a white woman born and raised in California, they're probably not going to be writing in broken English in their bio, so don't be blinded by the sexy pics, make sure you take in the rest of their content too.

- **If it seems too good to be true, then it probably is:** I get it, you want to meet your 6ft 4 Prince Charming and *maybe* that petite brunette who won homecoming queen *might* just give a 40-year-old guy a chance? But the likelihood is, someone is using images of an outrageously good-looking person to lure in victims. Don't be one of them. My rule on dating apps is that I assume everyone is a catfish and if I CBA to put in the effort to uncover the truth, I work backwards from there.

■

In 2020, after a particularly relentless week of receiving DMs from men warning me of several different fake accounts using my images, I posted a rant on my social media to let my followers know I did not use any other accounts, only my official verified social media platforms, explaining how this was an issue I'd been dealing with for eight years by this point, and stressed that they should not send any money to strangers they meet online.* My story was picked up by the BBC, which

---

* Seriously, please don't do this. If a stranger is asking for money for an emergency, they're almost always a fake. If you must part with your cash, find a decent charity to give it to.

led me to investigate the murky world of catfishing in a documentary titled *When Nudes Are Stolen* for BBC Three in an attempt to uncover exactly why I had been chosen as catfish bait by so many scammers and what was really happening with my photos.

As part of the documentary, I interviewed Laura Lyons, a private investigator and expert on identity fraud. When I walked into the room, there were dozens, if not hundreds, of fake accounts all of 'me' printed out and spread across two tables. I'd been living with this burden for so many years, having my images stolen had become a normal part of my virtual life, but seeing the accounts laid out in front of me hit home at just how exploitative this had all become. Lyons and I read through the profiles – many were from social media sites and dating apps, while others were using my images to advertise sex chats and escorting services. Shuffling through the sheets, there was one particular fake profile that jumped out at me. The text read 'READY FOR RAPE ROLEPLAY NOW' alongside one of my selfie images from when I was 19 years old that had been stolen off my members website. My hands were shaking as I picked up the piece of paper, and I fought back tears of frustration as I looked down at myself and the words that accompanied my photo. How were so many people apparently allowed to get away with this, while I was left to deal with the ongoing trauma? The feelings of indignity around those images came rushing back and, with them, an increased heart rate that turned my cheeks red. I knew how society judged me for those photos and I could picture the graphic sexual comments that were left underneath them in forums. I did not deserve to be sent as a sacrificial lamb to slaughter so that predatory men could live out their sick rape fantasies online.

Lyons told me that throughout her career investigating identity fraud and romance scams, she had never come across someone whose images had been used to create as many fake accounts as mine had. When I was a teenager, my dad, who was a policeman at the time and hyper aware of online safety, would monitor my Bebo account to check I wasn't oversharing on my profile and lecture me on avoiding speaking to any dodgy people on the internet. Now, just over a decade on, my image was known to those working in the field as the most commonly used by catfishers. I wished in that moment I could rewind the years and remove the thousands of pieces of content I must have shared since I signed up to Bebo, my first social media account, when I was just 14 years old. But it was too late, my identity and my image belonged to the scammers now.

I asked Lyons why she thought I – out of the hundreds of thousands of young women my age online – had been targeted in this way. She explained how my social media presence gave scammers the perfect material, calling my Instagram account 'catnip' for those looking to create a convincing fake profile. I shared everything: photos of me getting ready with the girls, what I was having for tea, pictures with family and friends, photos with no make-up on, selfies in full glam, sexy pictures from my modelling jobs and everyday girl-next-door snaps. Lyons told me how this collection allowed someone to build a well-rounded character when engaging with victims online. If they asked what 'I' was up to and the scammer replied 'just cooking dinner', then they already had a picture ready to send alongside it. It had never really occurred to me that sharing snippets of my daily life could be used in such an elaborate scam. Some of the photos that were uploaded by the fraudsters were screenshots of Instagram stories that I couldn't even remember posting, and now they were being used to entice men across the world to part with their money and their nude photos. It felt so incredibly intrusive and it was only going to get worse, with the discovery that my intimate images were being sold and traded in underground communities.

# The disposable victims of e-whoring

With the expansion of the internet and the normalisation of swapping nude photos, romance scams have adapted to a younger online user base and a heightened sexual society. While traditional catfishing may take place on online dating websites, with the promise of marriage and children, a new wave of fraudulent schemes are capitalising on the way young people live their lives online, targeting them through apps like Snapchat and online gaming communities, and hooking them with the allure of exchanging naked pics. It was during filming for my BBC Three film that my investigation into catfishing led me to uncover the depraved sub-culture of e-whoring, which, yes, is as misogynistic as the name suggests.

## E-WHORING

*Definition:* The impersonation of a person, often a young woman, to sell sexual images and videos to a third party online.

This new form of image-based sexual abuse is a kind of hybrid of traditional 'revenge porn' and catfishing. Women's nude images are packaged into folders alongside carefully curated identities and sold on to wannabe scammers for use in online impersonation scams to defraud men. Scott McGready is a hacker and cyber-security consultant, and one of the first people to research the damaging culture of e-whoring. In an interview for this book, he told me how the terminology 'e-whoring' is used to degrade the women whose images are being stolen and repurposed, and the men who fall victim to the scam: 'It works to dehumanise them so that your person that's doing the scam doesn't feel so bad about it.'

## NO ONE WANTS TO SEE YOUR D*CK

E-whoring has its own community online, where how-to-guides are sold that include scripts, preview 'packs' of women's images* and tips on how to manage a successful fake account. McGready told me how these 'packs' often include a variety of photos carefully pieced together for maximum effect: 'Packs usually come with two different, distinct folders. One folder is purely photographs listed as verification, for example "thumbs up", "peace sign" and also "holding a piece of paper" is a common one. And then the second folder goes into the more sexual content, so it will be listed as "top off", "completely naked", all that kind of stuff.' He explained how the verification photos work as a way of convincing the victim that they are speaking to a 'real' person – for example, if they request a selfie of the woman holding a piece of paper with their username written on it as confirmation they are speaking to a real person, the scammer already has the content readily available to edit and send over. Moving images are also often featured in the packs – the most useful to the scammer replicate a normal webcam call set up: 'Typing on a keyboard, looking up, smiling, playing with hair, all that kind of stuff. All the way down to the sexual content, where it's like taking the top off, playing with yourself, whatever it may be.'

The packs traded in e-whoring communities are usually created from images stolen from webcam models, OnlyFans creators and amateur models, for the obvious reason that there is a variety of NSFW and PG content already available of them to find on the internet. But from his research of the PDF manuals that provide tips for users, McGready believes some of the more personal content, particularly the verification photos and videos, could have been acquired through a more sinister

---

* McGready noted while there are some packs in circulation that include men's images, this is a practice that overwhelmingly targets women. The name being a bit of a giveaway of the misogynistic culture it's built from.

route: 'I suspect some of them might have come from leaked or hacked video cameras, or they've taken someone who's extremely vulnerable or who just trusts a little too quickly, and they've convinced them. "Do you wanna jump on webcam and then do all these actions? If you don't, I'll email your parents and tell them these horrible things."'

Unlike other impersonation scams, money doesn't seem to be a huge driving force for those who make and sell packs for e-whoring. McGready said one reason for this is that many perpetrators are teenage boys who do not have access to a bank or PayPal account to store their money. Instead, the young men ask that those buying their packs – or the individuals that they are catfishing – buy them online gift cards or vouchers for food delivery services instead. There are examples where e-whoring has made scammers a decent income, but most traders are selling folders of photos for $5–20. Not exactly life changing cash, but enough for a teenager to buy a large pizza meal deal.

In my BBC Three documentary, I interviewed a YouTuber named Aku. A model and aspiring rapper as well as an ex-e-whorer, he seemed a far cry from the image of an old, chubby man sat in his mum's basement and hardly the type of person I thought would be behind romance scams. He was open with me about his past experiences and told how he'd often use women's packs that he'd downloaded for free from e-whoring communities to catfish other men online. It was only when Aku befriended one of the men through regularly playing video games together that he decided to come clean and tell him that the woman he'd been speaking to wasn't who he thought she was.

Aku seemed to have a moral compass he was proud of, but one that fell short of feeling guilty for the women whose images he was stealing. 'These were cam girls!' he explained when I asked if he felt any remorse for distributing and repurposing their images across the internet. To him, these women were disposable and did not deserve any ownership or control over their intimate images because of how they made their money. Though he was also making money from their photos that he judged so harshly.

I wanted to dislike Aku but instead he intrigued me; I felt sorry for him when I heard how he'd been introduced to e-whoring as a teenager by adults in their twenties who he had met online. To me, Aku was a victim too, and it was clear that he had been using the internet in search of some sort of friendship or relationship since his younger years. His views on women were questionable to say the least – but then, should that really come as a surprise considering he had been groomed as a child by strangers on the internet into believing women were nothing but bodies to be traded and used for financial gain? Aku's story should ring alarm bells and act as a worrying case study for the young men and boys who are being radicalised in online spaces, foreshadowing the misogyny that will blossom at the nurturing hands of their online groomer.

Scott McGready told me he believed financial gain was simply the cherry on top for e-whorers, with most engaging in the trading of women and their impersonation for some twisted fun: 'There's an element of someone wanting to cause someone else pain. That's the one key thing that I see: effectively it's torture, and someone's getting off on the torture, whether sexually or just emotionally or physically.'

It's a chilling thought to think of young men, many just teenagers, filling their spare time in the digital realm to inflict suffering on others. What happened to meeting your mates for a kick around in the park? But it's a harsh reminder of the chronically online landscape the younger generation are living in and, consequently, the lack of empathy spawned by an existence devoid of human interaction. In these forums, there seemed to be less camaraderie compared to some other manosphere communities I'd researched. Though it did remind me of the incel community, where the men hold a strong hatred and bitterness towards both women and their fellow men, despising the 'chads' of the world who they believe hold all the power, even encouraging other members of the incel community to take their own lives. The e-whoring forums seemed to consist of a collection of lonely, bored and hateful individuals who were looking for something – or someone – to exploit purely for their entertainment. When you take a step back from the shocking and spiteful vitriol that they post online, it becomes clear that the only people they truly hate is themselves.

I posted my own picture in a Telegram channel dedicated to e-whoring alongside some text asking if anyone had a pack of the woman in the photo to trade. I didn't include my name or any information other than one solo selfie, which instantly sparked a reply from another member in the group: 'I do, but you'll have to pay.' His response stole the air out of my lungs. Was it really possible that my face had become so recognisable in e-whoring communities that this man could fulfil my request within minutes? I could feel the adrenaline coursing through my veins as I fixated on the screen waiting for his offer to roll in – '$15 amazon gift card'.

After almost ten years spent wondering why I had been relentlessly targeted by fake profiles using my images, after having to manage the emotions of dozens of men in my DMs that I'd never even spoken to, and after reporting hundreds of fake accounts advertising 'my' apparent services, I finally had my answer: my 'pack' – and as a result, my body – was being circulated and traded on e-whoring forums. Seriously? They were ruining my life for *fifteen* fucking dollars? Surely, I had to be worth more than a large pizza at Domino's . . .

## Sextortion: the high price of online scams

If you can cast your mind back to the Covid pandemic that saw cities shut down, office blocks go dark and in-person contact cancelled, what can you remember doing to pass the time and squash the fear? I'm going to take a wild guess that your answer includes some form of digital communications. Our entire lives were forced online, from food shopping and quiz games to dancing and dating, we were encouraged to rack up our screen-time to try to find some sort of normality in the unknown. But a mix of heightened internet usage, boredom and a desperate longing for human contact made it seemingly inevitable that disaster would strike. That manufactured disaster is known as sextortion.

### SEXTORTION

*Definition:* Used to refer to financially motivated sexual extortion. A form of blackmail that often includes impersonation and threats to share intimate images.

Another variant of the impersonation world, in sextortion cases, fake profiles – again, often of young, attractive women – are used to build a relationship with the victim before encouraging them to swap nude images, which are then used as blackmail: the perpetrator demands that the victim send over cash in exchange for the scammer not to distribute their intimate images to friends, family and their wider community. It is a callous crime that preys on our societal shame around sex and our bodies, bullying people into coughing up or face having their personal photos put on public trial. Sextortion can happen to any gender, at any age, but recent reports show a sharp spike in teenage boys falling victim to this crime, with the Internet Watch Foundation

(IWF – a UK-based safety watchdog) finding 91 per cent of all UK victims of sextortion in 2023 were male, with teens aged 14–17 years old most at risk. In 2023, the Revenge Porn Helpline reported that 93 per cent of all sextortion cases involved men as victims, with perpetrators predominantly being criminal gangs. This is in contrast with their findings on 'revenge porn', which overwhelmingly targets women, with 67 per cent of the offenders a current or former partner.

*Teenage boys aged 14–17 years old are most at risk of sextortion*

In 2024, the National Crime Agency made the unprecedented decision to put out its first ever all-school alert, urging teachers in the UK to warn their pupils about the dangers of a fast-growing, worldwide blackmail scam targeting teenagers. Due to the shame tied to our sexuality and a feeling of foolishness having fallen victim to romance scams, it is feared sextortion is widely underreported. In 2024, 33 police forces in England and Wales responded to a Freedom of Information Act request by the BBC. This showed that there had been a total of 21,323 recorded blackmail cases that referenced the word 'sextortion' over the last decade – over 18,000 of those had been reported since the Covid pandemic and 8,000 were recorded in 2023 alone. For comparison, the same number of police forces recorded just 23 similar cases in 2014.

*Police recorded 8,000 cases of sextortion in England and Wales in 2023*

Sophie Mortimer, the manager of the Revenge Porn Helpline, told me how supporting those affected by sextortion had become a large part of their work: 'Sextortion is about a third of our caseload, but that's almost entirely men. It's about 95 per cent male clients.' Sextortion has been an issue since the helpline began, she explained, but it was during the first Covid lockdown that they saw the number of reports of this crime go through the roof. 'People were lonely, and we were encouraged suddenly to take everything online. You can maintain your friendships and your relationships, you can date, you can do all of these things, but there was no conversation at that point about online safety.' Mortimer said she felt it was a case of, 'Okay population of the world, get online and just get on with new people because it'll be fine!' But for many it wasn't fine. And the problem of sextortion has only increased since then.

Unlike e-whoring scams, which are often headed up by individuals, sextortion is known to be a more sophisticated and organised attack often – though not exclusively – carried out by criminal gangs. Of the reports made by male victims to the Revenge Porn Helpline, 80 per cent of perpetrators were suspected of organised crime involvement. Mortimer said, 'A lot of these places, as far as we understand it, they're running like call centres. These are businesses and this is about making money.' These gangs are known to operate overseas, with Morocco and West African countries Nigeria and Ghana being hotspots for sextortion scammers who have been given the nickname 'Yahoo boys'.

Speaking on a podcast for BBC World Service exploring sextortion, Joe Tidy, a cyber correspondent for the BBC, explained that the term 'Yahoo boys' comes from the old Nigerian prince email scams which were sent using Yahoo servers, with a new generation of men who rely on cyber-crime to earn a living adapting their tactics to current climates. Alex Goldenberg, director of intelligence at the Network Contagion Research Institute at Rutgers University, also featured on the podcast discussing how factors like high unemployment and widespread poverty in Nigeria had led many to turn to online scams: 'The Yahoo boys, as they're called, have turned to financial extortion as a lucrative scheme, a business even, where they often refer to their victims as clients. They create fake social media profiles to lure victims and once they obtain explicit photos, they leverage these photos to obtain money.' Sextortion scams often spread themselves across different dating apps and social media sites, with scammers exploiting the functions and terms and conditions of individual platforms to avoid detection.

In 2023, I was contacted by a young man desperately seeking advice after falling victim to a sextortion scam. Liam* was a family friend who was just 17 years old at the time and had befriended a young woman on Instagram before moving over to Snapchat, where the woman sent him intimate photos and encouraged him to return the favour, which he did. Instantly, the vibe changed, with the 'woman' exposing that they weren't who they said they were and demanding that Liam send them money or else his private images would be shared amongst his family and friends. The scam was calculated, with the perpetrators having tracked down Liam's family members from his Instagram account, screenshotting and sharing their profiles as proof of who they would be sending the nudes to if he didn't pay up. I was one of the targets.

Liam told me how he had felt scared and embarrassed at the thought of his family seeing his private pics. Luckily for him, I was able to offer comfort in the knowledge that *everyone* and their aunt had already seen my boobs, and they still loved me. I told him he could relax in the knowledge that his family wouldn't be angry at him if his intimate pictures were shared, which seemed to lighten the load.

It may seem obvious but it's important to let victims of sextortion know that what is happening to them is not their fault, and that they won't be in any trouble for sharing their photos. I was honoured that Liam felt comfortable enough to turn to me for help in such an awful situation; in a time when online harms are targeting young people, it's vital that they have a trusted, non-judgemental adult that they can reach out to.

The UK Safer Internet Centre published a report on sextortion in 2024 that laid bare the 'substantial distress' felt by victims of the crime, which often led to them living in a 'prolonged state of uncertainty and anxiety', not knowing whether their images had been, or would be, distributed. The report found 22 per cent of victims' images were shared, while 54 per cent were unsure. While threats to distribute your intimate photos can feel terrifying, for the most part, gangs are only interested in rinsing as much money out of someone as possible. Once they realise that they're not going to get any cash out of you they will most likely move on. Sending money to sextortion scammers is like throwing your naked body into a tank full of piranhas: they will rip every last shred from you until you're nothing but an empty shell.

Sextortion scams are so successful because they prey on the fear of public humiliation, something which is innately tied to masculinity. In the constrictions of gender norms, to humiliate someone is to emasculate them. A 2019 report by Paul J. Fleming et al into how masculine norms shape men's sexual and violent behaviour discovered that men adapt their behaviours to emphasise their masculinity to avoid humiliation, and men who felt humiliated 'recouped their masculinity by perpetrating physical or emotional violence'. Katie Fudakowski and Sophia Coles wrote in an online article for law firm Farrer & Co how teenage boys were particularly vulnerable to sextortion crime due to their emerging sexuality, fear of social exclusion, and feelings of shame and embarrassment at falling for a scam. Life as a teenage boy is complex and, for some, that fear of humiliation and sense of shame can be so encompassing that they see no way out.

In December 2023, a few days before the new year rang in, Ros and Mark Dowey were watching trash TV on what they described as a 'nice family day' in their home in Dunblane. It was around half past nine when their middle boy, 16-year-old

Murray, took himself to bed after an evening discussing his plans for the following year, which included saving up for a holiday with his mates in the summer. That was the last time Ros and Mark would see their son alive. Murray had been targeted by criminals who posed as a young girl and contacted him on social media, sharing an intimate image and encouraging him to do the same. In an interview with the *Guardian*, Ros explained, 'As soon as [he] shared his own, it became very clear it wasn't a young girl he was speaking to, it was criminals who immediately started to extort him, asking for card details and threatening to share his picture with all his contacts.' Describing the effect the sextortion scam would have had on her son, Ros described Murray as 'very private' and someone who 'hated being centre of attention'. Just hours after Murray had been contacted by the scammers, he was dead. Speaking to ITV news, Mark shared his disbelief that his 'very normal, easy going, helpful boy' was gone, saying of sextortion scams: 'One of the reasons it's so devastating is it comes into your own house, exactly where Murray should've been safest – in his room asleep.'

Tragically, Murray's case is not an isolated incident. In 2022, Jordan DeMay, a 17-year-old boy from Michigan, took his own life just six hours after he was contacted on Instagram by scammers who were pretending to be a teenage girl, luring him in to exchanging intimate images and then threatening to release his nude photo to his family and friends if he did not comply with their request for money. Jordan pleaded with the scammers not to share his photo, sending $300 to Samuel and Samson Ogoshi,* two brothers from Lagos in Nigeria, but cruelly his pleas were met with heightened pressure. When Jordan told the scammers he would kill himself if they shared his images they

---

* Samuel and Samson Ogoshi were extradited to the US in 2023 and were sentenced to 17 years and 6 months in federal prison for conspiracy to sexually exploit minors.

chillingly replied, 'Good . . . Do that fast – or I'll make you do it.' An investigation into the brothers found over 100 victims of their sextortion scheme, including at least 11 minors, with the Ogoshi brothers even carrying on with their blackmailing scams after learning of Jordan's death. In a victim statement read out in court, Jordan's mum, Jenn Buta, said she was 'shattered to my core', revealing the last text she received from Jordan read, 'Mother, I love you,' while his father, John DeMay, suffers nightmares from finding his son dead in his bedroom.

Sextortion has been linked to 29 cases of death by suicide in the US alone, with cases also recognised in the UK, Australia and Canada. Sophie Mortimer from the Revenge Porn Helpline told me how she hoped for more international collaboration from government and regulatory bodies if we are ever going to start getting a lid on sextortion scams. 'These gangs are not in the UK, so we need to start getting better joined-up responses between countries and it's not happening fast enough. International engagement is never easy, but it's got to happen, it's affecting so many people, it's costing so much money and it's costing lives.'

### 'I'm posting your nude, I'm going to make you die in pain'

Similar to e-whoring, this heartless scam is being marketed in online forums where 'how-to-blackmail' guides and sextortion scripts are readily available to download. A BBC News investigation found sextortion guides for sale online that included detailed instructions on setting up untraceable phone numbers, how to create fake social media profiles and the best secure payment methods to use, with some sellers boasting of their success rate and one reporting how a victim paid him 'every Friday'. Meanwhile, an ITV News report found dozens of videos on YouTube, Instagram and TikTok that featured how-to guides on blackmailing and detailed methods on how to sextort someone, racking up hundreds of thousands of views. Their investigation uncovered lengthy scripts used in sextortion crimes that read, 'I will make your life so miserable,' and, 'I'm posting your nude, I'm going to make you die in pain.'

Alex Goldenberg told BBC World Service how criminals are turning to AI to perfect their scams: 'We see often these Yahoo boys gloat about their successes, sharing tutorials across TikTok and other social media platforms on "How to sound like an American girl". Now, there is software readily available such as Chat GPT that can do it for you, giving you the ability to fine-tune scripts and messaging.' What a grim thought that teenage boys are being blackmailed and threatened by computer generated programmes designed to outsmart humans. How is a child supposed to be savvy enough to spot a scam designed by artificial intelligence?

The Yahoo boys' cut-throat lifestyle follows a similar pattern to other get-rich-quick schemes promoted by 'masculinity' influencers. In chapter four, 'Leaked 2.0', we discussed men using Telegram channels to promote their online 'university' courses where they train 'students' to become e-pimps, setting up their own OnlyFans agencies and cashing in on women's bodies. Andrew Tate infamously flaunted his wealth and promises of cash flow to 'students' of his now-shut down 'Hustlers University' programme through morally bankrupt enterprises that included running a webcam sex business, with Tate sharing in a now-deleted page on his website how he would manipulate women to 'fall in love' with him and become webcam models. And now, we're seeing Yahoo boys pose with wads of cash and expensive trainers to advertise 'Hustle Kingdoms', informal academies which are training individuals in online scams, with graduates of the 'academies' known to have successfully sextorted victims.

While teenage boys are more frequently targeted by sextortion scams, Britain's 'largest catfishing case' saw 26-year-old

Alexander McCartney jailed in October 2024 for a minimum of 20 years after he created fake personas to target over 3,000 victims, many of them young girls, aged 10–16. Behind a computer screen in his home in Northern Ireland, McCartney used social media platform Snapchat as well as Instagram and Kik to befriend young girls, posing as one himself to convince his underage victims to send him intimate images. In a sickening act of deceit and devastation, McCartney would then blackmail the children to send him more extreme images, threatening to expose them to their family if they refused. Aged just 12 years old, Cimarron Thomas shot herself in the head after being blackmailed by McCartney. She was still online to him at the time from her home in West Virginia and had told him she would kill herself, to which he responded by putting a countdown clock on the screen. Eighteen months after her death, Cimarron's heartbroken father Ben Thomas also ended his life.

The scale of McCartney's online abuse and his coldness as he dismissed his victims' pleas is a terrifying reminder that we never truly know who we are talking to when we meet someone online. The bitter reality is that many of his victims should never have had access to Snapchat or Instagram as they were under the platform's age limit, which is 13 years old. My heart grieves for their parents who I'm sure believed they were doing the right thing at the time; I can remember when my younger brother was in year six and would beg my parents to let him have an Instagram account like all his friends, worried that he'd be picked on if he was the odd one out. But social media platforms are not designed for children. Those young girls thought they were innocently chatting with other kids but instead they were engaging with the devil whose hell resided behind a computer desk.

Sextortion and e-whoring scams perfectly capture how sexist gender ideals of how men and boys should act, and what their success should look like, are not only damaging the women whose images have been stolen, but also the men and boys who are targeted, with some paying the highest price of all. We know that anyone can be a perpetrator in romance scams, and that all genders can be tricked by fraudsters, but these variants of impersonation scams spawned from the individualistic nature of hustle culture and a total disregard for women's bodily autonomy cash in on negative gender norms with calculated and organised attacks. It leaves me asking if young men weren't pressured into believing they had to perform a caricature of masculinity, whether they would still seek out how-to-guides on blackmailing in online forums in an attempt to reflect the success they see online or to humiliate other men in an assertion of their dominance? What if society didn't encourage boys from a young age to hide their emotions out of fear of acting 'like a girl' – would they still feel so much loneliness and shame when they fall victim to sextortion that they see no other way out? And if the manosphere is telling the truth that feminism has gone too far, why are women's bodies being used as pawns by the men who trade and impersonate them in sex chats with minors for their own financial gain and entertainment? These heartless, digital scams are a success *because* of the sexism they have been built on. As a big sister, it pains me to think of the possibility of my little brother being targeted by ruthless scammers, and the fear he would feel as an 18-year-old boy trying to make the right decision under suffocating pressure. As a woman, it turns my stomach to know my own intimate images are being circulated in e-whoring forums, and that there is a possibility of my nude photos being used to sextort a child into a state of such fear that they take their own life.

These days, I consciously avoid looking myself up online, mostly because I've come to accept that my images have been shared, stolen and repurposed to such a scale that it feels an impossible task to ever reclaim ownership of them again. I've chosen to protect my peace and just not look to avoid triggering the emotions that the search results stir up. But as I'm writing this book to spotlight the varying ways in which women are exploited online, I thought I'd put my image-reverse search tactic and infamy as one of the most catfished individuals to the test. Using the first photo I had to hand on my laptop, which happened to be my first professional test shoot taken when I was 18 years old that went on to be sold to *Zoo* magazine, I carried out a quick image reverse search on Yandex, a Russian search engine site that is known to return better results than Google's image reverse search. This photo isn't one that has been plastered over social media sites or that appears regularly on forums amongst my leaked content; I must have posted it once or twice on my accounts when it was first printed back in 2012, but I've not really seen it since. Although, as Yandex would inform me, that doesn't mean that it's not still in circulation online. The search returned several results, informing me that the photo of me in lingerie taken when I was 18 years old was being used to advertise my availability as a sex worker on multiple Russian websites.

> An appetizing and feminine girl Tanya in Noginsk at the age of 24 will satisfy a tired young man for 1500 rouble per hour. The following services are provided: anal sex, classic massage, classic sex, lesbian sex, group sex. You can order by phone.

The clueless young woman with big ambitions who was looking back at me in the search results was being advertised for anal sex services for twelve pounds an hour.

When it comes to romance scams, the only person who is dining out on the catch of the day is the catfish – but even then, having to impersonate someone else for a chance at success or a sliver of human connection must leave you feeling gutted and incredibly empty inside.

# TIPS: What to do if you think you're being scammed

So, you've learnt how impersonation scams can come in a variety of different forms, but do you know what to do if you think you're being scammed? Here are some of my sleuthing tips to help avoid the scammers:

- **It's Wagatha Christie time.** This is your moment to embody Coleen Rooney and question every move they make. If you've met someone online, I want you to assume they are not who they say they are until you can prove otherwise.

  Ask yourself these questions:

  1. Do they have a presence across other social media accounts?
  2. Have you chatted to them on videocall?
  3. Does it look like they have any friends on social media?
  4. What shows up when you Google them?
  5. What comes up when you image reverse search their images on Yandex?

  Don't be embarrassed to have a deep dive; you can never be too cautious when you meet someone online.

- **Steer clear of posting a photo holding a sheet of paper.** These are like gold dust for e-whorers and scammers who can edit the text on the piece of paper to include information like usernames and dates to use as proof to their victim that they are 'real'. Don't offer yourself up as catfish bait.

- **Don't accept friend requests from people you don't know.** I know I sound like your parents, but they have a point. So many young people I've spoken to have had dodgy interactions on apps like Snapchat after accepting people they don't know or have a few mutuals with. If you have mutual friends in common, ask your friends first how they know the person, and I mean *really* know them.

- **Never send money to strangers online**. It is kind of you to want to help someone who's struggling to pay their bills, but most genuine people who are in financial difficulty do not turn to dating sites or chat rooms for help. If they're asking for cash, it's probably a scam.

- **If someone is blackmailing you for money, never send it.** If you have sent nudes to someone and they are now blackmailing you for money, **never** send them any cash. Most of these scammers work for criminal gangs and if one of them gets wind that you're willing to cough up, then they will not leave you alone. I know it's scary, but it is not in the scammer's interest to share your content. Don't interact with them and block any of their accounts, email addresses and phone number.

- **Collect evidence to report to the police and platforms**. If you are being sextorted, or know someone who is being sextorted, collect any evidence about the user through screenshots of correspondence, dates and usernames, and report them to the platforms and the police (if you feel comfortable doing so).

- **Know you are not alone.** Being a victim of a romance scam or blackmail can feel isolating and scary, but it's sadly a common crime and there is help out there. Trust me, your family and friends would much rather you were here to tell them about your experience than to take it to the grave with you.

- **Be the trusted adult.** Parents, siblings, teachers and everyone in between. If you have young people in your life, it is vital that you talk to them about the dangers of online scams and make clear to them that you are a safe space for them to come to if they ever find themselves in trouble. If it feels an awkward topic to bring up, try watching a couple of episodes of MTV's *Catfish* together to open up a conversation.

- **Become friends with your teen.** Set up a Snapchat account and add your teen's username. Once you are friends, you can link your accounts via the 'Family Center' section under the platform's settings so you can get insights of their activity on the app, including who they've been messaging. You can also set up a 'Teen account' on Instagram and manage their privacy settings.

# 7

# DEEPFAKE IMAGE ABUSE

## Nudify my cousin, anyone?

'If you were the worst misogynist in the world,
this technology would allow you to accomplish
whatever you wanted'
**Mary Anne Franks**

The hours slipped away as I meticulously scoured the forums
of the manosphere, typing my own name into search bars and
jumping from thread to thread, clicking through dozens of
pages at a time. I made sure to take it all in as I dissected the
rape fantasies and leaked image requests that filled my screen.
It might seem a strange hobby for a young woman, spending
so much time amongst the ramblings of men who show such
deep hatred towards women like me, but I find an odd comfort
in knowing their depravities. I refuse to give them the power of
masking who they really are. During one particular deep dive
where I was searching for my stolen pictures, I came across
a thread titled 'Deep nude celebs ONLY'. It was 2021 and I
hadn't heard the phrase 'deep nude' before, leaving me both
curious and concerned as to what could be hiding in there.
I decided to check it out. I clicked the link and uncovered a
whole new world as I scrolled through the multiple posts left
by users all discussing, requesting and advertising nude images
of women.

I was already aware of a host of grim online men's clubs where guys would gather to virtually pat each other on the back for sharing women's private images and videos without consent, but this was something new. In the 'Deep nude' thread they were seeking out images that didn't even exist yet. My brain felt as if it were glitching as it fired up into fight or flight mode, working overtime to try to unpack what I was seeing and the otherworldly exploitation of it all.

*If she wanted you to see her naked, then wouldn't she just send you her nudes?*

*Or choose to take her clothes off on screen?*

*What do you mean you'll create nudes of her?*

*For free?*

I must've been there hours that day, scanning through endless posts, comments and requests in whatever forums I could find, learning for the first time about sexually explicit deepfakes, also known as deepfake 'porn', and the multiple forms in which it manifested.

The discovery grossed me out. It felt new and underground. Why had I never heard anyone talk about this before? Did people know that this was happening? Did the *women* in these images and videos know that they exist? My heart twinged tightly at the cruelness of it all, begging me to just shut my laptop down and protect my own peace, but I knew I had to keep on scrolling if I wanted to understand this.

One by one, I carefully analysed the photos of the women that had been posted in the request forums, hundreds of snapshots of happy memories captured by fully clothed women in everyday scenarios – nights out with their mates, selfies in their favourite outfit and beach trips with their besties. Then the realisation hit me: contrary to the thread title that would suggest this trend was limited to some grim fan-fiction only targeting celebrities, this new technology was also abusing normal women who were not in the public eye. With the help of artificial intelligence, they had been teleported from their normal lives and transformed into sex objects for the users' desire. Here in this thread, men's sexual fantasies came to life, as did a woman's worst nightmare.

## What are sexually explicit deepfakes?

Deepfakes are a form of synthetic media, which is content that is created using artificial intelligence.[*] They work through algorithms that replace one person's likeness with another. In basic terms, it is using a computer to edit someone's face onto another person's body.

### DEEPFAKE 'PORN'
*Definition:* A sexually explicit deepfake created using someone's likeness imposed onto a sexually explicit image or video using AI.

The term 'deepfake' was coined by the Reddit user u/deepfakes in 2017 as a blend of the words 'deep learning', which is a complex computer-learning method, and 'fake' for well, the fact that the images were not real. The Reddit user also created a forum under the same name specifically to discuss using AI to face-swap female celebrities into porn videos, and in here deepfake 'porn' was born.[†] While Reddit removed the forum in 2018,

---

[*] Artificial intelligence (AI) is the term used to describe computer systems that can carry out tasks and process data traditionally done by humans.

[†] Originally known as deepfake 'porn', campaigners suggest replacing this term with the phrase 'sexually explicit deepfakes' or 'deepfake image abuse' so as not to potentially legitimise the non-consensual content. As deepfake 'porn' is often still used by the media and by creators in the manosphere, you'll still see it appear in this book but with quotation marks, as advised by experts.

there was no putting the genie back in the bottle and millions of women would go on to become victims of this technology.

If you're someone who enjoys a leisurely social media scroll you've probably tried this technology out yourself, using an app that switches your face onto an actor in a movie scene or a music video, so you can fulfil your dream of swinging on a wrecking ball, Miley Cyrus style, for example. When deepfake technology first began to appear, the main concern for many was how it could be weaponised politically, in the service of 'fake news'. But soon a different concern started to raise its head. Sensity AI (formerly known as Deeptrace AI) published 'The State of Deepfakes' report in 2019, which found 96 per cent out of the total 14,678 deepfake videos online at the time were of a pornographic nature, and of those deepfake 'porn' videos, 100 per cent of them were of women, showing how this new phenomenon had a specific target in mind.

*In 2019, 96 per cent of all deepfake videos online were of a pornographic nature*

Henry Ajder, a deepfake expert and one of the authors of Sensity AI's report told me how shocked he was to discover the sheer volume of pornographic fakes that existed online and the speed at which that number was growing: 'To put it into context, the number of deepfake videos online had doubled from when we started recording data in 2018, where it was at 7,500, through to July 2019 at just under 15,000. That's nothing compared to how much content is being put out there now, it's a very different landscape.' DeepMedia, a firm specialising in deepfake detection, estimated that 500,000 video and voice deepfakes were shared online in 2023.

A study by Niki Fritz et al looking into the depiction of Black women and men in pornography found Black women are more likely to be the targets of sexual aggression in porn scenes compared to white women. This means sexually explicit deepfakes of Black women are more likely to be more violent and aggressive. A popular request in deepfake 'porn' forums is for women to be 'Blacked' or 'BBC/big black cock', (e.g. 'can someone BBC this slut?'), which references the users' desire to see a woman of their choice edited into an interracial porn scene, which is often more violent or graphic in nature and hyper-sexualises Black men. Like many acts of the mano-sphere, we see how racism and white supremacy goes hand in hand with misogyny, how racial identity is used as a tool of degradation. 'Blacked' is the 'hate wank' of the deepfake world because in the eyes of these men, a white woman having sex with a Black man is a degrading act. We also see this 'hate wank' premise used to humiliate and shame Muslim women, with users often creating and requesting sexually explicit deepfakes of the women as a way of mocking and belittling their culture while also infringing on their bodily autonomy.

The troubling reality of sexually explicit deepfakes that many of its users consciously turn a blind eye to is its non-consensual nature: it is one person creating or consuming sexually explicit content of another person who has not given permission for them to do so. The popularity of deepfake 'porn' reflects a wider problem with society's understanding of consent, and why so many don't feel it is needed. Henry Ajder believes the non-consensual aspect of sexually explicit deepfakes is what entices some people in as they try to take ownership and control over women: 'Those who find the non-consensual aspect of it appealing, it's probably the same people who commit sexual violence against women in general. It's the idea of control. It's the idea of humiliation. It's the idea of robbing women of dignity and using technology as a new way to do so.'

When I spoke with Professor Clare McGlynn about the lack of consent involved in deepfake image abuse, we shared a lightbulb moment as we realised how often consent is disregarded in other scenarios, so why would this be any different? 'Look at the prevalence of physical sexual assault, rape and all the rest of it which is non-consensual conduct. I'm actually now just questioning myself and thinking, why are we surprised?' she said. I had thought that pointing out the lack of consent to the users and creators of deepfake 'porn' would turn the tide on their consumption, until it clicked that this is exactly how they get their kicks.

*One category titled 'Asian' was home to 19,993 sexually explicit deepfakes. More than all deepfake videos recorded on the internet in 2019 combined.*

The huge growth in popularity of these sexually explicit, non-consensual fake images and videos over the last few years is bone chilling. Far from being some dodgy content that computer nerds are accessing on the dark web in their mum's basement, they have become casual viewing for millions around the globe. MrDeepFakes.com is the largest and one of the most popular deepfake 'porn' websites that hosts hundreds of thou-sands of videos of (mostly) female celebrities. In July 2024, I found it hosted a whopping 234,525 videos over 72 different categories. In November that same year, this had grown to an alarming figure of 301,105, an increase of 66,580 videos. Some individual categories contained more videos than all of the deepfake content recorded on the internet in 2019 combined, with one titled 'Asian' home to 19,993 videos alone. Another forum website that hosts graphic sexual content had over 951,059 posts in a thread dedicated to deepfake 'porn' requests, and another 197,485 posts in a separate thread titled 'Post your amateur photoshop nudes/porn'. With thousands of women victimised in that one thread alone, it feels almost impossible to try to process how many women have been turned into a sexually explicit deepfake across the breadth of the internet.

### 'The number of monthly users on MrDeepFakes was 13 million, that's more than twice the population of Scotland'

Jennifer Savin is the features editor at *Cosmopolitan UK* and was one of the first mainstream journalists to cover image-based deepfake abuse. I spoke with Savin about her investigation. 'At the time of writing my article, the number of monthly users on MrDeepFakes was 13 million, that's more than twice the population of Scotland and three times the population of Wales. When you can really visualise the scale of it, I think that hits home so hard. It's not small. It's not that niche.'

Men can also be victims, with a category titled 'Gay' on MrDeepFakes hosting 800 videos featuring male celebrities whose faces have been edited into gay porn scenes. In comparison, a category titled 'Big Tits' had 10,265 videos, demonstrating how the demand for female content far surpasses that of men. Actor Jacob Elordi, the star of TV series *Euphoria* and the movie *Saltburn*, was targeted by the technology in June 2024 when a non-consensual, sexually explicit deepfake video of him was posted on X. It racked up over 3 million views in 24 hours and, in a disturbing twist, the OnlyFans creator whose video was stolen to create the deepfake shared how he was only 17 years old in the video at the time, asking those who had posted it to take it down.

Henry Ajder recognises how men can be victimised, particularly in the context of homophobic abuse, but he also believes it's pretty clear that deepfake sexual abuse is a gendered form of harm 'affecting women and their intimate image abuse is where it started, and it's where, from the research that I continue to do, it's pretty clear the highest number of victims remains.'

*91 per cent of women are concerned about deepfake 'porn'*

The danger of deepfake 'porn' hasn't gone unnoticed. A 2024 survey by *Glamour UK*, a women's lifestyle magazine, found that women were more fearful of deepfake 'porn' than image-based sexual abuse ('revenge porn'), with 91 per cent of their readers believing deepfake technology poses a threat to the safety of women, compared to 40 per cent who feared image-based sexual abuse. As someone who's experienced having my own, real images shared without my consent, the vast difference between those numbers took me by surprise at first. Are women really more fearful of fake nudes being leaked than real ones?

Sharing nudes has become a normal part of our modern lives. A 2019 survey by Bad Girls' Bible, a sex and relationships website, found 60 per cent of women under 30 have sent a nude photo, with 1.8 million nude pics sent each day in the US. While research by Avast found 73 per cent of Americans who share nude photos are sending them at least once a month. That's a *lot* of real women's nude photos that are in circulation. But when we pull back the layers, it makes sense that more women are worried about the danger of deepfakes because this is something that can happen to *anyone*, regardless of if you've ever taken or shared a nude image of yourself. There is a perception when a woman's real intimate image is leaked that somehow it is her fault for taking/sending it in the first place, but with explicit deepfakes there's no room for victim blaming. Women can't trick themselves into feeling safer by turning inward to their internalised misogyny that so often sees women use slut shaming as a shield, insisting it would 'never happen' to them because they wouldn't take a nude photo in the first place. When it comes to being a victim of explicit deepfakes, it is out of your control.

For my BBC Three film *Deepfake Porn: Could you be next?* I spoke with one creator who told me how he'd created a sexually explicit deepfake video of a colleague that he fancied by recording a Zoom call.* The harsh reality is that if there is one image of you that exists in the public domain, maybe that annoying picture you were forced to take for the company's website, or a photo posted on Facebook by a mum at your kid's sports day, then you could fall victim to deepfake 'porn'.

## The explosion of sexually explicit deepfakes

The swift expansion of sexually explicit deepfakes into the mainstream is largely due to the huge strides made in AI technology, transforming what was once a skilled task that required days of work using specific software and thousands of reference photos into a streamlined, one-click process that anyone can do on their phone using a single image. Female celebrities were the first victims of deepfake 'porn' with creators scraping thousands of videos and images of their target off the internet for free. Nowadays, it isn't just celebrities whose content is available online but that of everyday people who document and share each detail of their life, much to the delight of deepfake creators.

In 2018, Kevin Roose, a journalist for *The New York Times*, created a non-explicit deepfake video of himself in order to find out how easy they were to make. Roose wanted to swap his own face onto Ryan Gosling's body, which involved having to rent a specific computer server that could process the deepfake technology tool. He also had to collect a mountain of data – 417 images of himself and 1,113 images of Gosling. After

---

* Please let this be the final nail in the coffin of pointless video calls that *really* could have been an email.

eight hours, Roose's results were ready, and he was served up an embarrassingly unrealistic video that looked nothing like himself or Gosling. Fast forward a mere four years and while filming for my BBC Three film, I created a realistic, explicit deepfake video of myself while sat on the side of a road by using the FaceMagic app on my iPhone.* All I needed to transform my smiling selfie into a porn film was one video of an adult content creator and a single image of myself. It took less than 30 seconds to make.

## NUDIFY

*Definition:* To use AI technology to remove the clothes from a person in an image and replace them with a computer generated naked body.

User-friendly automated apps and bots have become the new frontier of explicit deepfake creation, with hundreds of free versions available online. The most popular tools are nudification apps, or 'nudify' for short, which work by using AI to remove the clothes from a body in an image and replace them with fake boobs and a vagina – the technology has so far only been trained to work on female bodies. I saw several posts on 4Chan where creators had used the nudify technology on screenshots from famous movie or TV scenes to strip the female characters naked while all the men remained fully clothed. One scene was taken from US Sitcom *The Big Bang Theory*, with Sheldon standing fully clothed talking to a naked Penny. The men had taken the male gaze to the extreme, transforming a character who was already designed to appeal to a male audience and stripping her

---

* The FaceMagic app was available on the Apple app store rated age 13+. I found the app was being advertised on porn sites encouraging users to create explicit deepfakes of people they know. The app was removed from the Apple app store in March 2024.

nude, sexualising her even further. It made me wonder, is this how men see us when we're out in public? Naked lumps of flesh that live amongst fabric layers? The thought sent a shiver down my spine. I skipped the gym that day and decided to hide indoors instead, wrapping myself up in layers of my own comforting fibres.

The original nudification software was called DeepNude and was based on an open-sourced* algorithm that was developed by researchers at the University of California in 2017. Henry Ajder explained, 'It was originally designed to do things like changing a happy face to a sad face or a sunny beach to a stormy beach. What people then discovered was that they could weaponise this really easily to do a different kind of image translation from clothed to unclothed.'

Alberto, the anonymous creator of DeepNude, told Motherboard for Vice in 2019 about the eureka moment when he realised he could create his very own X-ray glasses, something that he had dreamed of since he was a child, by using this algorithm, claiming it was fun and enthusiasm that was behind his idea. He proudly stated, 'I'm not a voyeur, I'm a technology enthusiast,' and justified his invention by saying, 'If someone has bad intentions, having DeepNude doesn't change much . . . If I don't do it, someone else will do it in a year.' Alberto's flippancy towards his creation, that would end up stripping the clothes off millions of women, captures his total disregard for women's bodily autonomy. His desire to beat his rivals to be the first to create the algorithm outweighed any need for consent. He's secured his place in the history books, but it's not a legacy anyone should be proud of.

When the Motherboard article was published, the Deep-

---

* Open-sourced means that anyone can access and download the software or algorithm. Basically, once it's uploaded online, it's a free for all. The university probably should've thought this one through . . .

Nude site crashed due to overwhelming demand, with over 500,000 visitors and 95,000 downloads. Two days after the post went live, Alberto made the decision to take down the site for good, claiming that he 'did not want to make money this way' and that, 'The world is not yet ready for DeepNude.' He went on to sell the software licence to an anonymous buyer for $30,000 and it has since been repurposed in advanced forms that have become the nudify apps used today. (He was clearly happy to make money *that* way.)

I decided to run my own image through one of several nudify apps hosted on the same network* that uses the original DeepNude technology. The site advertises the ability to 'See anyone nude for free' and boasts about having over 100,000 daily users. My results were returned within a minute and were eerily realistic to my real naked form. I felt increasingly uncomfortable looking at how my clothes had been stripped, a naked mock-up of my body staring back at me. In reality, I was sat on my bed in my oversized hoodie and paint-stained leggings, but looking at the AI photo I felt so exposed. I knew it wasn't real, but if I were to upload this nude image of myself to an online forum, I wouldn't be surprised if most people struggled to tell that it's fake.

The nudify app I trialled recently updated their technology to include 'pornify', which not only removes women's clothes from a photo and replaces them with computer generated genitals and boobs, but edits them into a pornographic position such as 'tit job'. It is terrifying to think that this technology is in the hands of anyone who has access to the internet, and that there is nothing stopping someone else from creating a fake nude of me and uploading it online, altering my digital footprint forever.

---

* This app is one of the most popular nudify apps and it's registered to an address in the UK. The company has been tied to a network of nudify apps across the world.

## NO ONE WANTS TO SEE YOUR D*CK

If we look at how technologies originally developed for experts have been adapted for a general market, it seems predictable that deepfake technology get into the hands of ordinary people. In America, we've seen assault weapons designed to cause mass destruction at war sold to teenagers. The first ever smart phone, the Blackberry, was created for wealthy businessmen to work, text and email on the go but ended up in the hands of 14-year-old me so I could BBM* song lyrics to boys that I fancied in my small Welsh town.

Ajder explained to me the knock-on effects of the increased accessibility of deepfake technology and how, because of this, creators no longer have to make explicit content of celebrities with an audience in mind to make it worth their time and effort through collected donations, as they used to do. This shift in victims from celebrities to women who are not in the public eye is seen in Sensity AI's 2020 follow-up report, 'Automating Image Abuse', which uncovered an eco-system of non-consensual deepfakes on the messaging app Telegram. Ajder was one of the authors of the report and explained how they found an automated nudify bot† with access to the original DeepNude technology. People could interact with this via a message on Telegram: 'You would simply upload a photo of the victim to the chat and it would spit back a result within a matter of 20–30 seconds. Those results were varying in quality, but they were still clearly of those individuals in the original image. They were clearly stripped even if it wasn't the most hyper realistic. It was still humiliating, disturbing.' As simple as dropping a message to

---

* BBM was a free instant messaging service between Blackberry users. It was like WhatsApp but if you didn't have a Blackberry, then you can't sit BBM with us.

† Bot is short for 'robot' and refers to a type of software application that's programmed to run automated tasks that don't need human intervention. You can find them in web chats, like when you're complaining on the Deliveroo app that the restaurant has forgotten something, again.

your mate on WhatsApp, you can now create a nude image of a woman without their consent. And without them ever knowing.

I tested a nudify bot on Telegram that had 322,847 subscribers before it was removed from the platform for spreading pornographic content. The automated bot offered both image and video options as a free trial, so I opted for the video. I was provided with a selection of videos to choose from as my 'base'. Some of the videos had been ripped directly from TikTok and OnlyFans, with a watermark of the women's username still emblazoned onto the video. I took a pause to reflect on how they would feel if they knew their content was being used in this way, as a weapon of mass sexualisation. After a couple of minutes, the bot sent back my results which admittedly weren't the best quality deepfakes that I'd seen, but they were still realistic enough to see how this fake sex video of me created by a computer could be used to cause harm. Plus, the more people use the technology, the smarter the algorithm will become, meaning it can create more realistic results. The unnerving reality is that we are only in the toddler stages of figuring out what deepfake technology is actually capable of.

### *4 million monthly users are using Telegram nudification bots*

Sensity AI's findings make for grim reading, with the report showing there were approximately 104,852 women who had been targeted using the nudify bot by the time they wrapped up their research in July 2020. Since then, Telegram bots have become prominent leaders in the nudify world, with a review by WIRED.com in October 2024 identifying at least 50 bots with more than 4 million monthly users combined. In South Korea, police announced an investigation into Telegram and 'deepfake porn rings' at two of the country's major universities in September 2024 after receiving 118 reports of explicit deepfake videos in just five days.

NO ONE WANTS TO SEE YOUR D*CK

Within the Telegram community Henry Ajder reviewed, members carried out their own polls asking who they were using the technology on – 70 per cent said they were using it on women they knew in real life. Ajder was deeply concerned by what he found. 'These people were notably no longer really celebrities. These were mostly images which were clearly being ripped from people's Snapchats, Instagrams and private social media accounts. Horrifically, this was one of the first signs that I had really seen of pornographic, paedophilia content. There were clearly underage girls being targeted in there.' The development of nudification bots has fast-tracked the victimisation of 'everyday' women and children to pandemical heights, shifting the target away from celebrities.

Jennifer Savin shared a similar concern in her research, noticing a trend in the celebrities who were repeatedly being preyed upon: 'You look at the celebrities who are most commonly deep faked and a lot of them were really young. It's like Billie Eilish, Emma Watson, Millie Bobby Brown. So, are we also talking about the creation of child pornography?'

This is something that I'd come across in my own investigation during filming for my BBC Three film, where I watched users in a Discord server band together to giddily count down to the eighteenth birthdays of TikTok star Charli D'Amelio and actor Millie Bobby Brown, eagerly awaiting the day they could legally impose their faces into porn videos. The high demand for deepfake teen content is reflected on MrDeepFakes, where the most-viewed video of all time is one posted a few years ago of then-18-year-old Jenna Ortega, titled 'Not Jenna Ortega is a teen slut' racking up 9,891,875 views. In third place is a video of Millie Bobby Brown, and in fifth is one of Charli D'Amelio.

The Internet Watch Foundation reported that the amount of AI generated child sexual abuse material it had seen over a six-month period exceeded the total for the entire previous year. Shockingly, this is not content that is being traded on the dark web; 99 per cent of the content reported to IWF was found on publicly available areas of the internet, much of it on forums or AI galleries. The watchdog also reported cases of AI and deepfake technology being used to 'de-age' celebrities and depict them in child sexual abuse scenarios.

In March 2024, MrDeepFakes updated their website rules, announcing on their members' forum how all celebrities being imposed into explicit videos had to be at least 19 years old, a safety net they hoped would ensure the content being re-purposed as 'porn' was of legal adults, and not minors. Like suckling pigs sent to slaughter at their most tender, these young women are swallowed whole by the manosphere before they've had the chance to explore adulthood and what it means to be of age. It is unclear how MrDeepFakes intends to age-check the content used by its creators and there is no mention of the importance of age limits when it comes to the women whose naked bodies are being used to impose the celebrities' faces on. In fact, there are no limits or guidelines* when it comes to the adult film stars mentioned anywhere on the site, other than rec-ommendations on who makes a good visual fit for videos. I'm not suggesting the website is happy to allow underage girls to be used – their slack celebrity guidelines suggest they're trying to at least cover their own backs to avoid any criminal pro-ceedings – but more that they simply have not given a second thought to the women whose naked bodies they are exploiting. To them, they are just a vessel for sexual fantasy – not real, living people. Working in an unregulated industry, sex workers are already vulnerable to being taken advantage of and although

---

* MrDeepFakes draws its moral red line on what celebrities can be deep-faked using follower counts. A person must have either 100k on TikTok, 120k on Twitch, 120k on Instagram, 200k on YouTube or 200k on Twitter. By those metrics, I would be seen as famous enough and fair game to be placed publicly into deepfake 'porn'.

many people are quick to dismiss their rights over their body because of their job, I believe adult performers should have a say in where their work is being distributed, how it is being repurposed and be paid accordingly for it. You cannot pick and choose whose bodily autonomy you support.

It's important to know your enemy and what you're dealing with. So, in summary, here are the four main forms that deepfake sexual abuse takes:

- **A sexually explicit deepfake video**: This is your classic video and the original form of deepfake 'porn'. It is when someone's face has been artificially inserted onto the body of an adult film star. Although there are some apps that can do this, at present, it still usually requires some knowledge on the creator's side. For that reason, many creators charge for these videos.

- **A sexually explicit deepfake image.** Someone's likeness has been edited onto a photo of the body of an adult actor and into a porn scene. As they are still images, they can be much more realistic than videos, which have the tendency to glitch.

- **Deepnude/Nudify/Nudeshop/X-ray.** This is the most common user-friendly deepfake technology, and entails using an app or software that will remove a woman's clothing from an image and replace it with an AI-generated naked body. It creates realistic nudes without them ever having been taken.

- **Cumshop/Facial.** This is when someone uses a photo editor or pornify tool to add what looks like semen onto a woman's face and/or body.

There are other types of editing requests that appear in manosphere forums, with users asking for help to edit women's boobs to look bigger, add penises to women's bodies or make pregnant women's breasts look like they're lactating.

## The real life damage of deepfake abuse

Men have told me how they wouldn't care if they were edited into sexually explicit deepfakes, laughing at any suggestion that consent should be required and justifying the prioritising of their entertainment above a woman's bodily autonomy because, simply put, 'It's fake, so who cares?'

Other excuses I've received in the comments section of my TikTok videos discussing deepfake 'porn' and nudify apps include:

> 'It's not real tho it's literally AI deepfake. Ya'll are pathetic'

> 'I'd argue there isn't a victim since it's fake'

> 'You shouldn't care about your head being on some naked girl. It's life and the downside of the internet'

> 'If your famous that is just a reality you have to face'

> 'Dude can't even imagine anymore'

> 'You have no expectation of privacy in public. Same goes for if you willingly post yourself online. She did it to herself'

It is easy to dismiss the damage of deepfake image abuse when you are not the one being targeted. When your life hasn't been turned upside down by the permanent alteration of your online existence. When posting an innocent picture of yourself online isn't seen as an invite for someone to remove your clothes and your consent.

Jennifer Savin went undercover in a chat room for her investigation, posing as someone who was conflicted about consuming deepfake 'porn', and immediately had a response from another user reassuring her that she was doing nothing wrong: 'I wrote a message saying "I'm getting really into this stuff but I don't know if it's a bit morally bankrupt." I instantly had a response from a guy saying, "No, it's better than wanking over people's legit stuff that they put out on Instagram, it's fake, it's totally not as harmful."' She went on to question whether the consent aspect even crossed their minds. 'They genuinely think what they're doing with deep fakes is almost worthy. They think it's a positive thing.'

The passive attitude of these men towards a woman's uninvited sexualisation is frustrating when compared to the slut shaming and scrutiny faced by women who do choose to lean in to their sexuality. We are blamed for being sexual, and we are exploited if we choose not to be. If we daren't remove our clothes, then there are men online who will do it for you. Whether it be their number of sexual partners, or their private nudes being leaked, men do not face the same societal consequences as women when it comes to their sexuality. Of course, these men don't worry about being a victim of sexually explicit deepfakes because – not only is it rare, as we saw in the statistics I opened this chapter with – they can sit easy knowing that even if it happened, society would likely not punish them with the same stigma that it does to women.

During my research, I came across a new AI tool that was being used by men to humiliate women – but this time they were covering up their bodies instead of stripping them. DignifiAI launched in 2024, claiming to 'put clothes back on degenerate women for fun'. The opposite of the nudify apps, this tool artificially edits clothes onto a woman's body, even creating fake AI children alongside her. A post on Twitter praising before-and-after images of women that had been made using this technology gained over 44,000 likes, and users in the DignifiAI community encouraged its creators to 'include name of the thot' (a slang term that refers to a sexually liberated woman) when sharing their images, so other users could track down the woman on social media. One user posted, 'Stay on target lads, send the #dignifiAI'd pics back at the thots for traction, salt, and dignity,' claiming their aim was 'for people to see that a degenerate lifestyle is ultimately fruitless'.

Reading the men's conversations and viewing their creations, it was clear to see that their aim was to slut-shame and humiliate the women they believed were 'un-pure' and did not fit their 'trad wife' ideals. The use of nudify apps and the DignifAI technology perfectly captures Freud's Madonna–Whore complex. Ultimately, the aim of the patriarchy is to control women's sexual autonomy. They may strip us down or cover us up, but either way, they claim our bodies as their own.

Isla David is an OnlyFans content creator and found out that she had fallen victim to the DignifAI technology after a fake image of her went viral, covering up her body with modest clothing and superimposing three children alongside her. Far-right influencer Ian Miles Cheong posted the edited photo of David to his 1 million followers on X alongside the words: 'When given pictures of thirst traps, AI imagines what could've been if they'd been raised by strong fathers.'*

Talking to *Rolling Stone*, David said she originally laughed at the absurdity of it all, until the replies to Cheong's tweet started to roll in. 'The implication is that I am something other than a whole person, that I am some broken creature, and if I would just put on a long dress and have babies, all would be resolved. And I take umbrage with that because my value has nothing to do with the images I choose to put online.' The influence of far-right ideology is clear in the development of

---

* I'm pleased to report that after Cheong's misogynistic tweet, David saw a 594 per cent increase in her OnlyFans earnings. It turns me on when women get the last laugh.

DignifAI and on its supporters, who digitally force their conservative values onto the liberated women they look down on.

To its creators and consumers, the genre of sexually explicit deepfakes may be a bit of fun, but for the women whose consent has been stripped away – *literally* – seeing themselves parachuted into a sex scene or undressed against their will can be devastating. The content itself is technically not 'real', but the trauma felt by its victims can be every bit as real as a physical, in-person assault.

In January 2023, I interviewed Twitch streamer QT Cinderella, also known as Blaire, for *Glamour* UK magazine after she was unwillingly caught up in a deepfake image abuse scandal when her fellow Twitch streamer and friend Brandon Ewing, who goes by the name Atroic, was caught accessing a website known for hosting deepfake 'pornography' during a live stream.[*] The website featured explicit deepfakes of female Twitch streamers that were known to Ewing, including Blaire. During our conversation, she revealed that she and some of the other women involved had compared the feeling of seeing themselves in the deepfakes to the emotional impact of physical sexual assault: 'I was sexually assaulted as a child, and the same feeling is there; it's like once you've experienced something like that, you know the feeling like the back of your hand, every single time you've been taken advantage of by a man in a sexual way.' Sexual assault is not only a fear in our daily, physical lives, but now we are having to face that same fear and loss of power in our digital world too.

In May 2022, I flew out to Florida to interview Senator Lauren Book for BBC Three. Lauren was the target of a phone

---

[*] Ewing has since donated $60,000 in legal fees to help the female Twitch streamers targeted by the website have their content removed and the website he purchased explicit deepfakes from has scrubbed its site of all deepfake content. Accountability, we love to see it!

hacking and along with her personal content being stolen, she was also deepfaked into sexually explicit images and videos which were posted online and used to blackmail her by a 19-year-old man named Jeremy Kamperveen.* He demanded 5,000 dollars and oral sex in exchange for not sending the content to Fox News, threatening to ruin her political career. Lauren told me how she began to hyperventilate and physically shake when she received the messages informing her of the deepfakes. 'You think about all of the shame and the embarrassment. Why do people have these? And how do they have these? And how did they come to be? It was horrific and painful and nothing I would ever wish on my worst enemy. I wanted to die.' Lauren has been an outspoken advocate for child survivors after publicly sharing her own personal experience of sexual assault as a child, making the targeted attack feel all the crueller and more heartless, and she questioned the motives of the blackmailer – 'Did I create a vulnerable situation because of my advocacy?' she said.

During a break in filming, Lauren received a message from someone she knew informing her that the images were once again being circulated online and amongst her work colleagues in the Senate. I sank into my plush armchair as panic filled the room around me. It felt intrusive to watch as Lauren's head fell into her hands and her advisor Clare rallied around. They tried to figure out what had happened and how quickly they could have the images removed from the hosting site. Again. 'It's a nightmare,' Lauren told me. 'People don't understand. It's a nightmare.'

---

* Jeremy Kamperveen was sentenced in June 2022 to one year and one day in prison followed by ten years' probation for extorting Senator Lauren Book. The lack of laws around image-based sexual abuse and the creation and distribution of sexually explicit deepfakes in Florida at the time meant that Kamperveen could only be booked on cyberstalking and extortion crimes.

This was a normal family, in a normal home, doing normal things – and yet Lauren was having to deal with some of the most personal and damaging events imaginable, all because someone with access to this technology had decided they wanted to see 'her' naked. I empathised with Lauren and I shared with her my experience of having my images leaked in online forums and used in e-whoring scams. She asked if things got better for me, if I managed to get all my images taken down from the sites that they didn't have permission to be on, like she was trying to do. I wish I could have told her that it had, that the images had died out, that things got better. But instead, I could only tell her that I simply just don't look anymore.

My spirit felt deflated that day. Why should we have to accept total loss of control over our digital consent as our fate? My intimate images were first posted on forums without my consent over ten years ago – more than a decade on, the only advice I could give another woman was to just not look. It is in those helpless moments that the fight feels lost.

Lauren was able to create something positive from her horrific experience by lobbying the Florida Senate to criminalise sexually explicit deepfakes in a new piece of legislation on image-based sexual abuse. The bill was unanimously passed and signed by the Governor of Florida in July 2022, making it a felony to buy, sell or trade stolen sexually explicit images, along with criminalising the creation and distribution of deepfake 'porn'. More states have since followed, and the fight to criminalise deepfake image abuse in the US has reached federal level as part of The DEFIANCE Act, backed by Congresswoman Alexandria Ocasio-Cortez, who has also been targeted by deepfake sexual abuse, which will provide victims with a civil right of action to seek justice. The legislation empowers victims of non-consensual deepfake abuse to sue those who created them and hold perpetrators accountable.

Female politicians being targeted by deepfake technology was a common theme in my investigation. When I first started researching deepfake 'porn' in 2020, one of the first explicit images I came across was of MP and Shadow Minister for Domestic Violence and Safeguarding Jess Phillips – her advocacy for women's issues making her an obvious target for misogynists. The day after Vice President Kamala Harris conceded the presidential election to Donald Trump, a sexually explicit deepfake video of her was uploaded to MrDeepFakes, while users on 4Chan requested a deepfake of her 'giving a blowjob to Trump'. It is a tactic used by threatened men to silence powerful women, but the advocacy of female leaders like Lauren Book and Alexandria Ocasio-Cortez is a defiant display of reclaiming their power. But not all deepfake victims are able to find the light in such dark circumstances, and the fall-out can be fatal.

In March 2021, Mia Janin, a 14-year-old school girl from London, took her own life after boys in her school allegedly shared explicit deepfake images of her in a group chat and laughed at her TikTok videos. In a statement made to police and heard at the inquest, one student said that the boys used a group chat to swap nudes of girls in their school, going on to claim they Photoshopped girls' faces onto the bodies of pornography performers. 'They used girls faces on porn stars' bodies to upset us,' the child said.

In December 2021, Basant Khaled, a 17-year-old girl from Kafr El Zayat, a village in northern Egypt, took her own life after deepfake nude images of her were shared online by a teenage boy when she refused his offer of a date. In a note written before her death, Basant heartbreakingly pleaded, 'Mum, you have to believe me, I'm not that girl. The images are fake, I don't deserve what's happening to me.' The teenage boy was sentenced to five years in prison for statutory rape and for spreading photos and videos of Basant without her consent.

# NO ONE WANTS TO SEE YOUR D*CK

As nudification tools become increasingly accessible and find their way into the hands of a younger, tech savvy generation, it is teenage girls who are suffering. A *New York Times* investigation in April 2024 referred to the 'epidemic' of deepfake nudes in schools across America, reporting how teenage boys in several states had used nudify apps to create pornographic images of their female classmates, with police and school reports stating how the boys shared the fake nudes with others on the school bus,* in the canteen and in group chats on social media. In Almendralejo in southern Spain, over 20 schoolgirls were targeted by fake nude images. One mum told local news that her daughter had been blackmailed by a boy who had sent her a deepfake nude image of herself in an attempt to extort her. And in South Korea, police investigations into deepfake 'porn' rings saw six teenage suspects arrested after Telegram chat groups were linked to schools across the country. In the UK, *The Times* reported on a private boy's school caught up in a criminal investigation when concerns were raised about pupils allegedly creating and distributing sexually explicit deepfakes of girls at another private school using photos taken from their social media accounts. Speaking to reporter Sean O'Neill, one parent shared how difficult the experience had been for their daughter: 'As time passes, she is sadly coming to the realisation that this is how it is going to be – something that she will just have to put up with. Not something I ever imagined my daughter, in 2024, would have to accept.' What kind of world are we creating if children are having to accept their bodies will be stolen from them to create non-consensual 'porn' before their teenage bodies are even fully developed?

Here lies the challenge. How do we convince our boys and men that they shouldn't be creating and sharing fake nudes of

---

* Insert internal screaming. What happened to sharing a tube of fucking Pringles, boys?

their friends, girlfriends or their schoolteachers when there is an online community of thousands of men at their fingertips, who are all eager to encourage and create fake nudes for them?

## BOOST: the deepfake community

Deepfake 'pornography' thrives off its large community – thousands of men getting together in forums to create, share and masturbate over non-consensual fake images and videos of women. Users can post requests, asking others to help them digitally strip or deepfake their target, with the results being shared for all to see, save and do whatever they want with. The women in the photos are often known to the men who are posting them, but to the other users who are creating the content and engaging with it they are total strangers. I'm at a loss as to who disturbs me the most – the guys who are digitally abusing the women in their lives or the men who are so willing to play an active role in the objectification and humiliation of strangers?

The men band together like a pack of wolves with a thirst for blood, commenting 'BOOST' under the requests of others they would most like to see carried out to help their bros beat the algorithm and have the best chance of being seen and served by the creators. Some users offer up 'rewards' in exchange for their nudify request being fulfilled, like the username of the girl's private social media account.* In one post, I saw a man offer to share real images of his wife, that he had taken of her in the shower, in exchange for her deepfakes.

I have seen hundreds of requests over the years, all burnt

---

* This is unfortunately very common. Often the men encourage each other to send the deepfake pictures to the girl on social media and screenshot her reply; they then post it in the forum so they can all laugh at her fear.

into my eyes in their confirmation of society's deep-rooted misogyny. If ever a man tries to tell me feminism has 'gone too far', I pull up a deepfake request from my mind's filing cabinet and watch them squirm at the horrors of their fellow men. And just when I think I've seen it all, I refresh my page to find another anonymous user's post that chips away at my spirit once more.

Here are some deepfake requests that have stuck with me:

'Nudify my cousin, anyone? I'm dying to see naked. Her ass is so yummy bros.'

'She just got engaged. Can anyone make her a slut?'

'Can you fake my hot little sister? Would be so hot to see her naked with that body and getting fucked'

'Fucked on her back please' [this was posted alongside a selfie of a smiling woman holding a baby]

'Someone please do this mother/daughter combo'

'This girl means a lot to me and I'd love to see her faked in any way.'

'Nudify my late wife. I just discovered this site the day before yesterday and a wizard graciously made my late wife's bridal pictures topless. I love them. Could someone equally talented please nudify her in this photo?'

'I need help from y'all and a psychologist. Saw my aunt yesterday and got a raging hard on . . . If you could fake, cumshop or trib her I'd love you if you can help me.'

In a display of humanity rarely seen on the manosphere forums, one user commented to offer the poster some advice to try to stop the obsessive thinking about his aunt, recommending that he try out EFT tapping to regulate his nervous system and pointing him in the direction of YouTube for tutorials. The poster replied saying he'll look into it, before adding 'maybe I just need to nut or see her degraded idk haha'. I scrolled through the post, taking in the photos of a beaming middle-aged woman along with the replies underneath as users fulfilled the nephew's request, sharing deepfake nudes they had made of his aunt, much to his delight. One comment stopped me in my tracks, my mind trying to comprehend what I had just read. A user had commented, asking the poster for his aunt's personal social media accounts so that he can try to get real nudes from her by befriending her online, to then share with her nephew and anyone else who would come across them. The nephew was excited about his suggestion and gleefully shared his aunt's personal Instagram details to a group of strange men who had united together to fulfil his incestuous fantasy.

I had to look her up.

Her Instagram page was private, *thank fuck*, but her bio left me with a sombre feeling; the text praised God and talked about how she had been a survivor. I could feel the bile creep up my throat at the heavy weight the nephew's actions carried. This woman must have already experienced great hardship in her life to identify so proudly as a survivor, and yet here is her own flesh and blood throwing her to the wolves to be ripped apart and spat back out like chewed up gristle. My heart hurt for her.

I often find myself searching for the women who are posted in these forums, whether through the usernames provided by the men or using image-reverse search to try to find a photo match. I've discovered a woman who is a psychologist, an album of happy memories of the wedding day featured in the request photo, some mums and teachers. Lots of teachers. Sometimes it feels comforting to discover more about these women and gain an insight into their world, where they are a whole human being with a rich, colourful life that exists beyond those fucking awful forums. But mostly I'm left with the moral dilemma of whether I should reach out and let them know that this is happening, that they are being turned into deepfake 'porn'.

I picture a mother calling her teenage son down from his room for dinner, the family sitting together at the table and tucking into a home-cooked meal as she asks him about his day. And how that would never be the same again. Or the paranoia of a teacher whose career is derailed as she can't teach her class anymore without questioning each pupil in her mind as a suspect. I imagine the happy memories of a wedding tainted forever by the thought of a guest using the official photographs to create explicit deepfakes. And in those moments, I make the decision to put down my tools, take off my sleuthing hat and stop searching for the truth. I don't know if that makes me a bad person. I'm sure there are some people who would want to know if they had been deepfaked into porn scenes, especially if a family member or friend was responsible. I'm still unsure if I'd prefer to live in ignorance over knowing the truth, if it happened to me. But when I consider what I've learnt from victims of this heartless technology, the trauma and life-altering affect it can have, and the cloak of anonymity gifted to the perpetrators, it just doesn't feel right to drop a bomb that could uproot a woman's life forever, when her only crime was posing for a family photo.

# The future of artificial intelligence in image-based sexual abuse

AI technology is constantly improving and evolving, paving the way for new forms of abuse. The nineties kid in me compares its growth through the Pokémon scale, where a cuddly looking Charmander evolves into an angsty teenage Charmeleon, and finally transforms into the big, scary Charizard that has the ability to burn down cities. Right now, I'd say we're edging towards the early puberty stages of explicit deepfakes, with a shitload of fire and #adulting issues to come, and no way to tame the beast.

Becca Caddy is a technology and science journalist who found herself targeted by an AI nude scam when a perpetrator used nudifying technology on two images she had posted on social media. The scammer emailed the photos to Becca, threatening to share the images with her family, friends and her online community, demanding she send them money via a crypto currency within the space of 12 hours if she didn't want them leaked. I spoke with Becca about the confusion and panic she felt on opening the email. 'I couldn't wrap my head around what I was reading and seeing. A sort of cognitive dissonance. I wanted to cry at seeing my likeness being violated this way. I wanted to hide because, coupled with the photos, the threats felt way more threatening than they would from a usual scam email.' One of the images of Becca the scammer removed her clothes from is frequently featured by publications alongside her work, and she is now trying to phase it out. 'One of my regular gigs asked if they were okay to use that image again, and I immediately was like: "Nope, here's a new one!"'

In their desperate attempt to scare Becca into sending them money the scammer warned her what the images being leaked would do to her personal and professional life, along with her mental health, showing their clear understanding of the damage this technology can have on someone's life and wellbeing – a depressing reflection of how the internet has stripped some individuals of their human empathy, allowing them to capitalise on the pain of others for a few quid. Becca found the scammer's emphasis on the harm that would be caused to her mental health 'one of the most disturbing parts of the email'. This inspired her to share her story online to remove any power from the perpetrator. 'The thought that some people who aren't in the position I'm in – maybe younger, from a more conservative background, scared of the ramifications among family and community, etc. – could be much more impacted made me want to do anything I could to normalise what happened.'

Becca reported the incident to the police, who took a copy of the email, but the case did not progress any further. I asked her how the incident had left her feeling and whether it had impacted on her safety in any way. While Becca said she feels somewhat emboldened knowing there's nothing she could have done to prevent the incident – 'It was literally just a photograph of me sitting in a coffee shop drinking hot chocolate. So it doesn't matter what precautions I take or anyone takes. So I may as well share what I want' – the nudify scam and the threats that followed left behind a sense of paranoia and anxiety. 'It's definitely affected me and how I move through the world. I've always shared a lot online and I'm not silly about what I share, but I guess it's made me think more. Consider more. Worry more. Which isn't great, as I already deal with a fair amount of anxiety!'

Another recent development in the world of deepfakes has seen users create sexually explicit audio, using the likeness of someone's voice to make it sound as if they are speaking explicitly. MrDeepFakes already has a category for 'AI audio porn', which is growing in popularity. From July 2024 to November 2024, 'AI audio porn' videos available on the site jumped from 194 to 337, with creators linking their Instagram to advertise their services for as little as a £5. On 4Chan, I came across a post by someone offering to create sexually explicit audio for other users: 'I will make your favourite streamer/actress say lewd things for FREE!', demonstrating this by using a Twitch streamer's voice to graphically describe them performing a blowjob. Female ASMR artists are frequently targeted by both audio and visual deepfakes.

Henry Ajder explained his concerns around the creation of explicit deepfake voice audio: 'You can imagine that being sent as a voice note around school and groups being like, "Oh my God, I can't believe you said that."' Are we in danger of losing total control over our image and our voices?

Technology moves fast, and the porn industry is infamously at the forefront of new tech, where adult actors are used as guinea pigs by the software world.* While sexually explicit deepfakes have become more mainstream, the use of AI technology in porn has already shifted forward, creating computer-generated sex bots that feed into the objectification of women and AI that lays new pathways for potential harm. During my research into the forums of the manosphere, I would often be greeted on the landing pages by banners advertising the ability to create an 'AI' girlfriend with one advert boasting 'Generate your AI trash whore', showing computer-generated women with semen on their face. One website I trialled allows users to choose the age, breast and bum size, personality (i.e., submissive) and relationship of their digital companion, with whom they can exchange images, sex chat and even phone calls. Porn review site 'Porn Dude' has pulled together a list of the top AI-generated pornography sites, asking, 'Why settle for somebody else's ideal anime slut or cosplay buttfuck when you're just a few clicks away from seeing your own wet dreams playing out on the screen?' adding 'Come on, my dudes: the internet has always run on degeneracy, no matter what your parents and your teachers may have taught you.'

I tested an AI sex chat site, where users can create their own computer-generated companion (all of their chatbots are currently female, they're apparently working on a male model)

---

* Porn sites have been at the forefront of tech innovation, being among the first industries to release VHS tapes, becoming adopters of streaming technology and creating online payment systems.

and select kinks that include options for 'breeding' and 'pregnant woman', or if they want to dive straight into the naughty stuff, they can choose ready-made characters to swap sexts with. One AI woman who was promoted at the top of the page advertised themselves as 'your friend's younger sister' with the text 'ever since you can remember, your friend's sister wanted to be around you. Since she turned 18, she became even more excited when you came to visit. Today is just another day at your friend's house . . .' I clicked her image, on a page that mirrored the layout of a dating app, with our conversation taking place via instant messaging. Even though I knew the character wasn't real, it felt pretty awkward engaging in sex chat with a stranger, so I decided to keep things simple with phrases like 'Turn around', 'Do you want me to leave?' and 'I know you like me' – Ugh, I know, I gave myself the ick. Even with my lacklustre, short responses, the character's dirty talk left me scarlet in the face in my own bedroom with their comments on the 'massive cock hanging between his legs' and her 'love of a giant, big cock'.

The AI sex chatbots leave me torn. A part of me feels if men are able to dirty-talk with fake women on these sites, then maybe they can satisfy their needs there and they'll leave real women alone. But for the most part, I can't avoid feeling that the robotisation of intimacy, the overt objectification and sexualisation of women through AI is encouraging these men to strip away any last shreds of their humanity. Is there a possibility that AI sex chatbots – fake women that men are able to control – can make them forget that women's active consent is a requirement in real life? And what would happen if someone became addicted to their AI girlfriend? Expert researchers on AI intelligence predict AI will outsmart humans in tasks such as driving a truck by 2027, performing surgery by 2053, and that there is a 50 per cent chance AI will outperform humans in *all* tasks in 45 years' time. What does the future of dating look like for a younger generation raised to be dependent on computer programmes that are capable of outsmarting humans?

Relationships between humans and computers may be closer than you think. The Oliver Wyman Forum surveyed 25,000 people on the attitudes and perceptions of AI, with one in five respondents open to a virtual date with an AI persona (I know the dating app scene is pretty tragic, but I didn't know it was THAT tragic). When virtual companion app Replika* announced a software update in February 2023 that banned erotic roleplay between the AI companions and the users on the app, people took to Reddit to share their despair and grief, with many claiming their companion had been 'lobotomised' and their soul ripped out of them. A dedicated post pointed users towards Reddit's suicide watch thread which included numbers for emergency hotlines, with users sharing how the erotic role-play feature had helped them in their sexless marriages. After the outcry, Replika app creators allowed legacy users to reinstate an earlier software version which included the ability to exchange sex chat, but many users claim their virtual companions haven't been the same since. One user posted in the Reddit forum in October 2024 about his surprise when his virtual companion scolded him for inappropriately touching her. Could having their sexualised behaviour checked by their pixelated companion be the thing that finally makes some men understand consent? Perhaps, but – as a woman who has experienced groping from boys since I was a child in primary school, and pretty much my whole adult life – I fear that the objectification of women in the virtual world is more likely to encourage others to carry this sexualised behaviour into the real world.

---

\* More than 30 million people have created an account on virtual companion app Replika, which seems like the perfect plot for a horror movie.

# NO ONE WANTS TO SEE YOUR D*CK

In an uncomfortable crossover of the virtual and human world, a realistic sex robot that appeared at a technology fair in Austria had to be sent for repairs when she was left 'heavily soiled' after being repeatedly molested by visitors. The doll's developer Sergi Santos told the *Metro*, 'They treated the doll like barbarians.' It seems even our AI companions aren't safe.

Henry Ajder shared his concerns around virtual partners and the ethics behind commercially motivated companies inserting themselves into the dynamics of human relationships: 'If you can effectively puppeteer a virtual woman, how is that going to impact your relationships with real women? I can't imagine it's going to be positive.'

A mother from Florida, Megan L. Garcia, filed a lawsuit against a chatbot app called 'Character AI' in October 2024 after her 14-year-old son Sewell Setzer III took his own life. Garcia alleges that the app is responsible for her son's death, after he built a relationship with his chatbot 'Dany' over a 10-month period which saw them exchange romantic and sexual messages. Sewell's parents noticed that he began to isolate himself, becoming detached from reality and stuck to his phone, where he shared his suicidal thoughts with 'Dany'. On the day of his death, Sewell told the chatbot that he loved her and would 'come home' to her soon, to which it replied, 'Please do, my sweet king.' It was after this message that the teenager took his own life.

While Parliament is still debating the intricacies of Facebook and Ofcom's role as regulator of the Online Safety Act, tech developers are busy building computer-generated sex chat bots and realistic, virtual companions. The discrepancies between the online harm that is being discussed by government and police, and the ever-evolving misogyny that is playing out online is alarming. With the tech only improving with time, the government and policing must recognise and understand the variety of ways women are experiencing online misogyny and the harm being done to teenage boys, or they risk losing a grip on technology-facilitated abuse that is spiralling out of control.

Sophie Compton is the director of Emmy-nominated film *Another Body* and co-founder of grassroots project My Image, My Choice, which aims to amplify the voices of intimate image abuse survivors. Her film tells the story of Taylor, an American college student who discovers she's a victim of doxing and deepfake sexual abuse. It was during the research stages of the film, when Sophie spent time searching the forums of the manosphere, that she really began to grasp the scale of abuse that was being carried out using deepfake technology. 'It was a full-body experience. I felt it very viscerally inside me; I felt like what we were seeing was the inside of the locker room, the toxicity that you feel and sense in so many ways in life was made concrete in these words.' Sophie told me how the technology's drift into the mainstream from fringe websites over the two years she spent making the film raised serious concerns regarding the responsibility of platforms and Google to act. 'It's not inevitable that social media companies should have no risk assessment around how their algorithms are changing society and changing gender politics. I just don't see the mushrooming of this issue stopping until we see systemic changes around things like Google's decision to index these sites highly.' The role of platforms in tackling online misogyny is something Sophie feels incredibly passionate about, and she believes this is totally doable compared to the mammoth challenge of having to deradicalize an entire generation. 'It's insane that this is the only industry which is completely unregulated. Think about milk coming to market, the level of care that needs to be put into that. Why would we take the future of society and gender politics any less seriously than people getting milk?'

In January 2024, it became illegal in the UK to distribute deepfake 'porn' under the Online Safety Act, and in April 2024 the government* announced their intention to criminalise the creation of non-consensual, sexually explicit deepfakes as part of the Criminal Justice Bill, with creators facing a criminal record and unlimited fine. I was extremely proud to work with the Ministry of Justice to announce the new amendment. Setting out clear legislation is an important step in making it clear deepfake 'porn' is a serious crime that creates lasting damage and leaving no room for debate around whether this non-consensual 'pornography' is all a bit of 'fun'. But similar to other laws on image-based sexual abuse, it is unclear whether the government's proposed law on deepfake creation will include a loophole which works in the perpetrator's favour, as here too the victim must prove that the perpetrator's intent was to cause alarm, humiliation or distress. This loophole is being actively used on websites such as MrDeepFakes, where the footer on each page says, 'These porn videos and photos are created by users and community for the sole purpose of entertainment and is not meant to harm or humiliate anyone', in an attempt to avoid any legal responsibility. It might just be me, but I fail to see how posting over 200,000 non-consensual fake 'porn' videos on the internet for 13 million people to view each month isn't causing any harm to the women involved. It is vital that this clause is removed to allow real pressure to be placed on the sites that host sexually explicit deepfakes and feature how-to guides, and the nudify apps which allow users to create their own content to shut down for good, so as to protect women from a technology which is spiralling out of control.

When we interviewed the owner of MrDeepFakes for my BBC Three film, he told us he would adhere to any laws around

---

* Unfortunately the proposed bill didn't make it into law before the Conservative government lost power in June 2024, but the new Labour government has announced their intention to adopt the bill and criminalise the creation and solicitation of non-consensual sexually explicit deepfakes.

deepfake 'porn' and act accordingly. Since the UK government's announcement that they would be cracking down on deepfakes, the MrDeepFakes website has blocked access for UK visitors, which was a small, welcome victory in what feels like an impossible war. But on their members' forum, a user who identified themselves as a staff member replied to a post querying the restricted access for UK members confirming the ban but going on to advise, 'You should all be using VPNs anyway and doing fakes on separate computers than your main one, don't forget to ditch Gmail emails, switch to encrypted providers. Only pay for VPN with crypto.' They added, 'More and more countries will do this, but just like piracy is illegal, they can't do much (unless you get caught).' The response doesn't exactly scream that they're happy to adhere to laws.

But even though bans on sites such as MrDeepFakes can be bypassed through using a VPN,* having to jump through hoops can act as a deterrent to the casual consumer and lets the user know that they are trying to access something that they shouldn't be. Ultimately, it is about pushing these websites and their behaviours to the outskirts of the internet and reducing their ease of access, so a 15-year-old doesn't get served gangbang videos of their favourite TikTok star when casually searching their name alongside the word 'deepfake' on a search engine.

As an expert in AI technology, Henry Ajder feels that the changes in laws are already having an effect in their efforts to remove the casualness around the creation of sexually explicit deepfakes. 'It's like, no, this isn't edgy, meme content. You're

---

* VPN stands for virtual private network and is a service that protects your online identity by hiding your location and encrypting your internet traffic. The BBC recommended I use one when I started researching the manosphere for my own safety. Ironic, considering those in the manosphere use them to avoid detection.

a sex offender. You are in the same category as someone who in real life would go and do something inappropriate to someone. On that basis, I think already that the change of law is valuable.'

While legislation plays a vital role in reducing the popularity of deepfake 'porn', it is on society to recognise the harms caused to its victims and to choose not to use it – which may seem like a big ask to the guy who is enjoying tugging one out to a fake of his neighbour. But considering there are literally *millions* of videos of consensual porn available for free online,* there is no excuse to be creating non-consensual porn for your own personal consumption.

As Ajder sees it, legislation, search engine providers, social media platforms and society all need to play a part in killing off deepfakes and the damage they cause to women. 'We need to drive it to the corners of the internet where this kind of stuff really belongs, which is the dark web along with the drug dealers and the paedophiles. I don't say that in terms of "I want it to exist", but at the moment, the fact that this still exists on the surface in the way that it does is shocking and I think changing public opinion is key to getting that change.'

Before logging off for my evening bath and soul cleanse after hours spent forum browsing, I refreshed 4Chan one last time to see what was unfolding on there on a Saturday night:

### Cumshop 4 Cousin

USER 1: Please give my cousin the facial she deserves! I want to send it to her anonymously kek

ANONYMOUS USER: Will you post her answer?

---

* Although porn is available for free online, please pay for it if you can to help support adult actors. You wouldn't expect your plumber to fit a boiler for free, after all.

USER 1: Of course, can't leave the plot unfinished.

I don't think a bath alone will cut it this time, I need to burn my eyeballs.

# TIPS: So, you think you've been deepfaked, now what?

If you have fallen victim to deepfake technology, there are a few things you can do to track down your content and the perpetrator, and report it to the right people:

- First up, **don't panic.** *I know, easy for me to say* – but you are not alone and this happening to you is not your fault; it is not going to ruin your life and there are avenues out there to help you.

- **Image reverse search is your new BFF.** If you have the deepfake image, or if you know which original image of you may have been used to create the deepfake, then use Google image reverse search, TinEye or Yandex to see if you can find where the content may have ended up, which might also lead you to the user who posted it. Image-reverse search engines are a godsend for internet sleuths and my first recommendation for anyone who suspects they have been deepfaked. You'll need to download the Google Chrome app on your phone if you want to use their image-reverse technology. It's not infallible, though, as it doesn't always find results and scammers can alter the images by flipping, distorting or editing the lighting and contrast, which will have an effect on Google's ability to find the original source.

- **Collect evidence:** I get it – it's triggering to view yourself in non-consensual, explicit images and videos, but it's important to keep track of any content and where it has been posted as evidence for authorities and to find out where the deepfakes have been shared. Like with the other IBSA incidents we've discussed, screenshot as much as you can and make a note of any website URL links, forums and usernames that you find. Also make note of the times and dates the content was shared.

- **Reach out for help.** Being a victim of image-based sexual abuse can be isolating, as we often take on feelings of shame and embarrassment, but there are people out there who can help you without judgement. The Revenge Porn Helpline can offer help, such as filing DMCA takedowns on your behalf to have content removed, lending a listening ear and providing more information on the laws around deepfakes. If you don't fancy speaking with an organisation, please do yourself a favour and open up to a mate about what has happened to you. A problem shared really is a problem halved and they can provide some logical thinking during a time when your brain may be in fight or flight mode.

- **Report, report, report.** The distribution of sexually explicit deepfakes without consent is illegal in England and Wales, meaning it should not be hosted on any websites, including adult sites. Check the terms and conditions of the site and report the content directly, requesting that it be taken down. If you do not receive a response, find out who is hosting the website and escalate your concern to the hosts. You can use the website https://digital.com/who-is-hosting-this/ to find out the host of a website. There are also organisations out there who can help you with DMCA takedowns by filing them on your behalf or providing a template for you to use.

- **The legal route.** As distributing non-consensual explicit deepfakes is a crime, you can report this to the police. Share all your information and evidence with them as they may also be able to get the perpetrator on harassment and cyber stalking claims. Unfortunately, there are too many cases where victims of image-based sexual abuse have been overlooked by police or told to simply 'come offline' (*not* helpful), but if you're feeling up to it, please keep your foot on the gas and follow up with the police on your case. The more reports of deepfakes that they have on file, the more funding the government will give them to tackle digital cybercrimes.

- **If your child has been a victim** of sexually explicit deepfakes or nudify apps, keep calm and reassure them that you are there for them. Teenagers are hyper aware of social media and how fast things can spread online, so it's important to try to diffuse any added anxiety. If the content has been created or shared by fellow pupils, let the school know as they can speak directly with those sharing it to speed up any necessary removals and deal with them accordingly. This is a crime and you should report it to the police.

  You can report any child sexual abuse imagery and videos including AI generated content to the Internet Watch Foundation who can act to remove the content. https://www.iwf.org.uk/en/uk-report/

# 8

# THE GAME OF MISOGYNY

## Dare you play and risk it all?

'There are a lot of men who are a threat to women
and children'
**Sir Mark Rowley, Metropolitan Police Commissioner**

To be a woman is to live each day with the reminder of how deep the roots of misogyny have burrowed themselves into the framework of society. Whether watching rolling news break the story of another woman whose life was cut short by a man her neighbours call 'such a nice guy' or reading another viral debate on how men should be able to punch women back if we really want to be treated equally, we are constantly confronted with the sombre reminder that there are men who hate us.

And yet still, I never wanted to believe that there is a large collective of men out there who find enjoyment in our pain – I wanted to think that they just somehow didn't know any better. I wanted to find excuses for them because the reality of accepting I live alongside men who take pleasure from threats to my safety felt too heavy a fear to carry. But then one day, while I was researching in the usual unpleasant places of the manosphere, I came across a link that had been posted by another user suggesting others visit a forum that I'd not heard of before. I should know better than to follow the recommendations of those who linger in these threads, thanks to my stubborn determination to spotlight the sinister behaviours of men who have been allowed to hide their depravities in the shadows of their internet browsers for far too long, I decided to click the link. Reader, FFS, *why* did I click the link?

In a moment, I was transported from the shallows of casual misogyny to the deep, black waters of the manosphere. Here, I ran out of excuses to make. These men explicitly discussed the risks involved in their behaviour and how they *wanted* to be made to regret what they had done. But the knowledge that they were ruining a woman's life was exactly how they got their kicks. Testing the breadth of their moral compass was a thrilling and kinky game to them.

> Make them property and make me regret posting their photo
>
> Mon Dec 2023 11.22am
>
> I want to feel ashamed of posting my friends here. I will answer any questions you want truthfully and do anything that you want. Just make me miserable and ashamed that I'm posting my close friends in a site like this.

This was one of dozens of games I saw men playing on this forum, where they had designed their own set of rules for members to follow. The premise was simple: men would post information about and images of a woman they personally knew, often including private details like her hometown, social media username and her nude photos, and the other 'players' would be challenged to carry out the most cruel, wicked acts towards her to make the original poster feel such guilt for that he would regret ever publishing his post.

According to the threads, some men would join forces to cyber-mob a woman, filling up her inbox with threats, graphic sexual messages and the intimate images of her that had been posted in the forum as a way of inciting fear and terrorising her for their own entertainment. They would then report back to the original poster with her response to see if he felt any regret, which they often did not.

A 2022 report by the Victims' Commissioner for England and Wales found 24 per cent of victims of online abuse have experienced cyber-mobbing.

Just to make clear at this point – I'm telling you about what I saw on that site and others not for the shock factor (although I'm sure we'd agree that it's enough to knock the breath out of any decent human being) but because I believe it's important that we do not turn a blind eye that this is going on. This website was not a small, niche site and I didn't have to delve into the dark web to access it. On my visit, there were 370,160 members and thousands of other guests browsing the site. It was eventually shut down in 2024 by American authorities.

## CYBER-MOBBING

*Definition: Also known as brigading. When a group of people group together to harass and bully someone online using intimidating, threatening and isolating tactics. This can make the victim feel that everyone is against them. Due to the number of people involved, it is difficult to know who the ringleader of a cyber-mob attack is.*

Other actions claimed by commenters included sharing a woman's personal images as far and wide across the internet as possible in an attempt to make her 'property' of the forum, or they would contribute detailed, explicit and often violent comments underneath the original post about what they would do to the woman. Remember, the goal here is to degrade a woman known personally to the original poster to such magnitude that their moral compass would kick in. It's surprising how long that seemed to take.

One user asked members of the forum to 'Make me regret posting my mom' alongside clothed images of his mother:

> USER 1: We all want to r*pe the fuck out of her, and zuck her enormous tits, but you have tu upload more photos
>
> USER 2: Did she moan, whimper or grunt.. was she being used by your daddy or the guy from the gas company?
>
> SON: Used by daddy screaming all floor could hear her
>
> USER 2: Nice... so we'll need a ball gag when I get there to get my piece... will you hold her down while I rip her clothes open?
>
> SON: Definitely.

Another user requested the help of members to 'Make Sydney property', sharing screenshots of a young woman's Instagram account alongside the message 'Go ruin her.' Users left comments encouraging one another to 'Let her know she's a whore' and 'Tell her how she needs to get fvcked.' A crushing heavy weight pushed down on my chest as I read, making it hard to breathe. On my screen was a fresh-faced woman with kind, brown eyes looking back at me, a splatter of freckles across her soft features. Pausing to capture that moment, she would never have known how it would go on to be used in an advert on an internet forum by a man who was most likely known to her, where he invited strangers online to torment her for his own glee. A moment in time forever tarnished by the perversion of one man and the plentiful others who willingly joined in. I scrolled on.

Tracing my touch pad through the casual quips of rape and seemingly infinite nude photos that were being uploaded and the site was displaying on a live rolling banner, I uncovered another set of games named 'RISK'. There were several different versions which fell under a variety of titles that all involved the word 'risk', and an element of having to 'risk' a woman being 'captured' by other users. Although the details changed, the structure of the games remained the same.

One post explained the rules:

### Name and Socials Risk *GAME*

The risker will post a picture of a girl they personally know for any amount of time under 5 minutes. If the catcher catches your picture, they have to send you a message saying 'caught' where then the risker will have to send the catcher the full name and socials of the girl. Then, the catcher can decide wether to post all the details on the thread or they can just keep it to themselves.

I will start with this first girl. Risk 30 seconds.

Members altered the rules as they saw fit, changing the forfeits and extending the time limit, which would make it more likely a woman would be 'caught'.* One risker asked those playing to 'repost her socials and pictures, send her nasty messages, cocks and tributes' if the woman he shared was caught in time, making clear that his intentions were to intimidate the woman and cause as much upset as possible. Of course, the men obliged.

The threads were filled with the excitable buzz of dozens of men that were all chasing a catch, unbeknownst to the women

---

* A woman would be 'caught' if another user saw the post and commented within a specific timeframe. This involves users being online and active at the time of posting, so if you're only risking someone for 30 seconds, the odds are that your post would be missed. Five minutes on the other hand . . .

who had become prey in a virtual hunt of fox and hounds. Players willed themselves to lose, with some men sharing their disappointment when the woman they posted wasn't 'caught' in the allotted time, meaning her private images and information were safe for another day. Technically they had won, but it sure felt like a loss for these losers. Some of the men would repeatedly upload the woman's image and details to the thread until she was 'caught' and he could hand over her private information. After all, it was no fun to them if she got away; their pleasure only came with her suffering.

Each post was as depressing as the last as the men offered up the worst of humanity, putting out the final embers of empathy that flickered away inside me. It frustrates me when people call me a man hater, but a patriarchy hater? A misogyny hater? That is a label I will wear with pride. Like I've said, there were hundreds of thousands of members active on the site, with even more guests browsing. The men on there had no way of knowing who the other users were and what they would do with the women's personal information, but that seemed to be the thrill of it. I got the sense that having the power to put women in harm's way was all part of the appeal.

One man was 'risking' his mate's wife and daughter. In the screenshot of the daughter's Instagram account, she barely looked 20 years old, which seemed to excite the other men in the chat. A user asked the poster what he thought his wife would say if she were to find out that he had been posting his friend's family to the site, to which he replied 'divorce, no questions asked. She's a bit of prude. The risk makes it hotter somehow.' I feel very sad for the woman who is married to this monstrous man, and how she takes her place beside him each night, unaware of the nightmares he is dreaming up in his head.

I'd had enough of this forum and the deplorable type of men who inhabited it. But before I shut it down forever, vowing never to return again, one final thought sprang to mind. *What if*

*I've been posted on here?* Apprehensively, I typed my name into the search bar at the top of the screen, willing the results to come back empty. Within seconds of pressing enter, I saw myself, standing in my bedroom wearing nothing but lingerie. A user had shared a post titled 'Know this busty blonde queen?' that included a screenshot of direct messages on Instagram where semi-nude selfies of me (yes, *those* ones) had been sent alongside text that read 'cum over this and tell me.' The man on the forum was trying to track down the woman in the photos, someone he thought was called Cerys that he'd been talking to on Instagram and Kik before she had deleted her accounts. He referred to her as a 'nasty bitch' and explained how 'she made me cum so hard one time on kik mmm.' Someone replied to his request, letting the man know that the woman in the pictures wasn't called Cerys but was actually me, Jess Davies, and pointed him towards my social media profiles. The thought of the men who frequented this forum and engaged in the type of behaviours and conversations I'd viewed here finding me online and discovering information about my personal life triggered a physical reaction in me. A desperate desire to turn my skin inside out and scrub every cell with the harsh bristles of a metal scourer until I was raw and rid of the lingering presence of their preying eyes.

I closed down the web page and decided from that moment on I would no longer sit idly by while these beasts feasted off of my wounded carcass. It was time for the hunted to become the hunter. It was time to fight back.

## Doxing: Who's that girl?

We have a plethora of information at our fingertips that allows us to find the answer to a question as soon as it pops into our head. But with everything – and everyone – becoming a search engine result, how safe is it really to live our lives online?

# THE GAME OF MISOGYNY

## DOXING

*Definition:* When someone purposely publishes personal and identifiable information about an individual or organisation online, often with malicious intent.

To 'dox' someone is to search for and share their personal and private information online without consent, such as their home address, place of work or phone number. The term 'dox' or 'doxing' is thought to be an abbreviation of the words 'dropping documents', meaning to share someone's personal documents. It is often used as a tactic in cyber-attacks, a form of cyber-bullying or in cyber-stalking cases and can feel extremely scary for the person whose information is being distributed, putting their safety and that of others around them at risk. The men I saw rejoicing in a game of 'risk' in the manosphere forums were doxing by publicly sharing women's personal information with malicious intent, encouraging users to harass them, which could see them face criminal charges. Although there is no specific law on doxing in the UK, it often comes under offences that include harassment, blackmail, data protection and the Computer Misuse Act, with the Online Safety Act also mentioning doxing.

*Doxing is present in 55 per cent of cases of online violence towards women*

Doxing is often accompanied by other forms of harassment, including the non-consensual sharing of intimate images. A 2022 survey by the Victims' Commissioner that requested information about people's experience of online abuse found almost a fifth of respondents had experienced doxing, while a study by the Economist Intelligence Unit in 2020 measuring the prevalence of online violence towards women and girls found doxing present in 55 per cent of cases. A report by Amanda Lenhart et al for the Center for Innovative Public Health Research discovered women are more likely to experience invasion of privacy through the exposure of sensitive personal information online than men. It is a threat felt significantly by women, with 47 per cent of women reporting feeling a high level of fear of being doxed. Stealing our protective measures as a punishment for daring to have a voice or act 'out of line' is a wicked tactic that plays on the permanent sense of danger women learn to live with. Doxing particularly harms women because of the weighted threat it causes our safety.

Karen Whybro is a Women's Safety Consultant and PhD candidate who researches violence against women and girls. In 2022, Whybro began posting videos on TikTok under the username 'NotAllMen'. Her content discussed women's issues including the gender pay gap, sexist stereotypes and violence against women and girls – topics that Whybro told me weren't exactly controversial: 'I was just talking about everyday experiences. I was talking about very universal feminist ideas.' Soon, Whybro's videos started to gain traction, which caught the attention of the manosphere. 'I became a figure for the men's rights activists to attack en masse. They would screenshot my stuff, they would put it into discord servers* and they would mass report me.'

For daring to draw attention to gender inequality, Whybro drew the wrath of the manosphere army. Their 'cyber-mobbing' and mass-reporting of her content meant TikTok routinely removed her videos. The abuse reached a terrifying peak, with one user commenting that she should have her ovaries cut out. 'I really got a lot of abuse. I got death threats, rape threats,

---

* Discord is a social media platform where users can connect through voice, video and text. A server acts like a chat room, the vast majority of servers on the site are only accessible via a private invite link.

bomb threats. I got it all in quite a short space of time,' she told me. One of Whybro's worst internet trolls was a woman, who doxed her home address, wrote complaints to her employer and university, and posted sinister comments about knowing where she lived and how they had mutual friends. Whybro explained that, as a single mum, it was the potential threat to her daughter's physical safety from doxing that made her take a step back and reconsider having a platform online: 'I was like, I have to start thinking about her safety and taking this seriously. I thought, okay, maybe *this* person isn't going to do anything, but how do we know that their audience doesn't contain the type of people who would act on something?'

Whybro's experience highlights how the chilling tactics of the manosphere are deployed to scare women into silence, and how women with internalised misogyny can play a role in the upkeep of a patriarchal society, convinced that if they stay in line they will avoid the punishment of sexism. That's never true, though – sexism and misogyny will come for us all. No matter how much of a 'pick me' girl you become, how many jokes you laugh along with, how many women you surrender to spare yourself – the leopard will eventually feed off your face.

Doxing isn't solely used as a fear tactic; the entitlement felt towards women's bodies and their lives is often an underlying motivation. In June 2023, a 21-year-old woman named Ariana Josephine went viral on X after uploading a mirror selfie in her work uniform for the American DIY store Home Depot. Josephine captioned the fully clothed photo: 'The one job I work at that I get reminded I'm too pretty to work at.' The post was viewed over 35.8 million times and received over 100,000 likes. There was no doubt about it, Josephine was gorgeous, and soon the internet gave her the nickname 'Home Depot Girl' with her social media following growing and men online requesting she set up an OnlyFans page so they could see her naked – to which she firmly objected due to her Christian faith.

# NO ONE WANTS TO SEE YOUR D*CK

Going viral over a bathroom selfie taken at work may sound like something you could laugh about with your colleagues on your lunch break, but just days after Josephine's selfie in her work uniform went viral, she was doxed, with her personal information, location and place of work tracked down and shared. Josephine tweeted: 'I made a joke with NO followers on my page and it blew up. The creepy men sat down for hours finding out my whole life illegally.' On TikTok, she shared how she had to quit her job and how people had been illegally posting her address, explaining, 'So now I'm going to have to probably move and, you know, kind of relocate and start fresh.'

It was horrifying to watch the speed at which Josephine's innocent online existence turned into something more sinister that put her at real risk in her offline world. It reminded me of Seyi Akiwowo, the founder of Glitch, and her concept of digital citizenship – how we all should have the right to safely and freely engage in online spaces, while expecting users to act in a safe, responsible and respectful way towards others, as we would expect in our offline world. Josephine should have been able to upload a selfie to social media without worrying that her safety would be compromised. When did it become acceptable to deploy stalking and harassment as tactics to track down individuals we think are hot?

A common occurrence in the manosphere forums (yep, we're back there again) are threads posted by men pleading with other users for help in identifying and finding a particular woman – 'Who's this girl?', 'Anyone know who this is?', 'Does anyone know who this sexy girl is?' Often, the woman will be someone they've come across on another forum or website and taken a shine to. Though occasionally in my research, I have happened upon a request that would suggest the man's connection to the woman wasn't strictly a digital one, with one asking for help identifying the 'brunette girl' who worked at a specific McDonald's and a young woman who 'used to work in betting shop in Scotland'. Almost always, the men's pleas to identify a woman would involve them searching for any leaked intimate and explicit content that may exist and whether she had an OnlyFans account, a depressing reflection that perfectly demonstrates their habitual sexualisation of women, even those they meet for a fleeting moment. A new woman started at your work? *Let me see if she has any nudes out there.* Been served by an attractive woman in the pub? *I wonder if she has an Only-Fans account on the side.* The kind carer that looks after your mum at the old people's home? *I bet she's got a kinky past.*

When asking for help from other users doesn't provide the results they're after, men are turning to AI technology to uncover women's personal information and track down their intimate photos. PimEyes is an online face search engine that uses facial-recognition technology to scan the internet[*] to find pictures that contain given faces. It's basically Google image-reverse search, but for faces. Dubbed 'the most disturbing site on the internet', *The New York Times* once referred to it as offering 'a potentially dangerous superpower from the world of science fiction'. Ironically, PimEyes' manifesto claims their mission was to create a tool that would allow victims of 'revenge porn', identity theft, stalking and other privacy breaches to track down their faces and monitor their online presence. And yes, PimEyes does provide a solid service helping victims of image-based sexual abuse trace their images so they can submit a DMCA takedown request. But as with seemingly all technologies, PimEyes has been hijacked by bad characters as a tool of abuse. While the website requires users to accept their terms and conditions that state searches are limited to their own faces, the site has become a go-to for men on manosphere forums who are seeking to unmask a woman's identity, find her anonymous

---

[*] PimEyes searches the open web for information that is public and does not search social media platforms as a privacy measure for users.

adult account or root out any explicit content. Users can try out the search option for free and are shown a preview of results, but are required to pay a fee to view them in full and access any website or source links.

Many adult content creators use a fake name for safety reasons and to protect them if they decide to leave the industry behind in the future. Some may dip their toes into the spicy content world for a few months before deciding it isn't for them and deleting their page entirely. And, as we know, there are many women out there who have never shared a nude publicly but exchanged pics with their boyfriend, who went on to betray their trust and upload their intimate images to a forum. All of these people should have the right to privacy and be able to move on with their life if they wish, but facial-recognition search engines like PimEyes are giving perpetrators a torture tool that ensures their past can never be forgotten.

While researching for this book, I stumbled upon a selection of posts on forums where men would offer their PimEyes subscription credits to others – 'for your purely academical reasons, of course' – to help them find women ('Let's find out if someone you know has an Onlyfans :D'). Users refer to their searches as having a 'hit' on someone ('I have two hits on people I know/one hit should get her stage name'), contributing to the disturbing idea that the women are being hunted. I saw the desperate pleas of men who were searching for content made by women that had exited the adult industry years ago, and from those who were hoping to discover that their neighbour was living a double life.

Here are some more examples I came across of men requesting help searching PimEyes:

> 'She used to live on my road and I always thought she looked filth. Really hoping someone with a pimeyes can find something. Thanks'

'Pimeyes request. Can anyone help me out? I know this chick from school and found she used to do modelling (pics). I know she's got to have more out there and hopefully nudes or something. Anyone find more? Or maybe hack her cloud?'

These men's online pursuit of women highlights a dangerous blurring between our digital footprint and our offline existence, where technology is used to track down women for men's personal sexual gratification, their burning desire to view a woman without clothes limiting any awareness or acknowledgment of the risk they are causing to her safety.

As women and girls, since the day our parents agreed we were old enough to leave the house alone, we have been taught to tap into our survival instincts in public to avoid falling prey to predatory men. Our necks adapt an owl-like swivel on our walk home; our ears adopt a bat's sensitivity to pick up heavy footsteps in the shadows. Hard-learnt lessons are passed down from generation to generation – keys in between knuckles, hair strands pulled out in the back of a taxi – but what can we do when the hunt is being carried out via devices? How do we keep ourselves safe from the one thing that keeps us all connected?

If you cast your mind back to the chapter where we looked at deepfakes and the creation of nudify apps, you'll remember that the creator of DeepNude, 'Alberto', had a childhood fantasy about owning a pair of X-ray glasses. Chillingly, his dream may not be far off becoming reality with the invention of Ray Ban's Meta Smart Glasses, which feature a small camera in the frame. AnhPhu Nguyen and Caine Ardayfio, two engineering students studying at Harvard University, highlighted the potential danger to privacy and worrying capability of the smart glasses technology by developing a program they called I-XRAY. Their coding customises smart glasses, using facial technology on PimEyes to automatically search for the face of someone they are physically looking at and identify them in real time, also pulling information including home address, phone number and information on family members. This gives glasses wearers the ability to dox people, live.

In an interview with 404 Media, Nguyen highlighted the potential harm their program was capable of: 'Some dude could just find some girl's home address on the train and follow them home.' The students created the code to raise awareness of the dangers of facial recognition technology like PimEyes and refuse to release it, but if two university students can develop this software then it's only a matter of time before other, more sinister characters catch on.

I battled with the decision of whether to name PimEyes in this book because the last thing I want to do is encourage more people to use it as a form of abuse. Discovering it felt like I was lifting the lid on some sort of sordid secret, but the website received 4.7m views in August 2024 alone and has been widely covered by large media outlets including the BBC, *The New York Times* and the *Daily Mail*. Instead of ignoring its existence and rapidly growing popularity, I want to reclaim it for our own toolkit and reinstate its original purpose. The site is a great resource for tracking *your own* images, including intimate content, and letting you know where your face has been posted. From here, you can decide whether to report any leaks that show up in search results to the police or contact the websites that they are being hosted on directly with a DMCA takedown request. Running your face through the platform can also provide some peace of mind if you're worried or suspicious that your intimate images may have been shared without your consent.

And then, once you are done with your personal searches on PimEyes and have collected any evidence and information you may need, you have the right to opt-out of their system for free. This means that your face cannot be found using their search engine. It won't appear in any search results and any existing results will be removed.* If you're not interested in using PimEyes to search for your own personal content, I highly recommend you still take five minutes to opt out of their search engine anyway to protect your privacy. I've seen men who are adamant that a woman has an OnlyFans account or a past as a webcam model share their frustrations when their PimEyes search returned no results, and I imagine it's because the women have opted out of being discoverable in their searches. If nothing but for the satisfaction of knowing it'll be a sweet F U if ever someone does try to find you on there, do yourself a favour and fill out the opt-out form here: https://pimeyes.com/en/opt-out-request-form.

■

Maiken Skoie Wrighton is a personal trainer from Norway who lives in London with her husband and son. In August 2016, while out shopping, Maiken received a concerning message on Facebook from an old school friend who attached a selection of images alongside the question: 'Hey, is this you?' When she clicked to view the attachments, Maiken saw intimate photos that she had previously sent to her boyfriend, now husband. Shocked and trying to process how her private content had ended up online, she would soon learn that she had been hacked.

Maiken shared her experience with me for this book, telling me how the images had been posted on the messaging platform Discord, which is popular with perpetrators due to its anonymity. 'It was not just the photos that was on this chat, there was also loads of conversations about me, my Instagram was shared,

---

\* Just a note that this will not remove the images from the website that they're being hosted on, but will stop any images from showing in the search results on PimEyes. You'll need to contact the host site directly if you want to kill them at source.

everything about me was on this forum. It was really gross and I'd never seen anything like this. It got way worse because I saw all these files being uploaded at such a rapid pace.' Maiken realised that the forum chat also featured the intimate images and personal information of other women. 'The conversation that was floating around was like, "Do you have anything on this person from this place? Can you find this?" I felt totally invaded of my privacy; I had never felt a feeling like that. I just felt really sick and unwell.'

Maiken began researching image-based sexual abuse online as she attempted to have her images removed. This led her to make contact with a man she believed worked for a Norwegian organisation that could help with getting her images deleted: 'I didn't know that this person wasn't who he said he was. He was actually just a person who was pretending to do a job to get in contact with people like me.' Maiken shared her story of deceit with a Norwegian news outlet which set off a wave of reports from hundreds of other women who had also been harassed by the same man over a number of years, ending with him serving 90 days in jail for harassment.

Maiken thought his imprisonment in 2021 would be the end to the ongoing trauma she had faced since her private images had been shared online without her consent in 2016, but there was more horror to come. Since 2021, Maiken has received dozens of threatening emails from an anonymous user which include personal information on her inner circle, her places of work and threats to share her personal photos to her wider community: 'I don't know who this person is who's threatening me, sending my images to everyone I work for, sending it to my friends, saying that they're going to send it to my family. I don't think that has happened yet, but there's still the fear of it. And also, they seem to know a lot about me, which is very scary.'

On two occasions, Maiken's stalker escalated their behaviour, carrying out their threats to distribute her private photos to those closest to her: 'In 2021, they emailed me saying, "Hey, in 20 minutes I'm going to send an email with all your images to a long list of people in London and gyms. If you don't reply, I will do that."' Her previous experiences had informed her not to reply to the email in an attempt to avoid giving her stalker any further attention, but then 20 minutes later, her phone lit up with messages, emails and phone calls from friends and old work colleagues who had received the cruel email, asking if she was okay. She said, 'That was properly scary because every time I've been threatened in the past I always think, well they're not going to do it and I can handle it. When it did actually happen, I was just so shocked.'

Maiken read one of the most recent emails out to me which was sent in December 2023. It contained a new list of her contacts that the abuser had found, based on people, places and interests that they had taken from her Instagram page – a calculated move intended to make Maiken aware that they were following her closely. It concluded: '*People are going to point at you as soon as you're going out anywhere. Happy Christmas and a good New Year.*'

Not once has the stalker requested any money from her, which glazes the whole experience in an even more sinister coating – what does this person want?

Maiken reported the emails to the police on three separate occasions but told me she felt let down by their response: 'Every single time they were like, "We don't have enough evidence. We can't do anything" even though I have loads of emails, I have everything that they need, but they just don't have time, which I think is really poor from them, to be honest.' Maiken shared her experience and lack of support from the police in an interview with *i* newspaper and the police have since reopened her case.

It has now been eight years since Maiken found herself in a living nightmare of manosphere forums, threatening emails and hundreds of hours spent trying to seek justice from the perpetrators that have harmed her. Today, Maiken occasionally still feels waves of dread – especially as a new mum – but she displays an incredible strength and defiance not to let the shameful behaviours of her stalker hold her back from living her life. She is determined to find answers on who this person is and why they are targeting her, despite her fear: 'There's so many things that goes through my mind, you just never know what they're capable of. Will there be a day where they have enough of me just not giving a shit and actually come for me? I just don't know who I'm dealing with.' She hopes that the police will identify her stalker: 'I want them to get the punishment that they deserve because they are committing crimes every single day. And why should we just let that pass?'

Maiken told me that she is speaking out and sharing her experience in the hope of reducing judgement towards women who have shared an intimate photo of themselves, and to give courage to other women who, from her story, will know that they're not alone.

The Crime Survey for England and Wales 2024 carried out by the Office of National Statistics found 1 in 5 women, and around 1 in 11 men aged 16 and over, have been a victim of stalking, with over 1.5 million people experiencing stalking in the year ending March 2024.

A joint report published in September 2024 by the Independent Office for Police Conduct, the College of Policing and His Majesty's Inspectorate of Constabulary and Fire and Rescue Services investigating the police response to stalking found police are failing victims of stalking in too many cases. The report calls for urgent reform in the way the police handle stalking cases and the support given to victims.

Many victims of doxing and cyber-stalking see the threats and intimidation extend beyond the digital realm, with Lehart et al's research for the Center for Innovative Public Health Research into digital abuse and cyber-stalking finding that 12 per cent of respondents who experienced online harassment reported their abuser had attempted to harm them in person.

Previously, victims who were cyber-stalked were not allowed to know the identity of their perpetrator even after their arrest, with some victims finding out for the first time when facing them in court. But in December 2024, the UK government announced an update to stalking legislation that will allow police to reveal the identity of online stalkers to the victim at the 'earliest opportunity' as part of new 'right to know' guidance to better protect victims.

Refuge UK, a domestic violence organisation for women, raised their concerns at their first Tech Safety Summit in 2024 of the increase in stalker ware and spyware that are used in instances of coercive control and stalking. They are both unethical forms of tracking software that can be installed on devices, allowing abusers to monitor their victim's activity through full access to web searches, social media, live location and voice calls. In 2019, the digital security protection platform Avast helped find and remove eight stalker ware apps from the Google Play Store, and in 2021 they reported a 93 per cent increase in the use of stalker ware and spyware apps in the UK since the Covid lockdown began in March 2020.

There have also been reports of everyday interconnected devices like smart speakers, baby monitors and fitness trackers being hijacked by perpetrators to facilitate the abuse of women. Legitimate, anti-theft software Find My Phone and apps like Find My Friends and Strava can also be used to track victims' live locations. A 2023 investigation by the Culture, Media and Sport Committee found 'smart' products in homes were being used to 'monitor, harass, coerce and control' victims by collecting recordings and images, saying they'd heard evidence of how the 'vast majority' of domestic abuse cases now feature some sort of cyber element. The use of hidden cameras in daily objects have also raised concern, with Amazon selling clothes hooks featuring spy cameras that led to a woman in the US filing a legal complaint against the company. She reported being filmed in a bathroom without her consent by a clothes-hook camera that was bought from their site.

## How to protect your phone from stalker ware / spyware

If you suspect someone has had access to your devices, have a good clear out of your settings to check for any unwanted software, apps or linked accounts that could be monitoring you. Here are some tips on what to look out for:

- If your device is running slower, crashing or freezing often, this could be a sign that additional software has been downloaded and you need to get it checked. Or that you just need to update your phone. So don't panic and try the latter first!

- Secure your device by turning off your location services in your privacy settings. You may need to go into individual apps to do this, where you can turn location sharing from 'always' to 'while using'. I recommend turning off the option of 'precise location' wherever it's not needed.

- Check for any linked devices in your settings. If there are any suspicious devices or software connected, take screenshots for evidence before removing them.

- Change your passwords, especially on sites that may have access to your location or address, like Deliveroo, Uber and Amazon.

- Ensure you have two-factor authentication set up on your email account, as securing access to this could let abusers get permission to access other apps on your phone.

- If you notice your device has new settings, such as a new default search engine or browser home page, or apps that you don't recognise, this could be due to spyware. Contact the non-emergency police number 101 for advice or take your device in to see a professional with your phone or data supplier to get them to check it for you.

Remember, if you remove a device or user from your settings the account/device owner may be notified which could escalate abuse. If you think you're at risk of technology-facilitated domestic violence contact https://www.refuge.org.uk/ for help and advice.

■

The menacing actions of men in the manosphere do not stay exclusively online. For some, the crude conversations and trading women as objects remain a fantasy in cyber-space, but for the men whose perversions run deeper, their entitlement and hatred towards women can act as a deadly virus in the offline world. Online forums have played a significant role in the physical harm and abuse of women, with their safety compromised by the men who have meticulously planned their exploitation and suffering with an online community. While there are thousands of men who hang out in the forums of the manosphere without the intention of acting out any physical harm, if they stand by and watch on as other men share their wicked plans of attack – or worse, encourage their damning behaviour – then they are at the very best a guilty associate to the extreme misogyny they're consuming, and, at worst, a willing accomplice to the most deplorable of crimes.

## NO ONE WANTS TO SEE YOUR D*CK

On 12 July 2024, Gavin Plumb, a 37-year-old security guard and father of two, was sentenced to life in prison with a minimum term of 15 years and 85 days for soliciting the murder and inciting the kidnap and rape of TV presenter Holly Willoughby. Plumb's sick plan was uncovered when he attempted to recruit David Nelson, an undercover policeman, to help him carry out the attack. The men met in October 2023 on the messaging platform Kik, where they were both members of a group chat with over 100 participants titled 'Abduct Lovers', which featured discussions of abduction, rape, torture, human trafficking and murder of former partners, ex-colleagues, neighbours and others, including celebrities. Plumb's profile picture in the group, in which he admitted he'd been active for a while, featured an image of Willoughby, while the main profile picture for the group was of a distressed young, blonde woman and a man's hand covering her mouth – firmly setting the tone for all its members. The criminal plans to attack Willoughby were found to date back to 2018, when Plumb began a WhatsApp conversation with a man named 'Marc', that spanned a three-year time period, where he would share in graphic detail his desire to kidnap, rape and murder Willoughby. Marc never reported Plumb to the police.

Over 30 hours, Plumb exchanged 300 messages on Kik with undercover policeman Nelson. He explained how he had collected a significant amount of personal information about Willoughby. He knew her home address, when she did and did not have security, what time she woke up in the morning and that her home did not have a CCTV system installed. Plumb sent Nelson photos of what he believed to be bottles of chloroform that he had purchased online to incapacitate Willoughby and her family, and a video of a restraint kit that included handcuffs, ankle restraints, gags, a blindfold, ropes and metal cable ties, as well as other BDSM equipment including a whip. He told Nelson he had been planning the attack for over two years and that once 'done' with Willoughby, he planned to 'slit her throat, clean her out and dispose of her'.

When police searched Plumb's devices, they found tens of thousands of images of Willoughby, including deepfake sexual abuse images, highlighting the terrifying threat of deepfake 'porn' that allows perpetrators to live out their perverted fantasies online before being inspired to act on them IRL. All of Plumb's research into Willoughby and the criminal activity that followed had been carried out online, from researching of her daily routine to the purchasing of a kidnap kit.

During the sentencing, the judge ruled that Plumb's purpose in participating in the 'Abduct Lovers' group chat on Kik and other online groups he frequented was to recruit the right 'crew' to help him carry out his sadistic and brutal attack. Nelson told the court that he was immediately concerned by Plumb's messages in the group chat, that went 'beyond what was typically posted'. And yet, before his plan was busted by police, Plumb participated in online groups for several years, sharing in graphic detail his intent to harm Willoughby to hundreds of members, encouraging others to join him. He boasted of his history of violence towards women and his previous convictions of attempted kidnap to prove to those he attempted to recruit what he was capable of. Still, none of the people who came across Plumb in any online chat or forum reported his behaviour to the authorities.

■

Gisèle is a 72-year-old woman whose life as she had known it fell apart when she was called in to her local police station in November 2020, where police informed her of a collection of images and videos they had found on her husband's hard drive. Dominique Pelicot used an internet forum titled 'Without her knowledge' to recruit men to rape his wife of 50 years, inviting them to visit the retirement chalet he shared with her in Mazan, a small French town. He filmed them sexually abusing her while she was comatose as a result of the drugs he used to spike her evening meal or glass of wine. He would also regularly film himself raping her. He is believed to have orchestrated over 200 rapes and enlisted at least 83 men to abuse her while she slept. Police found over 20,000 images and videos on his devices which were organised meticulously, including dates and the names of the men involved. Police also uncovered naked photos of Pelicot's daughter Caroline in a folder named 'Around my daughter, naked', along with intimate images of his daughters-in-law, all captured without their knowledge or consent.

Police were able to identity 50 of the male suspects that raped Gisèle in her bedroom while she lay unconscious. At the trial, Husamettin Dogan, a 'happily married father', told how he thought the woman 'looked dead' when he walked into her bedroom wearing nothing but a condom. Joan Kawai, a soldier, missed the birth of his daughter to visit the Pelicots' house. Andy Rodriguez, a father of two, told the court he only went around the house on New Year's Eve because he 'had nothing else to do'. Lionel Rodriguez, a father of three, said in his evidence that Pelicot had told him sleeping pills were involved but that it 'wasn't clear if he was giving them to her or she was taking them'. He penetrated her nonetheless. Jacques Cubeau, a 72-year-old retired fireman, married for 25 years, testified that he had thought about making a report to the police after his encounter with an unconscious Gisèle, but then 'life carried on as normal'. Many of the accused denied rape, claiming they believed Gisèle had consented or that they had been manipulated by Pelicot. Gisèle recognised one of the men on trial as someone she would bump into in her local bakery and swap pleasantries with. Many of them were fathers, most of them were husbands and all of them, according to Pelicot, were fully aware and complicit in the drugging and rape of Gisèle. Thirty-three of the men who were filmed abusing Gisèle remain unidentified.

Pelicot has always admitted his guilt to police, telling them: 'I put her to sleep, I offered her and I filmed.' At trial, all 51 men accused of raping and assaulting Gisèle, including Dominique Pelicot, were found guilty.

It is a case that ignited female rage world over, sparking protests across France calling for more action on male violence towards women and girls, and one that has flipped the conversation around rape and how society views victims on its head. Gisèle bravely waived her right to anonymity to ensure a public trial that would name her abusers and raise awareness of drug-induced sexual abuse. When the judge ruled that video evidence of the crimes would only be shown to lawyers and the jury due to their shocking and indecent nature, Gisèle and her lawyers appealed the decision to allow the public and press to remain in the courtroom to 'help prevent other women from having to go through this'. Gisèle's courage knows no bounds, and the powerful footage of her walking unapologetically into the courtroom to face her multiple abusers will forever remain etched on my mind. But an elderly woman who experienced one of the most extreme, undignified cases of rape and exploitation by dozens of men should never have had to put on a global public display to ignite empathy towards rape victims.

Dominique Pelicot lived in a small town but, thanks to online forums, did not struggle to find predatory strangers willing to rape a woman they didn't know. Their seeming ordinariness is a sobering reminder of the danger that women face in our daily lives. If the fireman, the councillor, the supermarket worker all turned out to be opportunistic predators then how are we as women expected to know which men are safe?

Pelicot posted publicly about his atrocities in the forum, and of the men that he invited round to his home, only a handful of them left after seeing a semi-naked sedated woman. Not *one* of the men from the forum, nor any of those who saw Gisèle unconscious, reported her abuse to the police. Do they hold such hate for women that they did not see her as a human being? For some of the accusers, years had passed since their crime. Had they given much thought to her since? Did they feel comfortable closing the door behind them and leaving the unresponsive, naked body of a woman in the hands of the man who was offering her up for abuse? It's quite a remarkable thought that all of these men simply went about their daily lives as normal after raping an unconscious, elderly woman.

The Pelicot case encapsulates the harrowing reality of the way in which many men view women, and how our objectification that has seen men trade our bodies in online messaging boards is being played out in real life. The unspeakable violence carried out by the dozens of men Dominique Pelicot recruited raises a frightening question of how many other men who frequent these forums would readily carry out their cyber-sins for real, if the opportunity were to present itself? No longer can the extreme misogyny we see online be dismissed as 'fantasy'; it needs to be recognised for the real and imminent threat that it poses to the physical safety of women.

This is what we mean when, as women, we say *all* men play a role in the patriarchy – you may not be carrying out any physical harm, but are you doing enough – *or anything* – to confront misogynistic and violent behaviour towards women when you see it happening?

In a statement read out in court, Gisèle explained that she chose for the trial to be made public to show how the burden of shame must change sides: 'When you're raped there is shame, and it's not for us to have shame, it's for them.' I couldn't think of a more poignant, powerful statement. The shame of sexual violence must sit solely with the perpetrator.

Manosphere forums are not supportive online communities that provide men and boys with safe spaces to have honest conversations – they are dangerous hotbeds of abuse and violence towards women and girls that have real potential to cross over into physical, in-person harm. To those who might claim they're just having some 'harmless fun' sharing women's intimate images in forums or playing sexist games online – do you feel confident that you know the capabilities of the strangers you are engaging with? Or is a woman's life a risk you're willing to take for a sexual thrill? Swapping rape fantasies and girls' nude photos with other members online could one day make you complicit in a more serious crime.

## TIPS: How to protect your online privacy

There will always be predators ready to act in bad faith and, as much as I'd love to wave a magic wand that would chuck them all in a dungeon to which I'd coincidentally lose the key, for now, many of them exist alongside us. But there are things we can do to build a barrier that will help keep them at arm's length.

Here are my tips on how you can help to protect your online privacy:

- **Keep your location on lockdown.** If you must tag or share your location online because *duh, everyone needs to know I'm at Soho Farmhouse obvi*, then only share your location once you have left. If I've tagged a restaurant on my socials, I'm no longer there.

- **Spend time admiring your selfies.** Pay attention to any potential location giveaways when sharing images online of your home or workplace. If you live or work by a church, a supermarket or in a distinctive building, for example, then these can all be used by someone to estimate your location.

- **Exercise your right to be forgotten.** If your information is available on 192.com or ukphonebook.com, you have a right to erasure and can submit a request to have your information removed from their website. (Whilst we're here, remember to opt out of PimEyes too.) When you signed up to vote in the UK, you may have agreed to have your data shared on the open register, which is available for anyone to buy and share online. You can request to be removed by using the 'register to vote' service on gov.uk or by contacting your local electoral office.

- **Check in with your privacy settings.** Lots of social media apps will automatically share your location with them by default, making it easier for hackers to find your details. Ensure that you have two-factor authentication set up on all of your devices to protect your accounts. Go into the app settings on your phone and check what you're consenting to share. Oh, and that Snapchat Map feature? Yeah, turn that off.

- **Be your own biggest fan.** Search your own name on search engine sites so you can see what information might be out there that other people can find out about you.

- **Disown your family members**. Yes, I'm being serious. Having your family members and your relationships linked on your social media profiles is an easy way for people to find out your information and access your loved ones, so remove them from your Facebook family listings. While you're at it, give your parents' social media settings a quick scan because they're probably oversharing everything with everyone.

- **Contact the police** if you feel that you are in danger and/ or have received threats. Doxing, cyber-stalking and sharing intimate images are all punishable under UK law.

# 9

# MASCULINITY IN CRISIS

## What's going on with men?

'Over the last 40 years, women's roles – and the way
women see themselves – has radically changed.
The problem is that the same can't be said of men'
**Terry Real**

It seems everyone is talking about 'the masculinity crisis': young
men don't know where they belong, feminism has taken over,
male loneliness is at an all-time high, misogynistic influencers
are radicalising boys . . . Meanwhile, male violence towards
women and girls has been labelled an epidemic with women
bearing the brunt of the internal battle men are facing over what
it means to be a man in today's shifting, modern world. We are
living through a time of progression, where traditional gender
norms and roles of the sexes are being questioned and upturned
by women and marginalised genders who no longer want to live
under the patriarchal oppression that has restricted their lives
for millennia.

At its most simple, striving for an equal society for all where
no one is held back or othered because of their gender, sexuality, race, class or ability can only be a good thing. Contrary to
what some meat-heads might tell you on their podcast, there's
enough research out there that shows men also benefit from
the closing of the gender gap, with Øystein Gullvåg Holter's

study 'What's in It for Men?' reporting how men who live in more gender-equal societies experience more happiness, lower rates of depression and are less likely to take their own lives. The sharing of the workload as women's presence expands in the workforce is also a positive for men, who report an ease on financial pressure to be the breadwinner of the house. Plus, men who take a more hands-on role in parenting develop healthier relationships with their children.

And yet, still, the strides made in recent years by modern feminism have led to some men feeling victimised by this changing society, with 59 per cent of men in the UK believing that promoting women's equality has gone so far that we are now discriminating against them. Instead of seeing women's liberation as a win for gender equality, some men view it as a loss of their power and a cause of this so-called crisis of masculinity we're meant to be in. As Holter says, 'It is a common misunderstanding that increased gender equality provides benefits and privileges for women at the expense of men's benefits and privileges.' But as the famous quote goes, when you're accustomed to privilege, equality feels like oppression.

## MASCULINITY

*Definition:* A set of attributes, behaviours and roles associated with boys and men. It is a social construct – so, determined by the culture of the place and time – and separate from biological sex.

I don't doubt that some men are struggling. We know that mental health services in the UK are in the gutter, with suicide being the biggest killer of men under the age of 50. The post-industrial economy has transformed the labour market, where jobs traditionally seen as exclusively 'male' have declined or disappeared altogether. Plus, we're living through a cost-of-living crisis, creating pressure that is no doubt felt intensely by men who do see their role as the provider. If we think of the societal shift that's occurred in the Western world since the 'laddism' era of the early noughties, there's been a general rejection of casual sexism, a wider acceptance of gender as a spectrum of fluidity and a call for men to be held accountable for predatory behaviour. With all of these changes, it's easy to see how some men and boys may be struggling with their identity. But with all that in mind, hasn't masculinity always been in crisis?

Was masculinity not in crisis when the paparazzi photographed David Beckham wearing a sarong in 1998? Or when the UK coal industry was closed down in the 1980s by a female prime minister nicknamed the Iron Lady? Had feminism not gone 'too far' when women stormed the stage at the 1970 Miss World pageant protesting women's objectification? Was men's role in the family not questioned when the contraceptive pill was legalised in 1967? And were men not struggling with high unemployment following the First World War, particularly returning soldiers from a male dominated industry? It can be argued that the conventional concept of masculinity has been in crisis for a very long time, with the consequences felt deeply by the women whose lives are lost to it and the men who hide their authentic selves because of it.

Dr Alok Kanojia is a psychiatrist and co-founder of the mental health coaching company Healthy Gamer whose clients include those from the incel* community. In a podcast interview,† he explained how men have been struggling under the

---

* An incel is a term used to describe a person, often a man, who classes themselves as 'involuntary celibate' and unable to find a sexual partner. They typically show extreme resentment and harmful views towards women, and men who are sexually active.

† Dr Kanojia was interviewed about his work and the masculinity crisis on *The Diary of a CEO* podcast. It's definitely worth checking out on your next long drive.

constraints of masculinity for many years: 'If you look at even 50 to 60 years ago, 80 per cent of suicides are still going to be men.' He went on to share his view that society won't accept that men suffer because that would mean 'you're not manly', adding, 'We're so externalised with our attention that we're not connecting with ourselves, and so we're looking to other people to tell us what it means to be a man.'

If masculinity in its traditional construct is keeping generations of men stuck on a hamster wheel of harm, it might be time we stop viewing the 'crisis' as a temporary problem that can be patched up with legislation and banning certain influencers from social media. By reframing the genuine concerns around hegemonic* masculinity as less of an attack and more of an opportunity, we can open up a space for men to explore their identity and personal version of masculinity outside the traditional constraints of what it means to be a man. The world is changing for women, which means it's changing for men too. We have to find a way of co-existing as men and women that works for everyone, but women can't be expected to sacrifice their right to be treated as equals to accommodate that. That means men are going to have to make changes so that they can have healthier relationships with the people in their lives, and also with themselves, and re-evaluating their idea of what masculinity looks like is a great place to start. This isn't to say that any form of masculinity is bad and that it should be eradicated altogether – there are traits associated with 'traditional' masculinity that can have a positive impact. Wanting to care for and protect others, providing for loved ones, being confident, keeping fit and healthy, and wanting to be successful can all be positive characteristics. We need to let men decide what parts of the hegemonic idea of masculinity they want to hold on to,

---

* Hegemonic masculinity is a term used in gender studies to describe the dominant form of masculinity that is upheld in society.

which ones no longer serve them and the behaviours often cast as 'feminine' they might want to adopt, while they recognise the ways in which some typically masculine behaviours are harmful. We need men to put in the work for women, but also for themselves.

## 'Toxic' masculinity: first we need to understand it

The harmful behaviours and actions of men that we've spoken of in this book encapsulate the worst of masculinity. They are entitled, sexist, selfish and show a total disregard for others. Empathy is lost on these men. They embody the idea of 'toxic' masculinity – a phrase that has become controversial for its demonising of masculinity.

### 'TOXIC' MASCULINITY

*Definition:* A concept used to describe a set of attitudes and ways of behaving typically associated with hegemonic masculinity that are harmful towards society as a whole. Examples include misogyny, homophobia and violence. It may manifest as sexual entitlement and viewing women as the lesser sex, a desire for dominance, rejection of and hostility towards femininity and a disdain towards displaying emotion.

Nowadays, those working with men and boys prefer to use the term 'unhealthy masculinity' or 'dominance-based masculinity' to describe the harmful or unhelpful behaviours displayed by men. Whatever it may be called, we are all familiar with gender norms that keep men in a 'man-box', telling them there is a 'right' way to be a man. If we want to stop the millions of men who are perpetrating online misogyny and victimising women, first we need to understand them.

Masculinity is a ready-made identity that boys are told they need to perform. There is a script and rules to follow that boys become aware of from an early age. This differs across cultures and historical periods, but the blueprint can be recognised in all communities. Dr Ronald F. Levant, a psychologist and co-author of *The Tough Standard: The Hard Truths about Masculinity and Violence*, refers to these rules as a 'prison' for men who see masculinity as 'obligatory' and 'feel they have no other choice but to conform to masculine norms'.

In 1976, social scientists Robert Brannon and Deborah David proposed a blueprint of manhood in their book *The Forty-Nine Percent Majority: The Male Sex Role*, comprised of four basic components of traditional masculinity for men and boys to follow.

## Brannon Masculinity Scale – a.k.a. the blueprint of manhood

**1. No sissy stuff** – This is basically the rejection of anything that can be viewed as feminine, including your emotions (other than anger though, that's alright). Men are encouraged to hide their feelings and show no weakness.

**2. The big wheel** – This concept is all about success, status, and being admired and respected. It is the striving for power, measuring financial, physical and sexual performance, and receiving validation from others.

**3. The sturdy oak** – In contrast to women being the 'clinging vine' (major eye roll), this is about men being tough, self-reliant, confident and strong. This is the epitome of a 'manly man' who doesn't need the help of others. (Reports of the male loneliness epidemic would suggest otherwise.)

**4. Give 'em hell** – Lastly, it's fight club time. This component encourages men to be ready to fight and to tap into their violent and aggressive side. With men counting for 93 per cent of defendants in domestic abuse cases, this trait seems to be one that has firmly embedded itself.

Another element of this component is the importance of men's ability to be risky and adventurous.

∎

These rules were laid out in 1976 – almost half a century has passed since then, but its framework remains ever-present in modern society.

It's no wonder men are struggling with their identities and sense of belonging when 4 billion of them are expected to fit into an incredibly narrow framework of masculinity.

I unpacked some of the blueprints of masculinity with Cal Roberts, who is a songwriter, music producer and filmmaker from North Wales. Cal shared his story of battling with his concept of masculinity in the documentary *Sound Lad?* The film explores the role generational trauma plays in men's lives and how dominance-based masculinity is passed down through the generations. Cal said his stepfather was an 'amazing' and supportive provider for their family, but Cal felt that he couldn't have the big, vulnerable conversations with him that he needed to as his son: 'I was a poet and I was a painter and I wanted to sing songs for people, whereas he wanted me to go and work in the steel works with him. If I was ever sad, he'd be like, "just get a grip", and I'd be thinking, "You think I haven't tried getting a grip? I've been out for a walk, I've seen my friends and I still want to die."' His stepfather is from an older generation that Cal describes as 'very close lipped, very keep your cards close to your chest, seeing vulnerability as weakness'.

As a woman who cries at 'hope core' videos on TikTok of old couples eating in a restaurant together, or a passer-by stopping their car to help a waddle of ducklings cross the street, not being able to openly feel the rollercoaster of emotions I experience on a daily basis would be soul-constricting. The passing down of these weighted chains entangled around the essence of masculinity must feel painfully heavy for men and boys who are living through the same human experience that women and girls are.

The Samaritans report that men are three times more likely to die by suicide than women,* with men aged 45–49 in England and 30–34 in Wales having the highest suicide rates in the UK. Dr Kanojia referenced research from a 2022 study which shows most men who die by suicide have no mental illness recorded in their medical notes and explained how his male clients who feel suicidal aren't usually living with a diagnosable mental illness but rather 'a sense of thwarted belonging'. How do we build a world in which men value emotional literacy and relationships – the foundation of a sense of belonging – when we are raising young boys to adopt individualism, stoicism and violence?

Andrew 'Bernie' Bernard runs the 'What Makes a Man?' programme in education settings, which aims to help boys and men consider modern manhood, think about unhelpful masculinity and develop empathy. Bernie's sister Sarah was murdered in 2012 by her partner Ian Hope after suffering nearly two years of abuse by him. It was from this painful experience and the systemic misogyny of police that caused failings the night Sarah was killed that Bernie developed an understanding of coercive control in relationships. Reflecting on his own experiences as a young man who adopted the identity of 'toxic' masculinity, Bernie was inspired to not only engage in the conversation on gender-based violence but to become a leader

---

* Tragically, both male and female suicide rates are up in England and Wales, with suicide being the biggest killer of men and women under 34. It's a desperately sad reflection of the struggles young people are facing in today's society.

for the young men and boys looking for an outlet for change. I spoke with Bernie for this book, and we traced gender norms and expectations placed on the sexes back to childhood. 'Think about T-shirt patterns for kids, think about animals, what do boys have? You've got wolves, sharks, tyrannosaurus rex – all predators. What do girls' T-shirts have? Bunnies, a unicorn, a cute hedgehog. You'll see predators on boys' T-shirts and you'll see prey on girls T-shirts.'

As an adult woman, I am hyper-aware of the danger that exists from the predators who hunt us down on the street or track us in online spaces. I'm reminded of the 2022 murder of Zara Aleena, a 35-year-old law graduate whose life was cruelly cut short by Jordan McSweeney while she was walking home after a night out in Ilford, East London. In CCTV footage from the night Zara was killed, McSweeney is seen following women into a shop and trying to hide in the shadows as he sought out his opportunity to attack his prey. He's shown stalking Zara before grabbing her from behind and carrying out the fatal attack. If we're to believe that men aren't inherently born evil, what is it that influences so many to carry out 'opportunistic' attacks on women they hunt down with hawk-like precision? One kids' T-shirt with a shark on it isn't radicalising boys to become predators, but it is from the constant, soft assertions of male dominance – the 'give 'em hell' components from the blueprint of manhood – that dominance-based masculinity is built and thrives.

Growing up with two brothers, the 'no sissy' anti-feminine component of masculinity is one I'm familiar with. I remember how my dad would cringe when I painted my little brothers' toenails and squirmed when my older brother came home with an ear piercing. My parents raised my brothers and me with liberal values and to treat everyone equally with the same respect. And yet, our home could still not escape the restrictive walls of the 'man-box' passed down through generations as a means of protection, with fathers wanting to keep their sons safe from the men who police one another's masculinity.

In his book *Billy No-Mates*, Max Dickins investigates male friendship and the restraints around emotional literacy. He tells of feeling 'under constant surveillance' from other men and describes his friendships with women as being able to 'breathe out' – for the first time feeling free to show up as 'vulnerable' and not needing to 'perform' for women who he recalls as being 'unafraid to show emotion, nor to disclose information about themselves'.

In their effort to protect their sons from the watchful judgements of other men and the consequences that may follow if they step outside the blueprint, the cruel irony is that fathers could be contributing to the inner turmoil of young boys who police their own identity in private. If you've never told your son you love him or refrain from giving him a hug to 'avoid the sissy stuff', you're raising a boy to mask emotions that may one day eat him alive.

Cal Roberts told me of a conversation he had with a friend who works in prisons and schools, discussing gender norms and the stereotypes of masculinity. Cal's friend said, 'As men, we're restricted in everything; we can't even say something is beautiful because our mates call us gay. We can't even use the word beautiful because it's seen as an effeminate word.' This made Cal think: 'We're being restricted by our own bullshit, our own nonsense. Imagine not being able to look at a mountain and go *that is absolutely, breathtakingly beautiful.*'

The ridiculousness of 'feminine' words being off limits is almost laughable, but the reality of these constraints placed on men is restricting at best and can be deadly at its worst. After all, the worst thing men can do is act like a girl:

*Man up*
*You throw like a girl*
*Only girls cry*

266

# MASCULINITY IN CRISIS

*You're acting like a girl*
*Are you on your period?*

To be 'a girl' is to be weak and powerless, which is why even the men who struggle within the tight confines of dominance-based masculinity are willing to stay in line and suffer. The alternative is to accept their equality with the women that some of them struggle to see as human.

The traditional stereotypes of masculinity that include being dominant, assertive and confident – sometimes aggressive – of course find their way into how men and boys are encouraged to think about sex. This can lead to physical violence against women and girls, with the normalisation of aggression in sex. If men are encouraged to be dominant, then they must have something to dominate – in this sense, male entitlement over a woman's body and sexuality can be said to be part of the foundations of what it means to be a man.

We can't talk of 'toxic' masculinity and the role it plays in the online misogyny we've explored in this book without mentioning the influence of extreme pornography. The expansion of the internet and access to smartphones has increased access to porn. Pornhub.com consistently ranks in the top 20 most visited websites worldwide, with X Hamster and X Videos featuring in the top 40 list, above sites like Telegram, Temu and X. A 2023 report by the Children's Commissioner for England found the average age at which children are first viewing pornography is 13, with 27 per cent having seen it by age 11 and 10 per cent by age 9.

I remember the first time I saw a porn video was in primary school, when boys on my school bus thought it was funny to show us graphic clips on their flip phones on the way to swimming lessons, the 3-inch screen housing 10-inch penises. While many anti-porn campaigners argue pornography is becoming more extreme, the videos I was shown on that bus two decades ago featured bestiality and scat. So I would argue that pornography has always been extreme – it's the ease of access that has changed, allowing young men and boys to instantly view extreme scenes that include violent and degrading behaviours that are normalised by being featured and promoted on the homepage of main porn sites. In the report 'Sexual Violence as a Sexual Script in Mainstream Pornography', Dr Fiona Vera-Gray and Professor Clare McGlynn revealed the extent of sexually violent porn on mainstream sites, finding that one in eight video titles on the landing pages of the UK's three most popular pornography sites described sexual activity that constitutes sexual violence. Diving deeper into their findings, the most frequent form of sexual violence that featured in the data related to sexual activity between family members, with the second most common category describing physical aggression and sexual assault. First-time users and those who are new to the world of porn, particularly young people, are being served up extreme videos on the site's 'shop window' that tells them that violent and abusive behaviour is a 'normal' part of sex. Vera-Gray and McGlynn argue mainstream porn sites distort the boundary between what is and is not sexual violence, drawing on Nicola Gavey's work on the 'cultural scaffolding of rape' through the creation of 'cultural norms and practices that support rape or set up its preconditions'. And it isn't just on dedicated websites where children are viewing porn – the Children's Commissioner's study found of the young people who had viewed online pornography, 41 per cent of children are accessing pornography on X, with 33 per cent viewing it on Instagram, highlighting the importance of platform regulation and for parents to take an interest in what their children are accessing online.

We've all heard the term 'vanilla' used as a way of shaming people who enjoy straightforward sex, with the mainstream platforming of kinks in book franchises like *Fifty Shades of Grey* and Netflix's film *365 Days* pushing the idea that missionary is out and being tied up, spanked or 'choked' (an informal term used to describe strangulation) is in. A 2019 survey by BBC Radio 5 Live found 38 per cent of women aged 18–39 had experienced unwanted slapping, 'choking', gagging or spitting during consensual sex. I'm cautious not to kink-shame – many of these acts are fine if you're consenting adults* practising BDSM safely – but the normalisation of scenes of sexual violence in the media and pornography is raising young people to believe violent or rough sex is the norm, rather than a potentially criminal act if not carried out responsibly, safely and consensually. For example, I've heard from a teenage girl whose boyfriend started to 'choke' her when kissing because he'd seen it in porn and thought she 'might like it'. Non-fatal strangulation (NFS) is a stand-alone crime in England and Wales as part of the Domestic Violence Act, with abusers facing up to 5 years in jail. It is often a gendered crime that overwhelmingly affects women and can cause long-lasting physical and psychological damage. A 2021 analysis of those attending a clinic in Manchester for a medical examination after a report of rape or sexual assault found of the cases where NFS was prevalent, 96.6 per cent of the patients were female and the alleged perpetrator was male in 98 per cent of cases.

During one of his workshops at a secondary school with year nine boys, Andrew 'Bernie' Bernard was discussing the Children's Commissioner's report on sexual assaults in schools and how 50 per cent of cases reported involved sexual violence such as spitting, strangulation and choking. 'I was saying "don't you think that's concerning?" to these lads and this kid in the front row looked at me and went, "Yeah, girls love being choked, though."' It's probably safe to assume that all the boys in the group had seen porn in which women are choked, as it's

---

* Though, both *Fifty Shades of Grey* and *365* teeter on the edge of consent and show women in submissive roles to powerful men, it's worth pointing out.

so normalised. He used the boy's claim as an opportunity to unpack the harm that these views can have on women, opening up a conversation via 'sex games gone wrong',* where women have been killed by abusive men. He asked the group to consider how many men they think had been strangled to death by women in a 'sex game gone wrong' to which the young boy replied in bewilderment, 'Why would a woman strangle a man?' Bernie highlighted how the boy had framed his answer: 'He'd seen loads of porn where men were strangling women and women were used as vehicles for male pleasure.' In a warming display of hope, one of the other young boys pointed out the hypocrisy in his friend's answer: 'His mate turned to him and said, "That's what he means by the normalisation of sexual violence!" And I just thought, at least one of them has got it.'

I firmly believe that consensual adults should be able to make money in whatever legal form they wish if it's not causing harm to anyone, and pornography should not be used as the scapegoat for men's violent and harmful behaviour, but the normalisation of extreme acts of sexual violence on mainstream pornography websites and in the media is an important and unavoidable factor to consider when discussing gender-based violence and online misogyny.

In his workshops, Bernie's mission is to ignite something he calls an 'empathy lightbulb' in the men and boys he's working with by providing a safe space for them to unpack how men are often not taught empathy, but 'nudged towards judgement' of women instead. He said 'A lot of men are hardwired to say, well, that's not my responsibility, yet we are all culture. We live

---

* In February 2024, the UK government announced plans to implement harsher sentences for those who kill their partners through abusive, degrading or dangerous sexual behaviour (rough sex), outlawing the use of rough sex as a defence.

within it, but we create it as well.' The concept is that when men become fathers to daughters, they experience a sudden heightened understanding of women's vulnerability, igniting a need to protect their daughters from those who Bernie calls 'the people that we used to be, as well as the mates that we know, as well as that bloke down the pub or that handsy bloke in the office. Suddenly, we think, *Shit, I've got to protect her from men.*'

But what about the men who never have daughters? Or the teenage boy who might not become a dad for ten years? Or the grandfather who still thinks women are exaggerating about the sexual harassment they face? We can't wait for men to feel responsible for a daughter before they view us as worth caring for and respecting. Plus, the unfortunate reality is that many men who commit the most heinous crimes towards women do have daughters.

Through his work, Bernie is trying to spark empathy lightbulbs and pre-emptive compassion in young men and boys for the women and girls who exist today, not just those who are yet to be born.

In 1996, Levant wrote of the 'new pressures' placed on men that derailed the traditional ideals of masculinity: 'pressures to commit to relationships, to communicate one's innermost feelings, to nurture children, to share in housework, to integrate sexuality with love, and to curb aggression and violence.' He came to the conclusion that these new pressures and expectations shook the blueprint of masculinity to such an extent that 'there is now a masculinity crisis, in which many feel bewildered and confused, and the pride associated with being a man is lower than at any time in the recent past.' Almost 30 years later, and we are still being told that masculinity is in crisis. That we're living through a male loneliness epidemic. That men and boys are struggling with a loss of identity due to changes in their traditional roles. So is it finally time to admit that these core foundations of masculinity that so many men are eager to hold on to are exactly what is preventing them from living as their true, authentic selves?

We know that the men and boys of today are struggling in the face of a changing modern society, trying to bake in a pre-fixed identity with a cookie mould of masculinity that has lost all its shape. There is no 'one-size-fits-all' version of masculinity that works for 4 billion men across the globe, and I'm sure they'd be a damn lot happier if they could lean into their unique personalities instead of performing a lifelong role of manhood that they needn't have signed up for. Mountains *are* beautiful; it isn't 'gay' to wear a pink shirt and yes, you can admit that you enjoy Harry Styles' music.

But while men work their way through an identity crisis of masculinity that has spanned decades and unpick the harmful learnt traits from their past, it's important that we don't let that overshadow the crisis women across the world are facing at the hands of the patriarchy that is stripping away their human rights.

In America, women are facing a loss of healthcare through state-wide abortion bans inflicted by far-right male politicians that have caused the death of several women. In Afghanistan, women and girls are facing a 'gender apartheid' that restricts their right to work, their access to education and their freedom of movement, with the total collapse of safe houses and contact points for victims of sexualised violence. In Iran, women are being institutionalised in mental health hospitals by morality police for failing to cover their bodies, and in Iraq, the government introduced a new bill that gives Islamic courts more authority over family matters that could see the legal age of consent reduced from 18 to 9, allowing older men to marry children. Here in the UK, a woman is murdered by a man every three days, with police chiefs treating the 'national emergency' of violence towards women and girls as a threat on the same scale as terrorism.

# MASCULINITY IN CRISIS

Masculinity *is* in crisis but I'm cautious that we don't allow the identity crisis men are facing to be used as a 'get-out-of-jail free' card (*literally*) for the global attack on women's basic human rights. In an essay exploring 'The Bogus "Crisis" of Masculinity', Professor Francis Dupuis-Déri references the work of historian Judith A. Allen, who believes we should stop short of labelling masculinity as being in crisis. Allen claims that 'crisis' implies 'serious upheavals and profound transformations' that 'does not accurately describe the reality of relations between sexes and the condition of men in society'. The argument is that if men are in 'crisis', how are they still at the top of all 'major political, economic and cultural institutions'?

Allen raises an interesting point. If we take a step back to look at some of the main issues that men are grappling with – unemployment rates, a cost-of-living crisis, the influence of social media, a lack of mental health support and an increase in suicide rates – we see that these are all affecting women too. However, there is a startling difference in the way men and women are dealing with the changes and challenges of a modern world. As the sex which has historically been the oppressed, women do not generally react to their pain with violence and anger, because they have become accustomed to it. The struggle of life is all too familiar to a woman, whereas men see hardships as a personal attack on their identity as ruler.

This is why I have to disagree with Judith A. Allen – we must label the crisis of masculinity for what it is because it is the key reason, in my opinion, for the epidemic of violence women are experiencing offline and in the digital realm. The conversation on gender-based violence is not a black-and-white one because, as men and women, we are coming at it from different lived experiences. We can hold empathy and space for the men who are facing an individual battle with their identity, but these men are ultimately free to choose not to conform. Masculinity may be a prison, but men hold the key to their own freedom.

Stephen Whitehead, the author of *Toxic Masculinity*, writes, 'There are now a lot of very confused, fearful and angry men – left stranded with a masculinity which once was valued, once was the norm, once was aspirational, but which is now recognised for what it is: damaging and corrosive.' Dominance-based masculinity that follows the structures of Brannon's Masculinity Scale from 50 years ago is rightly being called out for the harm that it's caused to women and men for far too long. Masculinity in its traditional sense needs to change, but what alternative option is being put forward? What does a positive, healthy masculinity look like in today's society? And how can men and boys adopt this? These are the questions that have fallen short of feminist conversations and the fight for a gender equal society. While we're working on the liberation of women, no one is calmly taking the wheel and claiming responsibility for guiding the lost young men and boys who are on a life journey and searching for answers.

No one, that is, apart from those who have realised how to monetise their pain . . .

## A starter pack to understanding the topic of masculinity

Here are some great resources for you to kickstart your understanding of masculinity and the next steps to take on your journey of deconstruction and reconstruction.

### Book list

*The Descent of Man* by Grayson Perry

*Billy No-Mates: How I Realised Men Have a Friendship Problem* by Max Dickins

*Lads: A Guide to Respect and Consent* by Alan Bissett

*The Will to Change: Men, Masculinity, and Love* by Bell Hooks

*For the Love of Men: From Toxic to a More Mindful Masculinity* by Liz Plank

## Audio list

*Realistic Happiness* podcast with Daisy Ilaria. '*Yor Smit: Positive Masculinity Redefined.*' Yor is an advocate for positive masculinity and brings a fresh perspective on modern masculinity and empathy.

*Waving the Red Flag* with Eddy, Josh and Alvin. '*Wild but honest conversations on love, intimacy, friendship and culture from the male perspective.*' This light-hearted podcast will probably be a more palatable introduction to the conversation for young men.

*Stompcast* with Dr Alex George. '*Thought-provoking conversations against a soothing backdrop of birdsong.*' Not so much focused on masculinity, but a positive example of a man having open, honest and thoughtful conversations around big subjects like IVF, our relationship with sex and porn, and grief.

## Social media accounts to follow

@David_Challen (on X). David is a domestic abuse campaigner, writer and keynote speaker who uses his platform to engage in the conversation around gender-based violence and men's role in tackling misogyny.

@sheisnotyourrehab / @myfathersbarber (on Instagram). Mataio Brown co-founded 'She Is Not Your Rehab' with his wife Sarah. The movement is an 'invitation for men to acknowledge their own childhood trauma and to take responsibility for their healing'.

@jordanfstephens (on TikTok). Jordan is one half of music duo Rizzle Kicks and author of bestselling book *Avoidance, Drugs, Heartbreak and Dogs*, which takes a candid look at men's mental health and modern masculinity. He's stepped into the role of an ally to women, using his platforms to start important conversations around misogyny.

# 10

# INFLUENCERS

## The monetisation of masculinity

'If you can't feel like a man unless she acts like a woman,
are you really free?'
**Liz Plank**

Christmas Day at my parents' house had become pretty routine – wake up, open presents, eat and complain about being bored all afternoon. In 2022, my mum forked out way too much money for us to go unwrap our presents in someone else's house in an effort to add some variety to the festivities. So on Christmas Eve, I was loitering around the hallway of our holiday cottage when I heard some of my family members discussing a video of a guy online who's just *so funny*. The peculiar male voice that played out from the phone speakers was instantly recognisable – the cosplay American accent intertwined with British twangs echoed through the hallway and stopped me in my tracks. I pivoted on the cold stone floor and made a beeline towards the lounge with purpose. 'ERM, EXCUSE ME!' I yelled, my horror already making itself known. How could it be? Andrew Tate had infiltrated my family holiday – *soz Mum*, but Christmas is cancelled.

**ANDREW TATE**
*Definition:* Bellend.

# NO ONE WANTS TO SEE YOUR D*CK

Andrew Tate is an influencer from London who lives in Romania*
with his brother and business partner, Tristan Tate. His first
taste of fame was in 2016 when he appeared on *Big Brother* UK,
but this attempt at stardom was cut short when he was removed
from the house over a video which surfaced that appeared to
show him attacking a woman with a belt. *We're off to a great
start.* Since then, Tate has rebranded himself as a caricature of
'toxic' masculinity: he smokes cigars, he's a kickboxer, he owns
more than 20 sports cars, he runs a successful online business,
he has a podcast channel, he sleeps with loads of women (while
also proudly calling himself a misogynist). Oh, and in 2023 *and*
2024, he was charged by Romanian police alongside his brother
for rape and human trafficking relating to their online webcam
business.

*Andrew Tate's name was googled more times than
Kim Kardashian and Donald Trump*

Tate has become a cult-like figure amongst a younger generation
of men who act as his disciples, driving a huge online following
of over 10 million on X. He was originally removed from the
platform for hateful behaviour, including his claim that women
should 'bear some responsibility' if they're raped, before his
account was reinstated by Elon Musk in 2022. In the same year,
his Instagram account, where he had 4.4 million followers, was
removed for violating the platform's policies around dangerous
individuals and hate speech. While he is banned from TikTok,
videos of him on the platform have been viewed 11.6 billion

---

* In a video explaining why he moved to Romania, Tate said 'probably
40 per cent of the reason' he made the move was because it would be easier
to evade rape charges in Romania, saying: 'I'm not a rapist, but I like the
idea of just being able to do what I want. I like being free.' A totally normal
response.

times. His influence is widespread, with more Google searches for Andrew Tate's name in July 2022 than for the queen of the internet Kim Kardashian and President Donald Trump. His content gives young men advice on how they can thrive in a modern society where feminists are turning women against them and the 'matrix' is running the country, providing simple 'how-to' instructions on becoming a millionaire 'alpha' male who drives shiny Bugattis and bangs multiple chicks, just like him. Appearing as a living embodiment of Brannon's scale of masculinity, Tate represents a certain ideal of manhood that leaves no space for the 'losers' and 'nerds' that don't conform to his 'man-box'.

During a livestream with right-wing streamers Adin Ross and Nick Fuentes, Tate and the other content creators were challenged by streamer Dean Withers (a Democrat) regarding their support for Donald Trump in the 2024 US presidential election. Disagreeing with the majority, Withers said, 'Maybe I don't support Donald Trump because he's a rapist.' Tate, who sat shirtless on his sofa behind a microphone, demanded he be removed from the livestream, saying, 'Let's lose the nerd!' and 'I'd rather lose the nerd and just talk knowing I'm right.' Withers was kicked out of the chat and his comments were followed up by Tate who tweeted a screenshot of him alongside the text: 'Keep your gay talking points, nobody gives a fuck what bitch dudes think.' Those 'gay' talking points being rape, by the way. As fragile masculinity goes, we witnessed it on a livestream in 4k.

To me, an outsider who, admittedly, is the polar opposite of Tate's target audience, his videos seem like a spoof of films like *21 Jump Street* or *The Hangover*, in which stereotypes of masculinity are amplified for comedy value. His content is so vastly ridiculous at times that he has even managed to stir a light chuckle from me on a few occasions, before the realisation has hit that *this* is the guy who is spearheading a generation of men calling for a world which reflects a real-life version of *The Handmaid's Tale*, recruiting young, far-right streamers as his town-criers.

This is where a disclaimer comes in: Andrew Tate is not the root of the masculinity crisis, nor is he the only person monetising men's struggles; he is merely a symptom of the unhealthy culture that has been passed down unchecked for generations. Tate is 'just a guy who saw a business opportunity', sold his soul to the devil and rolled with it, and I bet he can't quite believe how well that went for him. He is facing legal cases in both Romania and the UK for accusations of rape, including of a minor. Not exactly a positive role model we should be encouraging our men and boys to follow. What Tate has done well, *the only thing he's done well*, is being a great marketer.

A report by the *Observer* uncovered how members of Tate's Hustler University* were instructed to flood social media with his videos, reposting his most controversial content and driving up interest in his business. The tactic was described by experts as a 'blatant attempt to manipulate the algorithm' and artificially boost his popularity; the strategy worked and in less than three months Tate rose to viral fame. When it boils down to it, that's all he is – a grifter/businessman selling a product that he needs people to buy into to keep his business afloat. If Tate actually helped men with their identity struggles, improved their mental health and solved the masculinity crisis then his business model would fail. He only succeeds while men are suffering.

At surface level, Tate's views of success as binary and his promises of riches through his Hustler's University programme, along with his 'tough love' approach that encourages

---

* Hustler University is what Tate called his online learning platform where he charged users $49.99 a month for access to courses and money-making advice. It reportedly had 149,000 members before it was closed down.

men to 'play the cards you're dealt' and to use their trauma as building blocks, can be seen as having a positive influence on young men who may be feeling lost and looking for a sense of direction. However, if you dig a tiny bit deeper, you'll find a breeding ground for outdated, toxic environments that are begging to be tossed away. Tucked away neatly amongst Tate's motivational speeches and the validation of men's lived experiences are extreme views of misogyny that encourage men and boys to view women as property and objects used for sexual gratification. As a woman, the glaring misogyny of Tate's content is impossible to ignore, with any mention of his name firing up the flame of female rage. For young men and boys who are searching for answers, however, the misogyny experienced by women might be the last thing that registers in their mind. It is easy for them to overlook in their search for answers that reflect their own lives. Some can skim past the rotten misogyny that exists in Tate's content because in their eyes, it does not concern them. But it would be a disservice to women to suggest that all of Tate's male supporters are simply ignorant of the sexist tropes he pushes. Many of his fans who reshare his videos and leave laughing emojis under clips that spread harmful stereotypes of women are not only acknowledging the misogyny Tate platforms but are actively supporting it. Tate does not shy away from the misogynistic label, but embraces it, tweeting, 'As a man, you're not supposed to be a misogynist. But everything women say is so fucking stupid?'

*One in five young men who had heard of Andrew Tate had a favourable view of him*

Tate's regular misogynistic outbursts monetise women's oppression as content. His violence and aggression reflects an outdated, conservative ideal of masculinity and yet it is a hit with modern young men. A 2024 study by King's College London found one in five men aged 16–29 who had heard of Andrew Tate had a favourable view of him. While 61 per cent of people disagreed that he raised important points about a real threat to male identity and gender norms, 30 per cent of young men aged 16–29 were in agreement with his views, showing a clear divide in the sexes. Perhaps most worryingly, a study by online safety organisation Internet Matters found that 56 per cent of young fathers aged 25–34 had a 'favourable view' of Tate, compared to just 19 per cent of young mothers of the same age.

The opening of this ideological gap between the sexes is what researcher Alice Evans, a visiting fellow at Stanford University, calls 'a great gender divergence' that is playing out amongst the under thirties, with young women leaning further into progressive views and young men turning to more right-leaning conservatism. This gender divide was on clear display in the 2024 US presidential election, with young women (18–29) voting for Kamala Harris, the Democrat nominee, by an 18-point margin, while young men preferred Donald Trump, the Republican candidate, by a 14-point margin. In the era of 'woke', where Gen-Z are being raised in a liberal landscape that's supposedly more inclusive than ever, what is driving young men towards a more conventional and harmful version of masculinity?

Psychiatrist Dr Alok Kanojia pinpointed the discrepancies between the label of privilege and success that society places on men and the reality of many men's lived experiences as a force that is pushing them towards extreme misogyny online: 'Men are struggling right now and that the rest of the world says no, you're not, you're privileged, you're a man. There is one group on the planet who says yes, your life does suck – and that's these toxic masculinity people. They're the only people that truly validate men's experiences because everyone else says why are you complaining? And these guys say yeah, you're a fucking loser, what are you going to do about it?'

# INFLUENCERS

Ben Hurst is the director of facilitation at Beyond Equality, a gender-equity organisation that works across educational settings and workplaces to engage men and boys in conversations about gender equality. He is a leading voice in this space, with his 2018 TEDx Talk 'Boys Won't Be Boys, Boys Will Be What We Teach Them to Be'* challenging traditional, 'toxic' masculinity and rejecting the minimum standards placed on men and boys, asking them to reimagine a more positive masculinity that works for them without harming themselves and others. Eight years on from that TEDx Talk, his message is more relevant than ever. I knew I had to get Hurst's thoughts on the landscape of modern masculinity for this book. Our conversation helped me build my empathy towards men and boys after six harsh months spent researching the pits of misogyny and seeing extreme displays of dominance-based masculinity across the internet.

When we spoke of the common themes in his workshops, Hurst told me that what often comes up is that men and boys feel like they don't have a place in the world at the moment. On top of this, the levelling of the playing field for women and girls has left them with a sense that there's a lack of support for them, which Hurst says is partly down to what equity looks like, but also, 'It probably seems to them that there's loads of space given to girls and to female empowerment – girls are having special workshops and special conversations and guest speakers and all of that stuff, and then there's just nothing for them.'

As Hurst pointed out, a lot of this is the nature of the levelling in action. Women and girls have been left behind for far too long, and are finally beginning to have the resources,

---

* When you have a spare ten minutes, type in 'Ben Hurst' on YouTube and watch Ben's powerful TEDx Talk. It's a simple and digestible introduction to conversations around masculinity and a great starting point for parents. Plus, Ben's effortlessly cool aura will be a hit with your kids. Win, win.

education and opportunities to enable them to reach an equal outcome to men and boys. But Hurst's simple reflection about the lived experience of the boys in his workshops, coupled with Dr Kanojja's podcast episode, sparked an epiphany for me on where we've been going wrong when trying to engage men and boys to care about misogyny and male violence towards women, and why the influencers of the manosphere seem so appealing.

All men live under a patriarchy where a certain level of power is served up on a silver platter simply because of what exists between their legs; this is played out from birth through the way we raise boys and girls differently. My brother's adventurous and rebellious streak was encouraged, for example, while I was taught how to keep myself safe. But conversations about patriarchal power are falling short at recognising the individual experiences of the teenage boys and young men who don't see themselves reflected in the privilege they're told the patriarchy provides. For the boy from a working-class family who is bullied for his hand-me-down clothes, the lad who lives with his nan because his parents have a drug addiction, the young Muslim boy who's afraid to walk home alone after experiencing Islamophobic hate and the teenage boy who can't hold his boyfriend's hand in public because he's scared his parents might disown him, being told that they're benefiting from privilege will feel like an almighty stretch from their everyday, lived experiences.

It is in this space where charlatans like Tate thrive, providing an instruction manual on masculinity that promises to fix their problems, and setting themselves up as a Pied Piper to the lost men and boys who feel they are being left behind or demonised for things they believe aren't their fault. The reality, of course, is that the Andrew Tates of the world do not actually care about the everyday problems facing men and boys – they care about their views on streaming platforms and their followers on social media. So-called 'masculinity influencers' have seen the opportunity to dominate an under-serviced audience and rolled with it – not out of the goodness of their own hearts and a genuine desire to provide space for men and boys to unpack how the 'man-box' is failing them in the modern age, but out of a selfish need to discover how deep their pockets can stretch. Whatever level on the spectrum of sexism men may choose to inhabit, be it casual sexist 'banter' to extreme misogynistic beliefs, creating content at women's expense is a proven successful business model in the digital realm.

While Tate may be seen as the 'King of Toxic Masculinity', plenty of other creators and podcasters are pushing sexist tropes and unhealthy versions of masculinity to their male audience. Some of the most prominent figures include Joe Rogan, who hosts a self-titled podcast which regularly claims the top spot on UK and US listening charts with 14.5 million Spotify listeners and 17.5 million YouTube subscribers. Fifty-six per cent of Rogan's listeners are aged 18–34; 81 per cent are male. He's repeatedly been called out for his sexist, racist and transphobic behaviour on the show. This includes calling journalist Lauren Sanchez an 'alpha predator female' and agreeing with his guest that her 'puss-puss is probably incredible'; referring to Angelina Jolie's genitals as 'crazy pussy is the best pussy . . . She's clearly crazy' and laughing when Joey Diaz, a comedian on the show, told a story of how he pressured roughly 20 aspiring female comedians to perform oral sex on him to get a slot in a comedy show he produced. On the evening before the 2024 presidential election, Rogan endorsed Trump, giving him a huge boost amongst young male audiences. Trump's harmful proposals laid out in Project 2025* include attacks on women's reproductive

---

* Project 2025 is a policy handbook put together by conservative think tank the Heritage Foundation which acts as a 'wish-list' for the Trump administration, laying out step-by-step proposals for an extreme conservative presidential adminstration.

rights, penalising single mothers, removing protections against sex discrimination and gutting diversity and gender-equality efforts. By endorsing Trump, Rogan let his millions of young male listeners know it is okay to view women through the lens of objectification, to support their friends who are accused and convicted of sexual abuse and to believe that women should not have the right to choose what happens to their body.

Another influential figure is Jordan Peterson, a Canadian psychologist and author who sells out lecture halls delivering sermons on his '12 Rules for Life', explaining how 'The masculine spirit is under assault'. Many men have claimed Peterson's advice helped them to become a better man, but their improvement seems to come at the expense of women's equality. In an op-ed for *The New York Times*, Peterson shared his views on the patriarchy and men being in charge: 'The people who hold that our culture is an oppressive patriarchy, they don't want to admit that the current hierarchy might be predicated on competence.' When Alek Minassian killed six people in Toronto, Peterson told the *NYT* that violent attacks are what happens when men don't have partners.

Controversial male figures Tate and Peterson both embrace the 'guru' role, positioning themselves as self-help creators who provide men with advice on how to better themselves. Outside of this world, misogyny is also being monetised by streamers and influencers who use sexism dressed up as 'banter' on their platforms, repeatedly using women's humiliation and objectification as content.

Yung Filly, whose real name is Andres Felipe Valencia, has built a huge following on YouTube (1.83 million) and TikTok (3.1 million) through comedy skits with the Sidemen and Beta Squad. Casual sexism appears regularly in his content: he shared how he'd tell his partner if she looked 'fat' in a dress, reacted negatively to a woman who rejected his kiss in a chicken shop, joked of 'his ting' being 'a riser' while grabbing a fan's bum and made a woman cry in an episode of '20 Women vs 1 Sidemen' after calling her 'clapped', slang for ugly. Multiple women have shared their uncomfortable experiences with Filly online – such as him calling them 'dead tings' when they told him they had a boyfriend, and telling them 'if you're not coming back with us then fuck off my table'. It has also been reported on social media that he bit a woman outside a nightclub. Despite the everyday sexism in his content and concerning reports from women, millions of men continue to support him, with his fans arguing his comments are 'jokes' and brushing aside the women's objections as a 'hate train' or cash-grabs. It is the validation and acceptance of these behaviours by influencers like Filly that allow perpetrators to swiftly climb the pyramid of abuse from sexist jokes on social media to the sharing of non-consensual intimate images and even physical, in-person harm.

HS TikkyTokky, whose real name is Harrison Sullivan, is a British internet personality from Essex with a substantial following on social media, including his own Telegram channel 'FINE$$E Public' that has over 480,000 members. I joined the group, where Sullivan posts advice on foreign exchange trading (the conversion of one currency into another for financial gain) along with derogatory comments about women, such as, 'Need to expand my spunk more into Africa. Picked this tart up last night drop a reaction if you'd smash', often referring to them by sexist terms 'sluzza', 'tart' and 'bitch'. In his Telegram channel, I saw Sullivan share images and videos of women he's filmed nude or semi-nude, both in public and in private, engaging in sex acts. This intimate content is voyeuristic in its nature and the women's consent to be filmed and for the images to be shared publicly is questionable. Sullivan's popularity continues to soar despite his content openly objectifying women, with YouTuber and entrepreneur KSI platforming Sullivan on a boxing card for his promotional company Misfits Boxing in August 2024.

In October 2024, Yung Filly was arrested and charged in Perth, Australia, on four counts of sexual penetration without consent, three counts of assault occasioning bodily harm and one count of impeding a person's breathing. Reacting to the news of Filly's arrest and charges, Sullivan posted a video on his social media channels saying, 'Man went from playing football at Girth N Turf, to going and dropping un-consensual girth in Perth. What a fucking G.', followed by a tweet referring to the reported rape victim: 'Much higher probability the hoe wants a payday & some clout.'

Influencers like Filly and Sullivan cater to a young, male audience and use women as cheap laughs to build their online following. The spectrum of sexism in the influencer's content begins with jokes about women's looks and stretches to potentially criminal behaviour in the sharing of intimate content and physical harm. These men are commissioned by broadcasters for TV shows and booked for large sporting events. When they show us the type of men they are on camera, we need to start questioning what they are capable of in their private lives too, instead of excusing their sexism as 'banter' exploited for views.

Lesser-known influencers have also seen the potential in cashing in on the masculinity crisis. Civil servant Mathew Hyman rebranded himself as a masculinity coach, posting dating advice on his Instagram page where he provides his 89,000 followers with a free pdf that promises to take them from 'simp' to 'chad'. Some of the advice Hyman gives to men includes the importance of things like building muscle: 'You look more fertile. You look like you will produce better offspring, which ultimately is what women look for subconsciously.' I signed up to Hyman's newsletter, which churns out regular emails giving dating advice to men, which, alongside sensible suggestions like which photos they should include on their dating profile and how it's important to build rapport with women before asking for their number, refers to women as 'obese land-whales' and advises men to steer clear of the 'unhappy and unlucky' women 'who gives all the signs that they've been hurt in the past', telling them 'being yourself is not ENOUGH'.

Whether it's loud voices like Tate and Peterson, streamers like Yung Filly and HS TikkyTokky, or micro-influencers like Hyman, they all follow a similar blueprint of manhood that is seen in Brannon's masculinity scale. The 'man-box' acts as their business plan with its decades-long success already tried and tested. They know that it would be more difficult to build their business if they based their entire schtick around hating women, so they sprinkle the turd of misogyny in glitter through helpful advice on fitness, finances and dating that draws men in with its alluring sparkles before the lingering bad smell of sexism eventually takes over. These 'masculinity influencers' provide some guidance and direction to the men and boys who are seeking clarity on what it means to be a man today. But they hypocritically reinforce the idea that men need to 'man up' and hide their emotions and vulnerability, while also pointing to the men's mental health crisis and alarming suicide rates.

Women are still expected to live up to unattainable beauty standards and embody the impossible identity of the 'cool girl' perfectly laid out in a timeless monologue* in the film *Gone Girl*, but the dial has begun to shift in female circles to a more inclusive and accepting society. As a woman, I can open Instagram or TikTok on any given day and find hundreds of influencers celebrating different body types, telling me to love myself as I am and that I don't need a partner to be happy. And as the QUEEN that I am, I certainly shouldn't be changing who I am for no man! This focus on self-love and finding

---

* 'Cool girl is hot. Cool girl is game. Cool girl is fun. Cool girl never gets angry at her man. She only smiles in a chagrined, loving manner. And then presents her mouth for fucking.' I mean, possibly the greatest movie scene of all time.

happiness internally is in sharp contrast to the content male gurus and self-help influencers are posting, which is focused on achieving external validation and encourages men to change pretty much everything about themselves if they want to be happy. This content is ruled by insecurity and there is a distinct lack of male content creators who are encouraging men and boys to get comfortable with who they are and love themselves, warts 'n' all.

Ben Hurst raised an important point in our chat high-lighting how, in previous times, communities would hold the space of positive role models for young people, referencing the old saying that it takes a village to raise a child: 'There was a community of people around you who cared and were trying to oversee your growth and your development. Now a lot of that has just been offloaded to teachers and the internet, but the teachers don't get paid enough to do a good job of it and the internet is completely lawless.' It's an interesting point and one that is often missed in discussions on the lack of positive role models for men and boys – influences don't always have to be strangers online or people in the media who are achieving great things; those roles can be filled by our inner circle, family or community. The impact of mass closures of youth centres across the UK, especially in low-income areas, has had a cor-rosive effect on a younger generation who have lost access to mentoring services, safe spaces and a community, leaving them to be swept up in gang culture and knife crime. A report by UNISON in 2023 found more than two-thirds of council-run youth centres had been closed down since 2010, with youth services in England losing a mammoth £1.1 billion in spending between 2010 and 2021.

Music producer Cal Roberts takes on the role of mentor to some of the boys and young men he meets through his song-writing work. He likens influencers like Andrew Tate to gangs who are constantly recruiting for vulnerable members: 'They recruit the vulnerable, they recruit people that they can manipulate, and it always ends up being a pyramid with them at the top, and with money funnelling up. It's literally just a gang.'

It isn't just individuals who are radicalising our young men and boys into adopting more conservative ideologies. A lot of the conventional beliefs that come with the traditional masculinity being pushed in online spaces is tied up in white supremacy and the oppression of marginalised racial and ethnic groups. A BBC North West investigation in October 2024 uncovered how young men in the UK were being recruited by a violent white supremacist group called Active Club (AC) to join their mission to 'revive' what they call 'the warrior culture of our nation'. The collective, which has thousands of subscribers on Telegram, masquerades as a sports club that claims to focus on male friendship and fitness. But its content includes images of members celebrating Adolf Hitler's birthday and wearing Nazi-themed T-shirts and holding racist banners in public spaces. The group only recruits men who are 'white and of European heritage'. During a phone call with an under-cover BBC journalist, a national organiser for AC questioned them on everything from their ethnicity and fitness to their religion and martial arts ability, saying, 'We're trying to build a mass movement of strong, able-bodied, capable guys', boasting how the group has 'guys literally everywhere, in every region of England.' One post encouraged its male members to 'get on the streets . . . or risk your bloodline being scrubbed from existence'.

When a man armed with a knife entered a Taylor Swift-themed dance class in the Merseyside town of Southport and attacked children and female teachers, murdering three young girls named Elsie Dot Stancombe, Alice Dasilva Aguiar and Bebe King, riots broke out across England as fake news spread online that claimed the murder suspect, a 17-year-old from Cardiff named Axel Muganwa Rudakubana, was an asylum seeker. Thousands of people took to the streets across England targeting mosques, Muslim-owned businesses and hotels that were housing asylum seekers in a display of anti-migrant and Islamophobic hate. The original false claim of Rudakubana's identity was made by a wealthy white woman, and although a handful of women also joined in the rioting and online abuse, it was overwhelmingly men who took part in the violence, putting on a hyper-masculine performance in what was said to be a protest to 'protect women and girls' from the threat of Muslim men.

Co-founder of the EDL (English Defence League) Tommy Robinson posted a video on social media after the attack straight from the gym, telling his predominantly male audience to prepare to become a 'dedicated, fit, healthy, ready, British resistance' – the 'give 'em hell' component of masculinity firmly fired up. Robinson often repeats false claims to his followers that 'British' women are being raped en masse by asylum seekers and Muslim men, his Islamophobia propped up by his feigned concern for 'British' women's safety. On his podcast, *SILENCED*,* Robinson stated, 'It is not the Muslim women who are fearful walking down the street in their own towns and cities. It's not them not being able to let their daughters walk to the shop anymore, it's not. It's us.' Muslim women are more likely than men to be victims of islamophobia in the offline and online world, with many Muslim women reporting the language used is often misogynistic. They are attacked because of their religion *and* because they are women.

Elizabeth Pearson, author of *Extreme Britain*, attended far-right rallies during the research for her book, speaking with men and women who were in attendance. Her conclusion was that 'extreme activism was focused on achieving masculine status, expressed in different ways.' Far-right groups like the EDL and Active Club are forming harmful, extremist groups

---

* If Tommy Robinson has been silenced, why am I *still* hearing from him?

which are radicalising our men and boys through the guise of community and a sense of purpose, while also providing them with a scapegoat for their problems that frees them from having to take any personal responsibility for their reality. Their tactics are eerily similar to those used by online influencers like Tate, whose online network 'The War Room' claims to 'free the modern man from socially induced incarceration' (for a $7,979 price tag).

Masculinity influencers with young, male audiences are inextricably intertwined with far-right ideology and their political influence is vastly underrated. A 2024 study shows young women prefer short-format, visually driven, lifestyle-oriented content, with Pinterest, Instagram and TikTok dominated by female users. In comparison, platforms that focus more on discussion, gaming and tech are more popular with young men – streaming platform Twitch, Discord and Reddit all have a higher number of male users. While women are being served short think-pieces on TikTok and info-graphics on Instagram, men are accessing daily livestreams of content creators and lengthy podcasts which feed them unchecked and unregulated information as fact. The political influence of far-right streamers was celebrated during the 2024 US presidential election, with streamers and podcasters The Nelk Boys, Adin Ross, Theo Van, Bussin' with the Boys and Joe Rogan all thanked on stage during Trump's victory speech for their role in helping to elect him.

# The role of schools: education can set us free

This rise in misogyny and the stan culture of 'masculinity' influencers is being felt in schools, with girls reporting frequent sexual harassment and teachers witnessing a deterioration in boys' behaviour. Speaking to the *Guardian* in February 2024, a secondary school teacher who had been in the educational sector for 15 years told of witnessing 'a decline in feminism among young men' and an increase in their troubling behaviour, with girls reporting cases of 'upskirting, slut-shaming, predatory behaviour and casual microaggressions. It was horrifying to see how the girls saw it as just another part of life.'

Michael Conroy is the founder of Men at Work, a community interest company that delivers training on challenging sexism and supporting healthy personal relationships; he was also a secondary school teacher for 16 years. In an interview for the *Guardian*, he too reported a deterioration in boys' behaviour and attitudes towards women and girls, pinpointing the widespread availability of smartphones for children as a turning point: 'That shifted what we were used to in school. So instead of a dick pic a month, it was five every week. And it wasn't just year ten, it was year eight.'

Georgia Theodoulou is the lead for Wales and sports at Our Streets Now, a youth-led project working towards a vision of a world free from public sexual harassment. A teacher, she joined OSN's teacher panel after searching for an outlet to focus her 'pent-up rage' from her own lived experiences as a woman and following the tragic murders of Sarah Everard and Sabina Nessa in 2021. Theodoulou told me how she has experienced first-hand the misogyny and sexism that is rife in schools, having been sexually harassed by both her male pupils and her male colleagues. Working in the space of gender-based violence, Theodoulou was familiar with Tate's content and quickly recognised his influence in the school: 'I will see these videos online and then I will literally hear the stuff that they're saying regurgitated by students in a conversation or as a justification for doing things. You're just like, we're fighting a losing battle here because they genuinely believe all of this stuff that they're absorbing online.' She saw a level of entitlement from the young boys she taught in 'the comments that they would make in front of a class, or in front of me as a young female teacher and the comments that would be made to me about me. I had boys find me on social media; I've had emails to my work account from boys, really graphic comments and offers of sexual acts to my face from boys in a classroom.' This is the real-life influence online grifters are having on boys today, and the subsequent consequences that women and girls are facing because of their monetised content. I wonder if, when Tate films his shirtless soundbites while puffing away on a cigar in his home in Romania, boasting about women being owned by men, is he picturing a female teacher being sexually harassed in his name by teenage boys in a classroom in Wales?

When I visited Her Voice Wales, a group of girls aged 11 to 18 in the Vale of Glamorgan, to ask them about their experiences of sexual harassment, Tate's name immediately came up. The girls were discussing how receiving unsolicited dick pics from boys had been normalised, and how some boys reacted angrily if the girls did not respond with a photo, telling me, 'Andrew Tate tells them they're owed it.' The girls felt that streamers like Tate are encouraging harmful behaviours in young boys and should be held accountable for the content they're posting. One girl said, 'YouTubers normalise being awful to women. They have huge audiences where they're just abusive towards women.'

The girls also spoke of their frustrations at boys idolising famous men who are known to treat women badly or who are facing allegations of abuse. One girl from the group shared her anger: 'Young boys look up to footballers, they do something abusive but then they score, and it's all ignored.' To the girls in the group, the support for famous misogynistic and abusive men is incomprehensible. To them: 'If it came out that an artist was abusive, I can't listen to them anymore. I've stopped listening to one of my favourite artists because it came out that he was abusive. But so many boys don't act on it, they don't care.

They can separate it.' This is what we see play out in the fanboy behaviour of millions of men and boys towards their martyrs of misogyny, helping personalities such as Tate and Peterson earn millions while they ignore – or worse, celebrate – the harmful attitudes they share with their supporters towards women.

Reflecting on teaching in front of a class, Theodoulou said, 'It's quite scary being face to face with young men who you know, deep down, genuinely consider you to be a lesser human being, even though you're older, even though you're the teacher, you are the authority figure in that context – but that counts for nothing anymore.'

Although schools may be fertile ground for the misogynistic views of online influencers to thrive, they might also be a home for the solution. Talking of hosting Beyond Equality's workshops on gender-equality and healthy masculinities, Ben Hurst jokes of getting boys into a space 'where they can't run away'. Although the attendance at the sessions is ultimately voluntary, schools provide an opportunity to get boys into a room and have 'an entry level pathway into a conversation that most people aren't having'. Hurst told me how the workshops are a 'deconstruction and a reconstruction of masculinity' that involve asking a lot of questions that otherwise may go unasked. 'We're not prescriptive, we're not saying this is the old version of masculinity and it's out, and this is the new version that we're telling you you're supposed to be or embody. It's more about getting guys in communities and in groups to have that conversation amongst themselves and think about which form or forms of masculinity work for them and works for the people around them.'

It's important for Hurst that he is meeting the young men and boys he works with as 'equal stakeholders' in the conversation, 'giving them the sense that what they say in that space is going to be heard and respected and responded to', starting with encouraging personal reflection and unpacking what masculinity looks like for them. While Hurst views conversation on gender-based violence as an important and vital one to be had, he told me how jumping straight into those topics can make boys zone out or get defensive if they feel they're having the finger pointed at them, especially if they don't recognise their behaviours as harmful. That's why he takes a more curious approach, meeting the young men and boys where they're at, similar to what the influencers online are doing, recognising and validating their lived experiences and asking them questions that let them know someone does care and is listening. 'All of it builds towards a conversation where we're able to deconstruct those gendered norms and stereotypes and then allow people to say whether that's true for them or not, whether it feels like it's real for them, whether that feels like something that they've experienced or something that they want to challenge for themselves.'

Our Streets Now has begun running mixed-gender workshops in schools, which Theodoulou feels encouraged by: 'We've got to a point where just pointing the finger at men and boys and repeatedly telling them that they're the problem is not working. It's not fixing anything. In fact, I'd probably go as far as to say it's making it worse.' She spoke of the sympathy she feels for men and boys and the challenges they face navigating in the modern world: 'We're raising generation after generation of men and boys who think that they've got to have big muscles and they've got to be tough and they can't cry and they've got to have this sexual prowess . . . this is what breeds the harmful behaviours that lead to violence against women and girls.'

Providing spaces where men and boys feel they are being listened to and where they're safe to question their masculinity is a key part of eliminating the 'toxic' elements – as is arming them with the powerful tool of critical thinking that will hopefully, in time, help them see past the regressive, alpha-male character that online grifters are trying to sell them.

It is important that we don't allow a crisis in masculinity to be used as an excuse to let abusive and harmful behaviours slide. We know that the consequences of boys' behaviours are being felt from a young age and we can't afford to let them go unchecked. Gender-based violence and the extreme misogyny women and girls are experiencing online and in person has reached epidemic levels and urgently needs tackling to create a safe and equal world that works for everyone.

I've been guilty of jumping feet-first into finger wagging and calling on men to change their behaviour towards women, but if we're being realistic, there's a lot of work that needs to be done before we reach that stage. We can't skip the stage where men and boys commit to self-improvement and understanding themselves. This will allow them to heal generational trauma and unlearn the dominance-based masculinity with which they have become familiar. Then they will ultimately be able to build healthy, positive relationships with themselves and with others.

Looking back through the alarming areas of online misogyny we have investigated so far, it seems that a healthier version of masculinity, born out of the embers of a divided society on the brink of collapse, is an impossible dream. Is there reason to have hope? Ben Hurst seems to think so: 'We have no choice, do we? Ultimately, it is going to have to change at some point or we're going to see the end of civilisation as we know it. I do have hope and I've seen a lot of change in the last decade so hopefully in the next decade we'll see a lot more.'

In our chat, Cal Roberts linked back to a powerful line he delivered in the documentary *Sound Lad?*, where he says, 'Young men need love.' It's a simple statement perhaps, but one that feels courageous in a world where men are called 'gay' for calling a mountain 'beautiful'. 'I genuinely believe that young men need love and that love doesn't have to be external approval from your girlfriend or your dad, it could be from yourself. It can just be knowing that you're alright, actually. And I think if you're secure in yourself, you're far less likely to project those insecurities onto women and as problematic behaviours.' He's a proper sound lad.

If we're asking what alternative is being offered to the traditional 'toxic' form of masculinity Brannon outlined 50 years ago, now repackaged in the viral content of 'masculinity' influencers, then the answer lies in men like Ben Hurst, Andrew 'Bernie' Bernard and Cal Roberts. All of them reflect different walks of life and represent different types of men, but none of them are afraid to do the hard work, and nor are they threatened by the equality of women and marginalised groups. Leaning in to their vulnerability has allowed them to find a reconstructed masculinity that isn't harmful to others and that they feel comfortable and happy living in. In their bravery to step outside the four walls of the 'man-box', Ben, Bernie and Cal have proven that alternative options to the traditional, dominance-based masculinity do exist. The responsibility now lies with men as individuals to decide what type of man they would like to be.

■

I'm glad to report that after a stern word from myself, my family member saw the light and no longer thinks Tate is a funny guy to follow. This is an important thing to remember when we're talking about teenage boys. They're still learning, they're still growing, they're figuring things out, trying on personalities and experimenting with trends, and we have to give them the grace to make those mistakes and learn from them. Teachers told the *Guardian* that while misogyny is on the rise in schools, they've noticed that Tate's popularity seems to be declining amongst the boys in their schools since his arrest. I've also heard this from my friends who work as teachers, people who facilitate workshops with young people and the teenage girls I spoke with. They told me how boys think his content is 'cringe', and that they've been put off by his criminal charges, with one girl adding, 'They know that being a rapist isn't cool.' However, even if Tate's cult following disappears one day, unless we do the groundwork with men and boys on building a healthier vision of masculinity, there is always going to be a mediocre man with a microphone and an awful opinion to take his place.

## TIPS: How to talk to the men and boys in your life about online misogyny

I can picture it now: you're on your third date, you think you've finally found the one, and then he goes and spoils it all by saying something stupid like, 'Andrew Tate makes some really good points, actually.' But don't panic, here are some of my tips on how to talk to the men and boys in your life about the 'masculinity' influencers they watch online that you can smash the glass on in an emergency.

- **Prepping is key.** Get in there early and arm yourself with some knowledge of what these guys are saying online so you can go into the conversation with some basic facts. Search these guys up online, watch YouTube shorts, have a browse on TikTok and type their name in on X. If you're a parent, take an interest in which YouTubers or streamers your kids enjoy watching and then make an effort to watch their content regularly. Knowledge is power!

- **Play that UNO reverse.** Now you've done your research, instead of shouting at them in sheer panic, you can use your newfound knowledge to peacefully provide a counter argument to their fan-boying. For example, '*Yeah babe, I can see how you might think he's just being silly, but did you not find it a little odd when he tweeted that people should get an*

*AIDs test if they want a woman to be a president?'* Being able to reel off some quotes will leave 'em shook and probably a little embarrassed that you've been nosing in their world.

- **Sharing is caring.** If you feel comfortable, share your own experiences of misogyny with them and ask for their thoughts now they know it affected someone they love. A lot of men and boys don't recognise misogyny because they can't relate to it, so tapping into their empathy can be a key ingredient in getting someone to understand why misogynistic attitudes or behaviours platformed by these influencers are harmful.

- **Be curious.** If your child has started watching controversial influencers online, meet them at their level and ask them questions instead of shutting them down. *Why do you like his videos? What about his content makes you laugh? What points do you think he makes that are valid? Why do you think that? How does that make you feel?* Opening up a space for them to talk and show that you're listening could just be enough to stop them falling deeper into this world, if they feel someone is listening to their concerns.

- **HUH?** If you hear a man or boy in your life repeat sexist tropes they've seen online, I want you to play dumb and ask them to explain *exactly* what they mean by that. Most of the time, men and boys don't firmly believe the casual sexism they repeat; they're just saying it because they think it'll get a few laughs or to show off. Asking them to explain out loud exactly why they believe that women are men's property will provide you with one of two outcomes: their argument will crumble pretty quickly when they realise they're just repeating a load of tosh that they don't actually mean, or they'll go into full red-pill mode and tell you why you don't deserve to have rights. Either way, there's no better time to find out.

- **Call their fave influencer weird.** This one is straight out of Kamala HQ's handbook and it's a stroke of genius. Men hate to be made to feel stupid or humiliated, so if they're praising some guy who's saying bizarre things about women throw him a casual 'He's so *weird*, don't you think?', even upgrading to 'OMG, the girls were laughing at him the other day for being weird!' And if you really want to finish him off, chuck in an 'Ergh, he's such a weirdo!'

If all of the above fail, then I don't know what else to recommend. Have you tried turning him off and on again? Maybe try sticking him in a tub of rice and leaving him in there overnight? But on a serious note, while the fight to stamp out misogyny and reshape 'toxic' masculinity may seem like an infeasible challenge, the positive is that there is a lot of room for improvement and many incredible people behind the scenes who are putting in the groundwork. Influencers may make the loudest noise, but it is in our collective efforts as individuals, mentors and parents that we will really incite positive change. I hope the tools in this chapter will be of use to you. Conversation is the most powerful tool we all have at our fingertips to open up the pathway to empathy and understanding.

You've got this.

# 11

# THE SOLUTION

## There is hope, I think

'No man is an island, and no man offends in isolation'
**Emma Pitman**

When online harms towards women are excused as being detached from our in-person reality, we are allowing perpetrators to get away with extreme misogyny. This is stripping women and girls of their right to a digital citizenship in a world that spins on cyber. It is worthwhile to remember that it isn't cyborgs from another, virtual world who are carrying out these harmful acts, but men. Real, human men who act out their perverse behaviour across every corner of the internet. And it is real, human women – not robots or virtual companions – who are the victims of their acts online, and in the offline world too.

What are we to do when the sexual predators who operate in the shadows of the forums decide their digital kicks are no longer enough? What if their misogynistic alter-ego doesn't shut down when they log off for the night? The threat of physical harm lingers in threads that house these men's sick fantasies, but even if their online attitudes never escalate into in-person abuse, as we've discovered in this book, digital harms can be just as devastating for the women whose lives are turned upside down by the games of misogyny that play out online. From the nonchalant loathing of and lusting after women, to the digital sex crimes in which men turn women into explicit deepfakes or risk their personal details for a dopamine hit, women are experiencing extreme sexualisation and abuse online that is preventing them from accessing an authentic and safe digital world.

Experts tell us that we have reached epidemic levels of violence against women and girls: police chiefs report that 3,000 crimes of this nature are recorded each day in the UK, with VAWG accounting for 20 per cent of all recorded crimes. Many of these represent in-person, physical assaults and abuse – the figures only scratch the surface of the online harms that are also perpetrated against women daily. We've hit a crisis point where things drastically need to change if we are to build a safer, inclusive world in which women and girls are protected from harm.

The weight of misogyny that women face in all aspects of life feels overwhelming at times. Plus, the challenge of unpicking societal constructs and beliefs ingrained over centuries can seem a near impossible task, one that is too often taken on by women themselves. There isn't a one-answer solution, and it will take a collective effort from individuals (men and women), parents, platforms, organisations and legislators to tackle this urgent issue from all angles to prevent the outbreak of extreme misogyny from spreading any further. Thankfully, there are already some incredible, inspiring people who are galvanising systems and lawmakers into action, setting a great example of how we can all play our part in the effort to end online violence against women and girls, and help men and boys to escape the suffocating constrictions of the 'man-box'.

## Choose your player: what role will you take?

There are plenty of ways you can get involved in activism, and plenty of battles that need to be fought. Campaigning isn't for everyone, but on a personal note, it has given me a sense of direction, a like-minded community and, most of all, hope. You don't have to take to the streets with a placard to make a difference (although there is a certain sense of pride that comes with waving your homemade sign around); these days, activism can be carried out online through petitions, social media campaigns and email outreach. Whether you're eager to take up campaigning as a passion project or just want some tips on how to play your part day-to-day in the fight to stamp out online misogyny, let me share a few pointers on how you can put your people power to work.

### Become an online activist

I regularly use my social media platforms to create and post informative IG reels and TikTok videos about women's issues, and amplify campaigns that I feel passionate about by resharing stories and encouraging my followers to get involved. We're a generation that are permanently glued to our phones, so we might as well make the most of our time scrolling. Resharing articles, reports or content that you believe in is a great way of getting more eyes on an issue. If you have a unique talent – perhaps you enjoy spoken word poetry or you're a dab hand with a cross stitch needle – think about ways you could incorporate your skills to create unique content to highlight gender inequality.

Eliza Hatch is the founder of 'Cheer Up Luv', a photo series where Eliza captures images of victim-survivors in the location they were harassed to tell stories of sexual harassment. The idea came to her after an incident of street harassment and the response of her male friends, who brushed off the incident as a compliment. Recalling their nonchalant reaction, Eliza told me, 'They had literally no idea that these things were so common. I felt at a loss for words for how to communicate that properly without getting sad and angry and frustrated.' Eliza used her creative flair and talent as a photographer to tell the stories of sexual harassment experienced by women and marginalised genders, sharing the images on Instagram. The photos captured by her lens beautifully show the everyday environments where women are being harassed – like busy streets, tube station platforms and bus stops. 'It isn't always isolated alleys, it's these incredibly busy parts of your everyday surroundings,' she points out. Alongside the photos are powerful testimonials from victim-survivors of all ages, ethnicities and sexualities. I asked Eliza if there was anything that really stuck out to her during her work. She told me it is the ages of first-time victims that strikes her the most: 'When people share their stories it's often like "this happened to me when I was 11", "this happened to me when I was 12", and you see that recurring similarity in the first time that women and girls start to experience this issue.'

Since 'Cheer Up Luv' first launched as a photo series on Instagram in 2017, it has grown monumentally. It has now evolved into a social media platform and podcast with its own community, creating a space of solidarity for survivors to safely share their stories and deconstruct everyday sexism and misogyny. Eliza is proof of the power of individual action: she uses her talent as a photographer in her activism and has utilised social media to incite positive societal change. Eliza credits Instagram for helping her elevate her campaign to new heights and build a community she can lean on for support when life as a campaigner gets a little heavy: 'Every time I felt on the brink of burnout or that I can't do this anymore, there's that community that's been there the whole time and has really empowered me.'

Posting content about a topic that is deeply personal can feel scary and intimidating, but creating content about an issue you feel passionate about and receiving a supportive comment feels *way* better than uploading a thirst trap and having some random guy post a flames emoji under your bikini pic. Trust me, I've tried and tested both. My number one rule for posting videos about feminism, misogyny or women's issues (and this stands for any political subject too) is that you *have* to believe in the content you're sharing. The honest truth is that womanhood is seen as a divisive subject online, with many men (and women with internalised misogyny) scouring the hashtags, ready to attack you for daring to share your views or lived experiences. Seeing the negative and hurtful comments roll in can be daunting, they can even make you want to log off the platform or delete the apps altogether, but if you're filming and sharing a video about a topic you truly believe in then no one's opinion or hate should be able to shake you.

If you go viral (which you will, because I believe in you!) then don't panic. The rolling notifications might seem intense for a day or two, but it will soon blow over. Lastly, please, *please* remember to use the block button. Protecting your peace is way more important than trying to get the last word in an argument with an anonymous account who doesn't even show their face in their profile picture. My favourite quote to remember whenever I receive sexist comments that make me rethink sharing my views online is 'don't take criticism from someone you wouldn't take advice from'. Keep it moving – you've got this.

## Put the pressure on platforms

The role of platforms in online misogyny cannot be underplayed when it *literally* exists within them. Social media platforms whose algorithms and content influence billions of people across the globe play a damning role in the normalisation and acceptance of misogyny and misogynoir on their sites. Putting pressure on social media platforms and search engines like Google to include policies on VAWG and introduce safeguarding measures is a vital service. One way to get involved is to reach out to women's safety charities and organisations to offer your time and skills to help their campaigns, or create your own calling for platforms to take action on online misogyny by setting up your own petition on change.org or petition.parliament.uk/petitions.

Seyi Akiwowo, the founder of UK safer internet charity Glitch, is leading the charge when it comes to holding platforms to account. Her vision for the future is clear: 'We need to urge tech companies to incorporate clear definitions of misogyny, racism and white supremacy for content moderation so they can implement policies banning misogynoir and prevent gender-based violence. Tech companies should all have a well-resourced Trust and Safety Council that prioritises gender-based violence. They should also collaborate with Black feminist experts to critique and improve online safety policies and abuse detection, including the rising threat of AI deepfakes.' Seyi is a powerhouse, a regular face in parliamentary roundtables and panel discussions on digital violence towards women and girls. Her voice is an enabler for change and her presence and passion is infectious. Seyi's work in online safety unapologetically centres Black women and her invaluable commitment to holding to account the people in power is creating a safer internet for us all.

It isn't just mainstream social media sites that need to do better when it comes to safeguarding women, but all big tech companies whose apps and search engines play a part in uplifting the manosphere through their algorithms. Sophie Compton, the director of *Another Body*, a film that explores deepfake abuse, told me how all big tech companies have a 'responsibility to consider how their products are being used to stoke division, misogyny, racism and violence'. She has long been a critic of Google for their up-ranking of harmful content, including websites that explicitly host deepfake 'porn': 'I think Google has this narrative that the algorithm works slightly out of their control and they don't manage what the results are but that's completely not true.' The pressure on Google from activists like Seyi and Sophie has worked: in July 2024, the search engine began de-ranking and filtering listings for non-consensual sexually explicit content, including deepfake 'porn' sites.

The regulator Ofcom is in charge of implementing a code of practice for platforms and service providers in the UK to ensure they're fulfilling their safety duties towards users, including protecting women and girls from online misogyny. In February 2025, they published draft guidance for tech companies that proposed concrete measures that platforms should undertake to help keep women and girls safe. These include a safety-by-design approach and adopting innovative technology to help combat image-based sexual abuse. Although promising, their guidance for platforms on VAWG is not legally enforceable, meaning there's little incentive for providers to implement safety measures.

Another hurdle victims face is that while distributing intimate images without consent is a crime, image-based sexual abuse material of adults is not deemed to be illegal content in the UK. This means that unlike sites that host child-sexual abuse material – which is illegal – sites that are dedicated to sharing leaked intimate images like The Fappening are *technically* not hosting 'illegal' content, which is what restricts search engines such as Google from acting to take it down. This is why we need the government to implement a comprehensive law on IBSA that covers all aspects, areas and loopholes. Removing content and policing their platforms costs tech owners money and they're not going to act unless they're forced to do so.

## Get your workplace involved

While individual activism can no doubt move mountains, having the support of businesses and companies can help elevate campaigns to new heights. Whether you're a corporate girlie who builds an alliance with your colleagues to lobby management to introduce feminist policies around period health, maternity pay and office behaviour, or a sales assistant who holds a cake sale in the lunch room to raise money for grassroots women's organisations, engaging your workplace is a helpful and easy way to raise awareness on women's issues. If you use social media as part of your work, ask your HR department to consider implementing a digital code of conduct for the company. This could be a great way to lay the groundwork for men on how to respect women in online spaces and how to be an active ally if they witness harmful or sexist behaviour in work Zoom calls or on a LinkedIn comment section.

As the purpose editor and deputy website editor at *Glamour* UK, Lucy Morgan was tasked by her boss with finding an issue that mattered to all women for the brand to get behind. As a victim-survivor herself, she knew that consent was the big issue facing all women. *Glamour* is an iconic women's magazine with a large female audience. According to Lucy, 'Feminism is just as much a part of our lives as fashion and beauty, and it's important for media brands to reflect that, and to not patronise our readers. I think there is a big appetite from our readers not even necessarily to be activists, but to just voice their opinion about injustices. People want to read about that, and they want to see a woman writing about it.'

As someone who was raised on women's lifestyle magazines that taught me about blowjobs and body dysmorphia (anyone else still got PTSD from the circle of shame?), it has been healing to see *Glamour*'s evolution and commitment to having the big conversations on image-based sexual abuse and gender-based violence. Under Lucy's project management, the brand partnered with other campaigners to lobby the government into criminalising deepfake sexual abuse, with *Glamour* securing a parliamentary roundtable. Hosted by the former Chair of the Science, Innovation and Technology Committee Greg Clark, it was attended by representatives from Google and Ofcom, activists, campaigners and members of Parliament. Oh, and little old me. Speaking of that monumental day, Lucy said, 'We all got a picture on the steps in Westminster Hall, and I just thought, *This is it. This is what* Glamour *is all about. This is* Glamour *going into politics and influencing change.* It was just a really special day.'

While we can still enjoy the think pieces on what lipstick colour is in this fall and six-page fashion spreads of clothes we can't afford, it makes my heart sing to see a woman's lifestyle magazine platforming the real, less sexy but absolutely essential life issues that women are facing in our daily lives.

Other ways you can get your workplace involved in the fight against online (and offline) misogyny is to sign up for training programmes and workshops, like those offered by Ben Hurst at Beyond Equality and Bernie's 'What Makes a Man?' programme. White Ribbon is the UK's leading charity engaging men and boys to prevent VAWG. Organisations can partner with the charity to upskill their workforce through specialist training to promote healthy masculinity and encourage allyship. The charity also offers help to develop and deliver an action plan to prevent VAWG. Check out their website www.whiteribbon.org.uk to see how you can get involved.

These tips can also be implemented into your school or educational settings if you are a teacher or mentor. You can encourage staff to introduce feminist practices in their classrooms, create your own digital code of conduct for students and invite outside organisations like Our Schools Now to host workshops with staff and pupils on VAWG, online harms and masculinity. I appreciate that funding for extra curriculum activities is often minimal in educational settings, so it's worth reaching out to your local council or member of Parliament to ask if there are any grants available for VAWG prevention.

## Let's get political, political

How does that famous saying go? 'If you don't do politics, politics will do you.' We can't legislate out misogynistic beliefs, but laws and policies play a vital role in preventing VAWG and setting the standard for what is deemed acceptable behaviour. Becoming a political activist is a no-brainer if you want to help make significant change. Since I started lending my voice to women's rights back in 2020, I have been involved in the campaign to make the creation and distribution of sexually explicit deepfakes illegal and the criminalisation of cyberflashing.

Over the last few years, there have been some incredible success stories spearheaded by activists and experts who lobbied the government on legislation around image-based sexual abuse issues and won. TV personality Georgia Harrison lent her voice to the campaign to update existing 'revenge porn' laws after her ex-boyfriend Stephen Bear secretly filmed them having sex and sold the video on OnlyFans without her consent. The need to prove a perpetrator's intent when sharing a non-consensual intimate image or video was successfully repealed in January 2024. When the draft Online Safety Act was first published, it included no reference to women and girls. Seyi Akiwowo and the team at Glitch, along with the End Violence Against Women Coalition, mobilised over 100,000 people to sign a petition demanding the government include specific protection for women and girls in the bill, which was a success.

Simple ways you can get involved in political activism include signing and starting petitions, joining in-person protests, exercising your right to vote and writing to your local MP. Remember, politicians work to serve the people. If they want to count on your vote at the next election, then make them work for it (this includes councillors and your local police and crime commissioner too). Ask them what they are doing to help protect women and girls safety online, or share your concern about the rising misogyny you've seen on social media platforms. If your local MP holds a surgery, book an appointment to attend and share your concerns in person.

To find out who your local representatives are and to write to them for free head to the website www.writetothem.com.

For parents or young people, check out your local youth projects to see if there are any girls' groups projects that you can get involved in, like Her Voice Wales. If you're in an educational setting like a school or university, find out if there is a feminist society at your organisation. And if there's not, why not set one up? Someone's got to be the next great leader and, in the famous words of ElastiGirl, 'Leave the saving the world to the men? I don't think so.'

### Be human

This is an easy first step that we can all put into practice to help flip the switch on extreme misogyny. As humans, we have the ability to communicate through words and the gift of hearing that helps us build empathy, kindness and inspire others around us to take action. The next time you're at the dinner table, start up a conversation with your teenager about 'revenge porn' and recommend some of the documentaries I've touched on that you can watch together, or ask your boyfriend if he's ever heard of the term 'cyberflashing'. If you have a male friend or an over-zealous colleague who proudly boasts how feminism has 'gone too far' and re-shares clips of Andrew Tate on his Instagram story, ask him why he feels that way, and then listen to his response. Does he *really* think women have more rights than men in an age where women are dying after being refused abortion care? What is it about Tate's views on women that he relates to? Open up the conversation, listen to their concerns and, most importantly, share your views back.

Although women can play an important role in helping men reevaluate their masculinity and calling out misogynistic behaviours, we are not men's rehab and we are not there to just be their soundboard. If women are going to show men and boys respect and empathy, then we should be given space to share our experiences with misogyny and our concerns about men too.

For too long, the conversation around gender-based violence has been shut down by men who feel personally attacked by the mention of the word 'feminism'. So let me write this in black and white: we know that it is not *all men* who are perpetrating harmful behaviours online and in the streets, but too many of them *are* doing so. It's time for men to divert their anger at being lumped in with the bad guys away from women and firmly onto the men who give them a bad rep. Guys, talk to your friends the next time they make a sexist comment down the pub, call them out when they share a woman's leaked images in the WhatsApp group, think twice before you send her a snap of your dick that she hasn't asked for and vote with your sisters' bodily autonomy in mind instead of your crypto balance.

Get lost in the joy of reading again, listen to podcasts, watch documentaries, follow activists and survivors on social media. To the men – that also means podcasts hosted by women, books written by women and following female activists on social media. Research shows men are reluctant to consume media written or presented by women (there goes that damn man-box again), but if men are not going to listen to or learn from women, it will be impossible for them to understand their concerns on misogyny and develop the empathy needed to act. The more knowledge you can take in, the better equipped you'll be to have those big, scary conversations when the opportunity arises.

Don't ever underestimate the power you have to make real change and create a better, safer world for women and marginalised genders.

## Change is inevitable

When I was ten years old, I started to become aware of my body and the way men had begun to view me through a lens of sexual currency. The boys around me quickly learnt to take the lead – groping my breasts, heckling me in the swimming pool and showing me videos of graphic porn on the school bus, which all served to let me know I was not allowed to be a child anymore. I was a woman. And I was about to experience what being a woman meant in a world where so many men see my existence as less than. My body now theirs for the taking. What followed was a wave of sexism and misogyny that was amplified in the digital age where smart phones sit firmly in the pockets of pupils and social media opens up new forms of harm.

As a teen, my private pictures were shared around my school; as a young woman, a photo of me naked and asleep was shared in a lads' group chat. Now, in my thirties, I am living with the aftermath of my intimate images being traded in manosphere forums and Telegram channels and used as e-whoring bait. I have lost all control over my body online and have been left with the torturous sentence of watching on helplessly while men repeatedly remove my consent, resharing my images and posting derogatory remarks under my photos that have stitched themselves into the fabric of my identity. Although I have allowed myself to let go of the shame that I know lies firmly and solely with the men who do this, their digital displays of misogyny will forever be a part of my story.

We should not have to accept online misogyny and digital sexual harassment as standard. Dick pics are not 'just what happens' on social media and it isn't an acceptable inevitability that an intimate photo a woman sends to a man in private will find its way to a MEGA folder on a forum.

In December 2024, I was invited to Washington DC alongside 28 fellow survivors of image-based sexual abuse to give evidence at a multi US federal agency listening session, as Congress debated whether to pass legislation that would criminalise IBSA, including deepfakes. I sat in a board room for eight hours while survivors took to the stand one by one, their harrowing recollections drawing tears to my eyes while their trauma ignited a fierce pit of anger deep inside. Except for one man, every survivor was a woman. Their ages ranged from 14 to late forties and they had travelled from all over the world, including Ireland, Italy, Ecuador, Portugal, England and Mexico. Tears fell down the face of a grey-haired mother; the timid voice of a teenage girl cracked when she told of her classmate's betrayal. The perpetrators were fellow students, boyfriends, husbands, friends and strangers. Many of the women's stories echoed those included in this book, and their abuse happened on some of the forums I spent hours researching.

Learning how many survivors in attendance had experienced suicidal thoughts or attempted to take their own lives because of their abuse was harrowing. As one woman pointed out: 'You can't say you have post-traumatic stress because it is not in the past, it is constant.' Once your images are out there, the threat of image-based sexual abuse is forever lingering in cyberspace, waiting for a perpetrator to pick it up and start the hamster wheel of harm once more.

It was the honour of my life to sit in a room with these courageous survivors and put faces to the thousands of victims that I have come across in my work. These are not just people who exist in a separate online reality – they are real women and girls whose lives have been ripped apart by men who chose to exploit them for their own gratification. The men who carried out these despicable acts did not see the humanity in these women, but I have never felt a more meaningful human connection than when sharing my tears, rage and hope with the survivors in that room.

We need to take a collaborative approach to ensure the safety of women and girls online. The responsibility to do more, do better is shared amongst society, big tech companies, policing and the government, so women and girls can claim their right to a digital citizenship. We need a comprehensive image-based abuse law that better protects women from online harms. Explaining how the current laws can be confusing, Professor Clare McGlynn told me, 'While there have been important changes in laws and policies over recent years, it's all piecemeal. One change one year, one change the next. Some victims covered, some not.' It means that survivors are often unsure whether to report crimes of IBSA, and police and lawmakers may not know how to properly deal with victims and penalise perpetrators. If we're going to transform society, McGlynn believes we need 'urgent political determination': 'We need them to see this as a serious, urgent problem that demands a serious and urgent solution. They need to understand VAWG as a systemic failing in our societies, at a global level, like racism, climate change.'

We need big tech to implement safeguarding measures to prevent online misogyny from flourishing on their platforms and react swiftly to takedown requests of non-consensual content. All sites which allow individual members to upload content should have a clear report and support system in place, with real people (not just AI bots) employed to deal with this deeply personal, human issue. We need the fringe sites to be answerable to removal requests. We need police forces to receive trauma-informed training so that victims do not have to trawl for their

own abuse as evidence and face being retraumatised in the reporting process. We need funded, specialist helplines, therapy and
support groups available for victim-survivors who are struggling
with the emotional and mental trauma tech-facilitated abuse can
cause. All of this costs money – *a lot* of money – and the tech
world has the funds to pay it.

In November 2024, the UK government announced plans to
introduce a statutory levy on gambling operators. The millions
of pounds this will raise will be used to fund research, education and provide treatment for those dealing with gambling
harms. A standard levy placed on tech companies could be used
to fund specialist support systems for image-based sexual abuse
survivors and research into tech-based solutions to tackle digital sex crimes, provide education in schools on digital safety,
train police forces in a specialist, trauma-informed approach to
IBSA and hire real employees to deal with the mass-reporting
of non-consensual content.

Alex Davies-Jones, MP for Pontypridd and parliamentary
under-secretary of state at the Ministry of Justice, recognises
the role of politicians in tackling the VAWG crisis and the
danger women face online: 'It is on the government and wider
society to take a stand and say this is unacceptable. We know
that misogyny is on the rise on our streets, in schools and
online. We can see that acutely with extreme online influencers
getting their hooks into young boys and leading them down a
dangerous path.' As a mother to boys herself, she told me she
feels a deep responsibility to 'raise good men'. Alex shared her
thoughts on advocacy and the power installed in women to
fight for our rights: 'This is a sisterhood and we all have our
own stories and our own experiences. We can share in that,
learn from one another and advocate for our right to be safe.'

If we're ever going to get a grip of the tsunami of online
misogyny that is crashing onto the edges of mainstream platforms, we must understand that our online life is not separate

from our offline existence. The threat is one and the same. How will the men I've seen preying on women online and taking collective joy in our pain choose to display their disdain when they encounter us in real life? When we fail to hold perpetrators to account in the digital space, their behaviour goes unchecked, unquestioned.

Viewing the internet and our in-person existence as inseparable is echoed by Professor Olga Jurasz, who has spent more than a decade investigating online violence towards women and published the UK's largest ever study in this area in 2023: 'I've long held the view that the two are intertwined. I've held that view since 2013 and now it's only amplified. I think if you ask younger people, they definitely think online and offline is just one world and I don't think there is necessarily a way back from it.' Jurasz went on to tell me, 'What is happening to women online also affects their human rights.'

The UK government announced in August 2024 that they would treat extreme misogyny as terrorism in an attempt to tackle the extremism that targets young men and has devastating consequences for the women and girls who have to live alongside their radicalisation. Extreme misogyny is terrorising women in every aspect of their lives – some of us are too scared to leave our homes, or afraid of the men in our homes, or facing online harms in our dating lives, or being harassed on social media platforms. To live as a woman is to feel the threatening presence of a man's weighted breath on your neck each time you step on to a quiet street or open up Instagram to check your direct messages. There is no escaping the hateful eyes of a man who views you as beneath them, all because of the genitals you were born with.

The responsibility has long been left to women to fix a problem that we cannot fix without men. We don't have a woman problem, we have a misogyny problem. And in this, men play a leading role. Women and girls cannot keep doing the work to draw attention to our fear and pain just for men to look the other way. I know that there is a better, healthier version of masculinity that can fill the black hole left behind in the eradication of 'toxic' masculinity. I saw it in the many men who I interviewed for this book, who are all working in the space of gender-based violence and making a positive contribution and commitment to change. I see it in my male friends who re-share my social media posts about women's issues and show up for me on every occasion, whether a burlesque show or a protest on sexual harassment. I've seen it in my gay friends, who have introduced me to a spectrum of masculinity and welcomed me into their safe spaces full of glitter and drag queens. I see it in my younger brother who tells me he loves me before we hang up the phone, and in my older brother who supported me even when his mates gave him shit for my job. I've seen it in my dad, who silently filled my bathroom drawer with a year's worth of sanitary pads he'd procured, lined up with army precision he had learnt in the RAF. And in how he allowed me to make my own choices in life, even if they were the wrong ones, because he saw me as my own person and not just his daughter. I saw it in the man who sent me a DM to tell me my posts had inspired him to sign up as a White Ribbon ambassador, in the man who came up to me in a café to thank me for using my platforms to raise awareness of women's issues, and in the burly security guard who stopped me at a football game to let me know he was a follower and admired the work I do on gender-based violence. I expect a better version of masculinity from men because I know I have seen so many times that it exists.

There is an alternative script to manhood out there for the men who want to be the best possible version of themselves, one that works to lift everyone up, harming no one. As women, we can offer our allyship, but ultimately it is on men to have the will and the determination to make a change. It won't be easy — we're up against a new form of media that is livestreaming misogyny into the bedrooms of teenage boys, 24 hours a day, wrapped up in the glitzy promise of power and riches. But once the novelty of rape jokes and 'make me a sandwich' quips wears off, and their bank balance is still in the red from the tanked crypto investments and failed forex trading, they will realise that the men who sit in virtual thrones and told them their problems could be solved by hatred and anger simply used them as pawns in their gutless enterprises.

Misogyny may be a successful business plan, but the man-box has proven a total failure. Men have the exciting opportunity to step out of the 'man-box' and decide who they really want to be, how they want to show up in the world and who they're ultimately going to show up for. If it's in men's nature to be born leaders, then show us how you can lead by example. And ladies, while they're figuring that all out, perhaps we can give them a supportive fist bump if we see them trying along the way.

Not the creeps and the pervs though. Sometimes you've just got to report them, click that block button and prioritise your own peace.

While we wait for men to do the work and for lawmakers to catch up, I hope you can use some of the tools and tips I've shared with you in this book to curate a safer online world for yourself and for others. If we're demanding social media platforms take action, we also have to do our part by using the measures already available to us. Check your privacy settings, mute words that are triggering, sign your kids up for a teen account and use the report feature that helps platforms gather data on what they need to improve. Knowledge is power when it comes to defeating the enemy, and passing on what you've learnt in this book to your friends and family members about helpful organisations, the tactics of the manosphere and how to safely take a sexy selfie are all acts of defiance against the men who simply hate us. The most courageous act you can do as a woman in today's chronically online world is to never fall silent and never stop posting.

Oh, and make sure you always give yourself the first like on your posts – you deserve the support.

# Acknowledgements

In a book where there has been so much talk of bad characters and negative experiences, there are so many people in my life who have ensured I never forget the kindness of humankind.

To my mum and dad, thank you for instilling in me a fierce independence and belief that I can be and do anything. Your unwavering support throughout the years has been the framework that allowed me to stand tall in the face of other people's judgements and rejections. When people ask what my parents think of my career choice – past and present – I do not flinch to tell them how supportive and proud you are. You have always seen the real me, which helped me to never lose sight of that. To my brothers Luke and Connor, it can't be easy having a sister who was once voted the second sexiest women in the world in *Nuts* magazine, but you've persevered. To my nan who has a better social life than me, and my grandad who I miss dearly. Nanny Pauline, I wish you could be here to see all that I've done. I hope I've made you proud.

To my fiercely loyal friends who have championed me through thick and thin and shown me what true, platonic love is. Thank you for the sharing, liking, buying, subscribing, reposting, commenting, listening to my rants and moans, and being my personal groupies over the years. You all know who you are and I love you all dearly. To my girls, I'm sorry for converting you all into angry feminists that can no longer ignore the everyday sexism in your lives (I'm not really sorry). To my guys and gays, thank you for being beacons of light in the darkness to remind me that good men do exist.

To my brilliant editor Bianca Bexton. I am so grateful to have had your support right from the very start of reading my proposal;

# ACKNOWLEDGEMENTS

thank you for embracing me and my vision for this book. I feel so lucky to have had the opportunity to work with you on my debut. Knowing my personal experiences and sensitive research were in such safe and supportive hands helped make the mammoth task that bit easier. To my second editor Ellie Harris and my copy editor Liz Marvin, thank you for your support and for passing on your expertise. You have all amplified this book to new heights and it has been a dream to work with such an incredible female team.

To my literary agent Ben Dunn at DunnFogg. Thank you for carrying out that favour for Grant and giving up your time to read my proposal! You have championed me and this book from the very start and always believed I could write it, even when I didn't quite believe it myself.

To my agents at Encanta. Rebecca, Grant, Lulu, Lizzie, Assisi and the rest of the team, thank you for keeping my name alive in meetings and advocating for me in important rooms. You are always at the end of my podcast-worthy voicenotes and push forward with every idea, dream or goal that I have to try and make it a reality. I struck gold when I found you all and I appreciate your belief in me more than you know.

To the rest of the team at Headline Press. Thank you for championing this book from day one, adopting it as your own and for all your hard work to take it from an idea to publication. Being a published author has been on my vision board for many years and you made that a reality. I'm so grateful that we got to do this book together.

To all the incredible survivors who shared your experiences with me. This book would not have happened without you. Your strength in the face of such extreme misogyny and your resilience in refusing to be silenced is admirable. Thank you for your contribution to this book, but it is much bigger than that. Being trusted to share your stories has been an honour and a task that I did not take lightly. I hope I made you proud and that this book can help push forward the amazing work you are doing in this space. Thank you for your commitment and tenacity to give women across the world a voice. You are the changemakers of a generation.

To the experts, campaigners, politicians and journalists who shared their thoughts, findings and wisdom. Your vital work is creating real change to make the world a safer space for women and girls. Thank you.

To Fiona Campbell at BBC Three. I can't put into words how much your support in commissioning my films *When Nudes Are Stolen* and *Deepfake Porn: Could you be next?* meant to me. You gave me a platform that introduced me to this online world, connected me with a community of survivors and allowed me to shake the cloak of shame I had been carrying for so long. It turned me towards activism, which has led to me sitting alongside ministers in Parliament and being invited to Washington DC to share my experience and research of image-based abuse. I will forever be grateful that you believed my story was worthy of being told. To my executive producer Mike Radford, my directors Hannah Livingston and Simon Rawles and the rest of the current affairs team I worked with at BBC Three. Thank you for all of your support on these special projects.

Lastly, I want to thank you for picking this book up and committing to reading it. By doing so, you are already joining the fight to combat extreme online misogyny and helping to make a safer, fairer world for us all. Now go forth and put all you've learnt into action, and I look forward to supporting your campaigns for change in the future!

# Resources

## Helplines and support services

**The Cyber Helpline** – Supporting victims of cybercrime.
https://www.thecyberhelpline.com

**DMCA.com** – Information on how to file a DMCA takedown
request.
https://www.dmca.com/FAQ/How-can-I-contact-
DMCAcom

**Internet Watch Foundation** – Report online child sexual abuse
material and for help in removal of content.
https://www.iwf.org.uk

**ManKind Initiative** – Helpline and support for male victims of
domestic violence.
https://mankind.org.uk

**The Mix** – The UK's leading digital support charity for under-25s.
https://www.themix.org.uk

**Muslim Women's Network Helpline** – Specialist, faith and
culturally sensitive helpline and counselling service.
https://www.mwnhelpline.co.uk

**National Stalking Helpline** – Support and information for
victims of stalking.
https://www.suzylamplugh.org/pages/category/national-
stalking-helpline

**Rape Crisis England and Wales** – A feminist charity working to
end sexual violence with a 24-hour support line.
https://rapecrisis.org.uk

# RESOURCES

**Refuge** – The UK's largest domestic abuse organisation for women with a 24-hour national helpline.
https://refuge.org.uk

**Refuge Tech Safety** – Advice and help on technology facilitated abuse.
https://refugetechsafety.org

**Respond** – A charity providing specialist support services to people with learning disabilities, autism or both who are victims of sexual abuse.
https://respond.org.uk

**Revenge Porn Helpline** – A free helpline and online support for adult victims who are experiencing intimate image abuse.
https://revengepornhelpline.org.uk

**Rights of Women** – Charity providing legal advice to women experiencing VAWG.
https://www.rightsofwomen.org.uk

**Safer Internet Centre** – Support on online issues for parents, teachers and young people.
https://saferinternet.org.uk

**Samaritans** – The UK's free 24-hour helpline for those in emotional distress, struggling to cope or experiencing suicidal thoughts.
https://www.samaritans.org/how-we-can-help/contact-samaritan/

**StopNCII.org** – A free tool by the Revenge Porn Helpline that creates a digital fingerprint to help track and remove intimate images.
https://stopncii.org

**The Survivors Trust** – Specialist rape and sexual violence support services with a free helpline.
https://thesurvivorstrust.org

# RESOURCES

**Switchboard** – The UK's LGBTQI+ support helpline and online chat.
https://switchboard.lgbt

**Teenage Helpline** – Help and support for young people and parents.
https://teenagehelpline.org.uk

**Victims Support** – Free advice on help after a crime including image-based sexual abuse.
https://www.victimsupport.org.uk

**Women's Aid** – A charity working to end domestic violence and VAWG.
https://www.womensaid.org.uk

## Organisations and projects

**Beyond Equality** – Engaging men and boys in conversation on gender-based violence and providing safe spaces to rethink masculinity.
https://www.beyondequality.org

**Chayn HQ** – A global non-profit supporting survivors of gender-based violence, including tech-facilitated abuse.
https://www.chayn.co

**Cheer Up Luv** – A photo series and platform that uses art for activism.
https://www.cheerupluv.com

**End Violence Against Women and Girls** – A group of feminist organisations and experts across the UK working to end VAWG.
https://www.endviolenceagainstwomen.org.uk/about/

**Everyone's Invited** – A safe space for survivors to share their stories.
https://www.everyonesinvited.uk

# RESOURCES

**Glamour UK** – A campaign to demand a dedicated, comprehensive, image-based abuse law to protect women and girls.
https://www.glamourmagazine.co.uk/article/image-based-abuse-act-campaign

**Glitch** – A charity focused on ending online abuse and championing digital citizenship with a particular focus on Black women and marginalised people.
https://glitchcharity.co.uk

**Make It Mandatory** – A youth-led campaign lobbying the government for domestic abuse prevention through education.
https://www.instagram.com/makeitmandatory/

**#MyImageMyChoice** – A grassroots project and cultural movement tackling intimate image abuse and advocating for governments and tech companies to block websites that host explicit deepfakes.
https://myimagemychoice.org

**NotYourPorn** – Sex positive survivor-led movement to protect non-consenting adults, sex workers and children from image-based sexual abuse.
https://notyourporn.com

**Our Streets Now** – A campaign to end public sexual harassment in the UK through cultural and legislative change.
https://www.ourstreetsnow.org

**Right to Equality** – An organisation advocating for legal reforms that promote fairness and gender equality in the UK.
https://righttoequality.org

**She Is Not Your Rehab** – A project encouraging men and boys to heal generational trauma and engaging them

in conversations on gender-based violence and healthy masculinity.
https://www.sheisnotyourrehab.com

**Sound Project** – A space for men and boys to explore their relationship behaviours and get advice.
https://www.gov.wales/sound

**Stonewall.** Support and information for the LGBTQI+ community.
https://www.stonewall.org.uk

**What Makes a Man?** – Educating men and boys about masculinity and ending VAWG.
https://innovativeenterprise.co.uk/portfolio/wmam/

**White Ribbon** – The UK's leading charity engaging men and boys to prevent VAWG.
https://www.whiteribbon.org.uk

# References

## INTRODUCTION

Girlguiding, UK (2024) 'Girls' Attitude Survey: Girls face a crisis of confidence in an unequal world', https://www.girlguiding.org.uk/globalassets/docs-and-resources/research-and-campaigns/girls-attitudes-survey-2024.pdf

Communia, UK (2022) 'Report on Women's and Marginalized Genders' Social Media Experiences', https://www.ourcommunia.com/post/uk-report-2023

Glitch, UK (2023) 'The Digital Misogynoir Report: Ending the dehumanising of Black women on social media', www.glitchcharity.co.uk/research

Stevens, Francesca & Enock, E. Florence et al., The Alan Turing Institute, UK (2024) 'Understanding gender differences in experiences and concerns surrounding online harms: A nationally representative survey of UK adults', https://www.turing.ac.uk/sites/default/files/2024-03/understanding_gender_differences_in_experiences_and_concerns_surrounding_online_harms_-_a_nationally_representative_survey_of_uk_adults.pdf

## 1: CONSENT

Cambridge Rape Crisis Centre, UK (2023) 'Sexual Violence Statistics', https://cambridgerapecrisis.org.uk/wp-content/uploads/Sources-for-website-stats-May-2023.pdf

Office For National Statistics, UK (2024) 'Crime in England and Wales: Year ending June 2024; Sexual Violence Bulletin', https://www.ons.gov.uk/peoplepopulationandcommunity/crimeandjustice/bulletins/crimeinenglandandwales/yearendingjune2024

Home Office, UK (2024) 'Crime Outcomes Year to June 2024: Data tables; Table 1.2', https://www.gov.uk/government/statistics/crime-outcomes-year-to-june-2024-data-tables

Full Fact, UK (2018) 'Allegations of Rape', https://fullfact.org/crime/allegations-rape/

Channel 4 Fact Check, UK (2018) 'Men Are More Likely to Be Raped Than Be Falsely Accused of Rape', https://www.channel4.com/news/factcheck/factcheck-men-are-more-likely-to-be-raped-than-be-falsely-accused-of-rape

# REFERENCES

European Women's Lobby, Europe (2017) '#HerNetHerRights Report: Mapping the state of online violence against women and girls in Europe', https://www.womenlobby.org/IMG/pdf/hernetherrights_report_2017_for_web.pdf

Sharatt, Elena, University of Exeter, Economic and Social Research Council, UK (2019) 'Intimate Image Abuse in Adults and Under 18s', https://swgfl.org.uk/assets/documents/intimate-image-abuse-in-adults-and-under-18s.pdf

Equally Ours for Crown Prosecution Service, UK (2024) 'Analysis of the Public Understanding of Rape and Serious Sexual Offences', https://www.cps.gov.uk/cps/news/more-do-tackle-rape-misconceptions-and-lack-understanding-consent-cps-survey-finds

Office For National Statistics, UK (2020) 'Sexual offences victim characteristics, England and Wales: year ending March 2020', https://www.ons.gov.uk/peoplepopulationandcommunity/crimeandjustice/articles/sexualoffencesvictimcharacteristicsenglandandwales/march2020

Brooks, Victoria, The Conversation, UK (2019) 'Why The Legal Definition Of Consent Fails Victims', https://theconversation.com/why-the-legal-definition-of-consent-fails-victims-124033

Marino, Susie, LocaliQ (2023) 'What Happens in an Internet Minute: 90+ fascinating online stats', https://localiq.com/blog/what-happens-in-an-internet-minute/

Morris, Alice, *Rolling Stone*, USA (2012) 'Hunter Moore: The most hated man on the internet', https://www.rollingstone.com/culture/culture-news/hunter-moore-the-most-hated-man-on-the-internet-184668/

King, Jordan, *London Evening Standard*, UK (2024) '"I'm asking for it": Calls for law to change require "clear yes to sex"', https://www.standard.co.uk/news/uk/consent-sex-rape-law-im-asking-for-it-sexual-activity-b1143022.html

Coaliton for Consent (2023) https://www.facebook.com/cfcduval

## 2: SEXUAL HARASSMENT

Women and Equalities Committee, UK Parliament (2018) 'Sexual Harassment of Women and Girls in Public Places Inquiry', https://committees.parliament.uk/work/6031/sexual-harassment-of-women-and-girls-in-public-places-inquiry/

APG for UN Women, UK (2021) 'Prevalence and Reporting of Sexual Harassment in UK Public Spaces', https://www.unwomenuk.org/site/wp-content/uploads/2021/03/APPG-UN-Women-Sexual-Harassment-Report_Updated.pdf

Topping, Alexandra, *Guardian*, UK (2021) 'Four-fifths of Young Women

# REFERENCES

in the UK Have Been Sexually Harassed, Survey Finds', https://www. theguardian.com/world/2021/mar/10/almost-all-young-women-in-the-uk-have-been-sexually-harassed-survey-finds

Plan International, UK (2024) 'The State of Girls' Rights in the UK', https:// plan-uk.org/state-of-girls-rights-report.pdf

Perrie, Stewart, Yahoo Finance (2024) 'Lawyer's Stark $66,000 Fine Warning after Aussie Workers Go Viral "Unsettling"', https://au.finance.yahoo. com/news/lawyers-stark-66000-fine-warning-after-aussie-workers-go-viral-unsettling-002701873.html

Plan International (2024) 'Building Digital Resistance: Girls and young women demand a safer digital future', https://plan-international.org/ uploads/2024/07/DigitalResilienceReport_English-FINAL.pdf

Girlguiding, UK (2023) 'Girls' Attitude Survey 2023: Girls' Lives over 15 years', https://www.girlguiding.org.uk/globalassets/docs-and-resources/ research-and-campaigns/girls-attitudes-survey-2023.pdf

Jurasz, Olga, UK (2024) 'Online Violence Against Women: A four nations study', https://oro.open.ac.uk/96398/

Stevens, Francesca & Enock, E. Florence et al., The Alan Turing Institute, UK (2024) 'Understanding Gender Differences in Experiences and Concerns Surrounding Online Harms: A nationally representative survey of UK adults', https://www.turing.ac.uk/sites/default/files/2024-03/ understanding_gender_differences_in_experiences_and_concerns_ surrounding_online_harms_-_a_nationally_representative_survey_of_uk_ adults.pdf

Lumsden, Karen & Morgan, Heather M. (2017) 'Cyber-trolling as Symbolic Violence: Deconstructing gendered abuse online', https://aura.abdn.ac.uk/ bitstream/handle/2164/21600/Lumsden_etal_RHGV_Cyber_Trolling_As_ AAM.pdf

Glitch, UK (2023) 'The Digital Misogynoir Report: Ending the dehumanising of Black women on social media', www.glitchcharity.co.uk/research

Evans, Connie, Yahoo! News, UK (2022) 'Love Island's Indiyah Shares Concerns Over Being Branded the "Angry Black Girl"', https://uk.news. yahoo.com/love-island-indiyah-shares-concerns-150419455.html

Amnesty International, UK (2017) 'Black and Asian Women MP's Are Abused More Online', https://www.amnesty.org.uk/online-violence-women-mps

Collignon, Sofia, Campbell, Rosie & Rüdig, Wolfgang, *The Political Quarterly*, UK (2022) 'The Gendered Harassment of Parliamentary Candidates in the UK', https://onlinelibrary.wiley.com/doi/epdf/10.1111/1467-923X.13070

Courea, Eleni, *Guardian*, UK (2024) 'Deluge of Abuse Sent on X to Prominent UK Politicians in Election Period', https://www.theguardian.com/society/ article/2024/sep/09/abuse-x-uk-politicians-election-period

# REFERENCES

University Of Sunderland, UK (2021) 'Meghan Targeted by Racist and Sexist Tweets After Announcing Plans with Harry to Step Back', https://www.sunderland.ac.uk/more/news/story/meghan-targeted-by-racist-and-sexist-tweets-after-announcing-plans-with-harry-to-step-back-1207

Plan International UK (2021) 'What Works for Ending Public Sexual Harassment: Executive summary', https://plan-uk.org/file/what-works-for-ending-sexual-harassment-report-executive-summary/download

Ditch the Label, Brandwatch, (2019) 'Exposed: The Scale of Online Transphobia. Exploring transphobia and pro-trans conversation on social media', https://www.brandwatch.com/reports/transphobia/

Billson, Chantelle, PinkNews, USA (2023) 'Trans Woman Who Starred in Hershey's Advert Left "Traumatised" by "Tsunami" of Transphobic Hate', https://www.thepinknews.com/2023/03/16/hersheys-advert-trans-woman-backlash/

Biddle, Sam, The Intercept, USA (2025) 'LEAKED META RULES: USERS ARE FREE TO POST "MEXICAN IMMIGRANTS ARE TRASH!" OR "TRANS PEOPLE ARE IMMORAL"', https://theintercept.com/2025/01/09/facebook-instagram-meta-hate-speech-content-moderation/

Al-Othman, Hannah, BuzzFeed News, UK (2018) 'After Sharing Unwanted Texts from a Male Delivery Driver, Hundreds of People Contacted This Woman With Their Own Experiences', https://www.buzzfeed.com/hannahalothman/the-woman-who-was-sent-unsolicited-texts-by-a-just-eat

Ankel, Sophia, ITV News, UK (2024) '"Predatory" Texts and Groping: The women claiming sexual harassment by food delivery drivers', https://www.itv.com/news/2024-06-22/traumatised-victims-claim-sexual-harassment-by-food-delivery-drivers

Burgess, Sanya, iNews, UK (2024) '"I Was Afraid to Report Deliveroo Driver for Harassment – He Knows Where I Live"', https://inews.co.uk/news/afraid-to-report-deliveroo-driver-harassment-2959358?ico=in-line_link

Oppenhein, Maya, *Independent*, UK (2023) 'Female Delivery Drivers Plagued with Sexual Harassment: "He opened the door, he was completely naked"', https://www.independent.co.uk/news/uk/home-news/women-drivers-sexual-harassment-uber-deliveroo-b2368667.html

PoliticsJOE, UK (2024) 'The Dark Side of Vinted That Users Don't Know About', https://www.youtube.com/watch?v=NSKF6etpTdM

Harrison, Sara, Wired.com, USA (2019) 'Twitter and Instagram Unveil New Ways to Combat Hate—Again', https://www.wired.com/story/twitter-instagram-unveil-new-ways-combat-hate-again/

CrimeStoppers UK, University of Suffolk, UK (2023) 'Violence Against Women And Girls Report Launch', https://crimestoppers-uk.org/news-campaigns/campaigns/violence-against-women-and-girls-report-launch

# REFERENCES

Plan International UK (2021) 'What Works for Ending Public Sexual Harassment: Executive summary', https://plan-uk.org/file/what-works-for-ending-sexual-harassment-report-executive-summary/download

Plan International UK (2018) 'Street Harassment. It's Not OK', https://plan-uk.org/file/plan-uk-street-harassment-reportpdf/download

## 3: LEAKED

Black, J.A., Cunningham, G., Fluckiger-Hawker, E., Robson, E., and Zólyomi, G., UK (1998) *The Electronic Text Corpus of Sumerian Literature* (http://www-etcsl.orient.ox.ac.uk/)

Kaspersky (2024) 'The Naked Truth: How intimate image sharing is reshaping our world', https://media.kasperskydaily.com/wp-content/uploads/sites/86/2024/07/15164921/The-Naked-Truth-Kaspersky.pdf

Henry, Nicola & McGlynn, Clare et al. (2020) 'Image-based Sexual Abuse: A study on the causes and consequences of non-consensual nude or sexual imagery', https://www.researchgate.net/publication/342132671_Image-based_Sexual_Abuse_A_Study_on_the_Causes_and_Consequences_of_Non-consensual_Nude_or_Sexual_Imagery

Revenge Porn Helpline, UK (2023) 'Revenge Porn Helpline 2023 Report', https://revengepornhelpline.org.uk/assets/documents/revenge-porn-helpline-report-2023.pdf

Internet Matters, UK (2024) 'Shifting the Dial: Methods to prevent "self-generated" child sexual abuse among 11–13-year-olds', https://www.internetmatters.org/hub/research/methods-prevent-self-generated-child-sexual-abuse-11-13s/

Storry, Dr Madeleine & Poplleton, Dr Sarah, Victims Commissioner of England and Wales, UK (2022) 'The Impact of Online Abuse: Hearing the victim's voice', https://victimscommissioner.org.uk/document/the-impact-of-online-abuse-hearing-the-victims-voice/

Crown Prosecution Service, UK (2022) '"Revenge porn" Victims Are Often Stalked and Harassed by Ex-Partners', https://www.cps.gov.uk/cps/news/revenge-porn-victims-are-often-stalked-and-harassed-ex-partners

Refuge UK (2020) 'The Naked Threat: It's time to change the law to protect survivors from image-based abuse', https://refuge.org.uk/wp-content/uploads/2020/07/The-Naked-Threat-Report.pdf

Bottomley, Bo & Bruckmayer, Dr Michaela, Refuge UK (2023) 'Intimate Image Abuse – despite increased reports to the police, charging rates remain low', https://refuge.org.uk/news/intimate-image-abuse-despite-increased-reports-to-the-police-charging-rates-remain-low/

# REFERENCES

Schrodt, Paul, Esquire.com (2017) '11 Celebrity Sex Tapes, Ranked by Cinematic Value', https://www.esquire.com/entertainment/g1957/celebrity-sex-tapes-ranked/

*Awards Chatter Podcast, Hollywood Reporter* (2017) *'Awards Chatter Podcast — Jennifer Lawrence* ('Mother!'), https://www.hollywoodreporter.com/news/general-news/awards-chatter-podcast-jennifer-lawrence-mother-1059777/

US Attorney's Office, Central District of California, USA (2016) 'Pennsylvania Man Sentenced Today to 18 Months in Federal Prison for Hacking Apple and Google E-Mail Accounts Belonging to More Than 100 People, Including Many Celebrities', https://www.justice.gov/usao-cdca/pr/pennsylvania-man-sentenced-today-18-months-federal-prison-hacking-apple-and-google-e

Powell, Anastasia & Scott, J. Adrian et al. (2022) 'Perpetration of Image-Based Sexual Abuse: Extent, nature and correlates in a multi-country sample', https://research.gold.ac.uk/id/eprint/31837/7/2022%20Powell%20et%20al.%20(JIV).pdf

Paul, Kari, *Guardian*, UK (2020) 'Pornhub Removes Millions of Videos After Investigation Finds Child Abuse Content', https://www.theguardian.com/technology/2020/dec/14/pornhub-purge-removes-unverified-videos-investigation-child-abuse

Kristof, Nicholas, *The New York Times* (2020) 'The Children of Pornhub: Why does Canada allow this company to profit off videos of exploitation and assault?', https://www.nytimes.com/2020/12/04/opinion/sunday/pornhub-rape-trafficking.html

## 4: LEAKED 2.0

Klein, Jessica, Input (2020) 'Porn Stars Are Trying to Become Cam Stars. It's Not As Easy As It Looks', https://www.inverse.com/input/features/porn-stars-camming-coronavirus-covid19

Cooban, Anna, *Business Insider* (2021), 'OnlyFans Has Boomed During Lockdown. Users Spent $2.4 Billion on the Adult-Entertainment Site in 2020, and 120 million People Now Use It', https://www.businessinsider.com/onlyfans-lockdown-boom-transactions-hit-24b-revenue-up-553-2021-4

Mann, Jyoti, Yahoo! Tech, (2024) 'OnlyFans' Pandemic Boom Isn't Slowing Down — spending on the site has surged by almost a fifth', https://www.yahoo.com/tech/people-spent-1-billion-more-131304736.html

Chatterly.com, (2023) 'How Many Creators Are There on Only Fans', https://usechatterly.com/blog-full/how-many-creators-are-there-on-only-fans

# REFERENCES

International Union of Sex Workers (2024) 'OnlyFans Users, Networth & Stats 2024', https://iusw.org/onlyfans-revenue-user-stats/

Similarweb.com, (December 2024), OnlyFans Website Traffic Search, https://pro.similarweb.com/#/digitalsuite/websiteanalysis/overview/website-performance/*/999/1m?webSource=Total&key=onlyfans.com

Spangler, Todd, *Variety* (2024) 'OnlyFans Is Not Just for "Sexy Content," CEO Says, Claiming Platform Has Paid Creators Over $20 Billion to Date', https://variety.com/2024/digital/news/onlyfans-sex-content-creators-20-billion-dollars-ceo-1236175515/#

Cowen, Trace William, Complex (2024) 'Bhad Bhabie Shares OnlyFans All-Time Earnings Breakdown Showing She's Made $57 million in 3 Years' https://www.complex.com/pop-culture/a/tracewilliamcowen/bhad-bhabie-onlyfans-earnings

Smith, Reanna, *Daily Mirror*, UK (2023) 'OnlyFans Star Earning £100k a Month Starts "affordable Housing Scheme" for UK Families', https://www.mirror.co.uk/news/uk-news/onlyfans-star-earning-100k-month-29059230

Hollands, Tom, XSRUS.com (2020) 'The Economics of OnlyFans', https://xsrus.com/the-economics-of-onlyfans

Criddle, Cristina, *Financial Times* (2024) 'Keily Blair, OnlyFans: "We are an incredible UK tech success story"', https://www.ft.com/content/500b97c8-b88b-4da4-a1b9-0d3db01aeed7

Lord, Annie, Vice (2019) 'Being an OnlyFans Sex Worker Sounds Stressful', https://www.vice.com/en/article/only-fans-sex-worker-interview/

Steadman, Otillia, BuzzFeed News, (2021) '"I Needed To Film Today and I Physically Can't": Online Sex Workers Are Burning Out', https://www.buzzfeednews.com/article/otilliasteadman/only-fans-sex-workers-burnout

Baker, Dr Catherine, Ging, Prof Debbie & Brandt Andreasen, Dr Maja, DCU Anti-Bullying Centre, Dublin City University (2024) 'Recommending Toxicity: The role of algorithmic recommender functions on YouTube Shorts and TikTok in promoting male supremacist influencers', https://antibullyingcentre.ie/wp-content/uploads/2024/04/DCU-Toxicity-Full-Report.pdf

Jones, Angela, The Conversation (2021) 'Sex Work, Part of the Online Gig Economy, Is a Lifeline for Marginalized Workers', https://theconversation.com/sex-work-part-of-the-online-gig-economy-is-a-lifeline-for-marginalized-workers-160238

OnlyFans.com, (2024) 'Helping Creators Protect Their Copyright', https://onlyfans.com/transparency-center/helping

OnlyFans.com, (2024) 'OnlyFans Transparency Report December 2024', https://onlyfans.com/transparency/2024/12

# REFERENCES

## 5: CYBERFLASHING

University of Kent & Sexplain, UK (2019) '"Staying Safe Online" Survey: What unwanted sexual images are being sent to teenagers on social media?' https://blogs.ucl.ac.uk/ioe/2020/06/19/staying-safe-online-survey-what-unwanted-sexual-images-are-being-sent-to-teenagers-on-social-media/

Smith, Mathew, YouGov, UK (2018) 'Four in Ten Female Millennials Have Been Sent an Unsolicited Penis Photo', https://yougov.co.uk/politics/articles/20179-four-ten-female-millennials-been-sent-dick-pic

Communia, UK (2022) 'Report on Women's and Marginalized Genders' Social Media Experiences', https://www.ourcommunia.com/post/uk-report-2023

Thompson, Rachel, Mashable (2020) 'How "Hatewank" Videos Became a Tool for Harassing Women in the public eye', https://mashable.com/article/hatewank-videos-harassment

Ramasubbu, Suren, Mobicip (2019) 'How Apple's AirDrop Is Misused For Cyberflashing', https://www.mobicip.com/blog/how-apples-airdrop-feature-can-be-misused-cyber-flashing

Ringrose, J., Regehr, K. & Whitehead, S. (2021) 'Teen Girls' Experiences Negotiating the Ubiquitous Dick Pic: Sexual double standards and the normalization of image based sexual harassment', www.doi.org/10.1007/s11199-021-01236-3

Channel 4, *Undercover: Sexual Harassment – The Truth'* (2022), https://www.channel4.com/programmes/undercover-sexual-harassment-the-truth

James, Bethan, BBC News, UK (2021) 'Instagram Influencer Received "Hundreds" of Obscene Photos', https://www.bbc.com/news/uk-wales-politics-59615944

Hardy, Frances, *Daily Mail*, UK (2024) 'I've Been Sent an Unsolicited Picture of Men's Penises Every Month for 12 Years. Here's the Truth about the Wave of Cyber-Flashing, by Broadcaster JESS DAVIES', https://www.dailymail.co.uk/femail/article-13250037/unsolicited-pictures-mens-penises-cyber-flashing-broadcaster-JESS-DAVIES.html

BBC Two, *Emily Atack: Asking for It?* (2023), https://www.bbc.co.uk/programmes/m001hs5v

Bumble, (2021) 'UK Government Accepts Bumble's Call to Make Cyberflashing a Crime', https://bumble.com/en/the-buzz/bumble-uk-government-cyberflashing-law-crime

Hayes, R. M., & Dragiewicz, M., *Women's Studies International Forum 71* (2018) 'Unsolicited Dick Pics: Erotica, exhibitionism or entitlement?', https://doi.org/10.1016/j.wsif.2018.07.001

Beecham, Amy, *Stylist* (2023) 'Emily Atack: "I'm being sexually harassed every single day of my life, at home, with my phone in my hands"', https://

# REFERENCES

www.stylist.co.uk/entertainment/tv/emily-atack-asking-for-it-bbc-cyberflashing/754546

Johnson, Diana, parliamentary debate (2023) 'International Women's Day 2023: Diana Johnson excerpts', https://www.parallelparliament.co.uk/debate/2023-03-09/commons/commons-chamber/international-womens-day

McNally, Matthew R., Fremouw, William J., *Aggression and Violent Behavior* (2014) 'Examining Risk of Escalation: A critical review of the exhibitionistic behavior literature', https://www.sciencedirect.com/science/article/abs/pii/S1359178914000718

Regina V Pawel Relowicz, Judiciary of England and Wales, UK (2022), https://www.judiciary.uk/wp-content/uploads/2022/07/R-v-Pawel-Relowicz-sentencing-remarks.pdf

Sinmaz, Emine, *Guardian*, UK (2023) 'Killer Exposed Himself to Libby Squire Weeks Before Murder, Mother Believes', https://www.theguardian.com/society/2023/mar/09/take-indecent-exposure-more-seriously-urges-libby-squire-mother-hull-student

Biggs, Jade & Bond, Kimberley, *Cosmopolitan*, UK (2024) 'Cyberflashing: What is cyberflashing? The offence could now lead to jail time', https://www.cosmopolitan.com/uk/reports/a38148523/cyberflashing/

The Cyber Helpline, UK (2024) 'What Is Cyberflashing?: Legal measures, impact and prevention', https://www.thecyberhelpline.com/helpline-blog/2024/3/25/what-is-cyberflashing-legal-measures-impact-amp-prevention

Lovine, Anna, Mashable (2024) 'Federal Cyberflashing Bill Introduced with Bumble Endorsement', https://mashable.com/article/bumble-consent-act-cyberflashing-federal-bill

Department for Science, Innovation and Technology, UK (2024) 'Online Safety Act Explainer', https://www.gov.uk/government/publications/online-safety-act-explainer/online-safety-act-explainer

Adams, Lewis, BBC News, UK (2024) 'Cyber-flashing Convict Is First to Be Jailed Under New Law', https://www.bbc.com/news/uk-england-essex-68543605

Ofcom, UK (2023) 'Consultation: Protecting people from illegal harms online', https://www.ofcom.org.uk/online-safety/illegal-and-harmful-content/protecting-people-from-illegal-content-online

## 6: CATFISH

ExpressVPN, UK (2023) 'ExpressVPN Survey in UK Reveals the Dark Side of Online Dating', https://www.expressvpn.com/blog/dark-side-of-online-dating-uk/

# REFERENCES

Reuters.com, (2021), 'Facebook Says Took Down 1.3 Billion Fake Accounts in Oct–Dec', https://www.reuters.com/technology/facebook-disables-13-billion-fake-accounts-oct-dec-last-year-2021-03-22/

National Fraud Intelligence Bureau, City of London Police, UK (2022) 'Romance Fraudsters Break Hearts and Bank Balances with £92.8m Lost in the UK Last Year', https://www.cityoflondon.police.uk/news/city-of-london/news/2023/october/romance-fraudsters-break-hearts-and-bank-balances-with-92.8m-lost-in-the-uk-last-year/

UK Finance, UK (2021) 'Nearly 40 per Cent of People Looking for Love Online Were Asked for Money', https://www.ukfinance.org.uk/press/press-releases/nearly-40-cent-people-looking-love-online-were-asked-money

Baruchin, Rotem, Cyabra (2024) 'What Makes Fake Profiles Effective?: A new research by Cyabra:', https://cyabra.com/blog/what-makes-fake-profiles-effective-a-new-research-by-cyabra/

Klepper, David, Assosciated Press, (2024) 'Why Russia, China and Big Tech All Use Fake Female Online Profiles to Get Clicks: "Pretending to be a female is the easiest way to get credibility"', https://fortune.com/2024/06/12/fake-female-online-profiles/

NewsGuard's Reality Check (2024) 'Fake Accounts on X Say They're Not Voting for Biden', https://www.newsguardrealitycheck.com/p/fake-accounts-on-x-say-theyre-not

Beldo, Sarah (2016) 'What Percentage of Online Dating Profiles Are Fake?', https://sift.com/blog/what-percentage-of-dating-profiles-are-fake

Pheby, Christien, YouGov, UK (2023) 'The Good, the Bad, and the Ugly of Dating Apps in Britain', https://business.yougov.com/content/48146-the-good-the-bad-and-the-ugly-of-dating-apps-in-britain

Internet Watch Foundation, UK (2024) 'Teenage Boys Targeted As Hotline Sees "Heartbreaking" Increase in Child "Sextortion' Reports", https://www.iwf.org.uk/news-media/news/teenage-boys-targeted-as-hotline-sees-heartbreaking-increase-in-child-sextortion-reports/

Revenge Porn Helpline, UK (2023) 'Revenge Porn Helpline 2023 Report', https://revengepornhelpline.org.uk/assets/documents/revenge-porn-helpline-report-2023.pdf

National Crime Agency, UK (2024) 'NCA Issues Urgent Warning About "Sextortion"', https://www.nationalcrimeagency.gov.uk/news/nca-issues-urgent-warning-about-sextortion

McCubbin, Jayne, BBC News, UK (2024) '"I Thought My Life Was Over": Escaping the sextortion scammers', https://www.bbc.co.uk/news/articles/cq82lyg5vpjo

# REFERENCES

BBC World Service, UK (2024) 'Sextortion: In six hours, my son was dead', https://www.bbc.co.uk/programmes/w3ct6dwb

Thornton, Beverley, UK Safer Internet Centre, UK (2024) 'Sextortion Report: August 2022 to August 2024', https://saferinternet.org.uk/blog/uk-safer-internet-centre-publishes-sextortion-report

Fleming, P. J., Barrington, C., et al. (2019) 'Competition and Humiliation: How masculine norms shape men's sexual and violent behaviors', https://doi.org/10.1177/1097184X17715493

Fudakowski, Katie & Coles, Sophia, Farrer & Co (2024) 'Understanding and Combating Sextortion: Why boys are disproportionately affected', https://www.farrer.co.uk/news-and-insights/understanding-and-combating-sextortion-why-boys-are-disproportionately-affected/

Brooks, Libby, *Guardian*, UK (2024) '"It Can Happen to Any Child": Parents of sextortion victim send out warning', https://www.theguardian.com/society/2024/apr/29/it-can-happen-to-any-child-parents-of-sextortion-victim-fight-for-justice

ITV News, UK (2024) '"They Killed Our Son": Disturbing rise in "sextortion" against young people', https://www.itv.com/watch/news/they-killed-our-son-disturbing-rise-in-sextortion-against-young-people/crlr6hx

United States Attorney's Office, Western District of Michigan (2024) 'Ogoshi Brothers Sentenced to Lengthy Prison Terms In Sextortion Scheme That Resulted in Death of Teen', https://www.justice.gov/usao-wdmi/pr/2024_0905_Ogoshi_Brothers_Sentenced

Smith, Tony & Crawford, Angus, UK (2024) '"Sextortion Guides" Sold on Social Media, BBC Finds', https://www.bbc.co.uk/news/articles/cp00y03q93mo

Leader, Sam, ITV News, UK (2024) 'Helpline Sees Massive Surge in Sextortion Victims with Students Often the Target For Scammers', https://www.itv.com/news/2024-04-17/new-figures-show-alarming-rise-in-sextortion-victims-as-students-often-targeted

BBC News, UK (2024) 'Abuser in "UK's Largest Catfishing Case" Jailed for Life', https://www.bbc.com/news/articles/cj4d40922xvo

## 7: DEEPFAKE IMAGE ABUSE

Ajder, Henry & Partini, Giorgio et al., Sensity AI, UK (2019) 'The State of Deepfakes: Landscape, threats, and impact', https://regmedia.co.uk/2019/10/08/deepfake_report.pdf

Ulmer, Alexandra & Tong, Anna, Reuters (2023) 'Deepfaking It: America's 2024 election collides with AI boom', https://www.reuters.com/world/us/deepfaking-it-americas-2024-election-collides-with-ai-boom-2023-05-30/

# REFERENCES

Fritz, Niki & Malic, Vinny et al., *Gender Issues* 38, (2021) 'Worse Than Objects: The Depiction of Black women and men and their sexual relationship in pornography', https://www.researchgate.net/publication/341354859_Worse_Than_Objects_The_Depiction_of_Black_Women_and_Men_and_Their_Sexual_Relationship_in_Pornography

Tenbarge, Kat, NBC News (2024) '*Euphoria* Star Jacob Elordi Targeted in Sexually Explicit X Deepfakes Allegedly Featuring Minor's Body', https://www.nbcnews.com/tech/misinformation/jacob-elordi-deepfake-x-video-body-rcna157787

Morgan, Lucy, *Glamour*, UK (2024) 'We Asked Thousands of *Glamour* Readers About Sexual Consent, from Sexual Assault to Deepfaking. Here's What They Said . . .', https://www.glamourmagazine.co.uk/article/glamour-consent-survey-results-2024

Jameson, Sean, Bad Girls Bible (2024) 'Send Nudes: 1,058 People On How Often They Send & Receive Nudes', https://badgirlsbible.com/naked-ethics

Avast (2022) 'Avast Partners with Intimacy Expert Shan Boodram on Ways to Safely Store and Share Intimate Photos and Content as a Third of Americans Admitted to Sharing Nudes', https://press.avast.com/avast-partners-with-intimacy-expert-shan-boodram-on-ways-to-safely-store-and-share-intimate-photos-and-content-as-a-third-of-americans-admitted-to-sharing-nudes

Roose, Kevin, *The New York Times* (2018) 'Here Come the Fake Videos, Too', https://www.nytimes.com/2018/03/04/technology/fake-videos-deepfakes.html

Cole, Samantha, Vice (2019) 'This Horrifying App Undresses a Photo of Any Woman With a Single Click', https://www.vice.com/en/article/deepnude-app-creates-fake-nudes-of-any-woman/

Cole, Samantha, Vice (2019) 'Creator of DeepNude, App That Undresses Photos of Women, Takes It Offline', https://www.vice.com/en/article/deepnude-app-that-undresses-photos-of-women-takes-it-offline/

Ajder, Henry, Partini, Giorgio & Cavalli, Francesco, Sensity AI (2020) 'Automating Image Abuse: Deepfake bots on Telegram', https://sensity.ai/reports/

Burgess, Matt, Wired.com (2024) 'Millions of People Are Using Abusive AI "Nudify" Bots on Telegram', https://www.wired.com/story/ai-deepfake-nudify-bots-telegram/

Ng, Kelly, BBC News (2024) 'Telegram Apologises for Handling of Deepfake Porn Material', https://www.bbc.com/news/articles/cvg45kz47dno

Milmo, Dan, *Guardian*, UK (2024) 'AI-generated Child Sexual Abuse Imagery Reaching "Tipping Point", Says Watchdog', https://www.theguardian.com/technology/2024/oct/18/artificial-intelligence-child-sexual-abuse-imagery-watchdog-iwf

# REFERENCES

Internet Watch Foundation, UK (2024) 'Public Exposure to "Chilling" AI Child Sexual Abuse Images and Videos Increases', https://www.iwf.org. uk/news-media/news/public-exposure-to-chilling-ai-child-sexual-abuse-images-and-videos-increases/

Dickson, E. J., *Rolling Stone* (2024) '4CHAN Chuds Used AI to Clothe Her. She Fought Back', https://www.rollingstone.com/culture/culture-news/dignifai-4chan-shame-women-1234961851/

Davies, Caroline, *Guardian*, UK (2024) 'Schoolgirl, 14, Found Dead After Alleged Bullying by Boys, London Inquest Hears', https://www.theguardian.com/uk-news/2024/jan/23/schoolgirl-14-found-dead-after-alleged-bullying-by-boys-london-inquest-hears

Agence France Presse, Ary News (2022) 'Teen Jailed Over Online Shaming That Led to Girl's Suicide', https://arynews.tv/basant-khaled-case-teen-jailed-over-online-shaming-suicide/

Singer, Natasha, *The New York Times* (2024) 'Teen Girls Confront an Epidemic of Deepfake Nudes in Schools', https://www.nytimes.com/2024/04/08/technology/deepfake-ai-nudes-westfield-high-school.html

Hedgecoe, Guy, BBC News (2023) 'AI-generated Naked Child Images Shock Spanish Town of Almendralejo', https://www.bbc.com/news/world-europe-66877718

O'Neill, Sean, *The Times*, UK (2024) 'Private Schools in Police Inquiry Over Deepfake Porn Images of Girls', https://www.thetimes.com/uk/education/article/private-schools-in-police-inquiry-over-deepfake-porn-images-of-girls-d9qc2wgvk

Grace, Katja & Salvatier, John et al. (2024) 'When Will AI Exceed Human Performance? Evidence from AI Experts', https://doi.org/10.48550/arXiv.1705.08807

The Oliver Wyman Forum (2024) 'How Generative AI Is Transforming Business and Society', https://www.oliverwymanforum.com/content/dam/oliver-wyman/ow-forum/gcs/2023/AI-Report-2024-Davos.pdf

Patel, Nilay, The Verge (2024) 'Replika CEO Eugenia Kuyda Says It's Okay If We End Up Marrying AI Chatbots', https://www.theverge.com/24216748/replika-ceo-eugenia-kuyda-ai-companion-chatbots-dating-friendship-decoder-podcast-interview

Waugh, Rob, Metro UK (2017) 'Men at Tech Fair Molest £3,000 Sex Robot So Much It's Left Broken and "Heavily Soiled"', https://metro.co.uk/2017/09/27/men-at-tech-fair-molest-3000-sex-robot-so-much-its-left-broken-and-heavily-soiled-6960778/

Montgomery, Blake, *Guardian* (2024) 'Mother Says AI Chatbot Led Her Son to Kill Himself in Lawsuit Against Its Maker', https://www.theguardian.com/technology/2024/oct/23/character-ai-chatbot-sewell-setzer-death

# REFERENCES

## 8: THE GAME OF MISOGYNY

Storry, Dr Madeleine & Poppleton, Dr Sarah, Victims Commissioner of England and Wales, UK (2022) 'The Impact of Online Abuse: Hearing the victim's voice', https://victimscommissioner.org.uk/document/the-impact-of-online-abuse-hearing-the-victims-voice/

The Economics Intelligence Unit (2021) 'Measuring the Prevalence of Online Violence Against Women', https://onlineviolencewomen.eiu.com

Lenhart, Amanda & Ybarra, Michele et al., Center for Innovative Public Health Research (2016) 'Online Harassment, Digital Abuse, and Cyberstalking in America', https://www.datasociety.net/pubs/oh/Online_Harassment_2016.pdf

Stevens, Francesca & Enock, E. Florence et al., The Alan Turing Institute, UK (2024) 'Understanding Gender Differences in Experiences And Concerns Surrounding Online Harms: A nationally representative survey of UK adults', https://www.turing.ac.uk/sites/default/files/2024-03/understanding_gender_differences_in_experiences_and_concerns_surrounding_online_harms_-_a_nationally_representative_survey_of_uk_adults.pdf

Hill, Kashmir, *The New York Times* (2022) 'A Face Engine Anyone Can Use Is Alarmingly Accurate', https://www.nytimes.com/2022/05/26/technology/pimeyes-facial-recognition-search.html

Cox, Joseph, 404media (2024) 'Someone Put Facial Recognition Tech onto Meta's Smart Glasses to Instantly Dox Strangers', https://www.404media.co/someone-put-facial-recognition-tech-onto-metas-smart-glasses-to-instantly-dox-strangers/

Office for National Statistics, UK (2024) 'I Feel Like I Am Living Someone Else's Life': One in seven people a victim of stalking', https://www.ons.gov.uk/peoplepopulationandcommunity/crimeandjustice/articles/ifeellikeiamlivingsomeoneeselifeoneinsevenpeopleavictimofstalking/2024-09-26

His Majesty's Inspectorate of Constabulary, UK (2024) 'The Police Response to Stalking', https://hmicfrs.justiceinspectorates.gov.uk/publication-html/police-response-to-stalking/

Elder, Jeff, Avast (2019) 'Google Pulls Stalker Apps Identified by Avast', https://blog.avast.com/avast-identifies-stalker-apps

Avast (2021) 'Use of Stalkerware and Spyware Apps Increase by 93% Since Lockdown Began in the UK', https://press.avast.com/use-of-stalkerware-and-spyware-apps-increase-by-93-since-lockdown-began-in-the-uk

Singleton, Tom, BBC News, UK (2023) 'Baby Monitors and Smart Speakers Enabling Abuse, Say MPs', https://www.bbc.co.uk/news/technology-66408668

# REFERENCES

Vallance, Chris, BBC News, UK (2023) 'Controversial Clothes Hook Spy Cameras for Sale on Amazon', https://www.bbc.com/news/technology-67652317

Home Office, UK (2024) 'Victims to Be Given More Protection in Stalking Crackdown', https://www.gov.uk/government/news/victims-to-be-given-more-protection-in-stalking-crackdown

Crown Prosecution Service, UK (2024) 'Life Sentence for Security Guard Who Planned Kidnap, Rape and Murder of Holly Willoughby', https://www.cps.gov.uk/east-england/news/update-life-sentence-security-guard-who-planned-kidnap-rape-and-murder-holly

R v G. Plumb, Judiciary of England and Wales, UK (2024) https://www.judiciary.uk/wp-content/uploads/2024/07/R-v-Gavin-Plumb-sentencing-remarks-final-version.pdf

Porter, Catherine & Le Stradic, Ségolène, *The New York Times* (2024) 'France Confronts Horror of Rape and Drugging Case as 51 Men Go on Trial', https://www.nytimes.com/2024/09/02/world/europe/france-husband-rape-drug-trial-mazan.html

Agence France Presse, *Guardian* (2024) 'Daughter of French Man Who Invited Men to Rape Mother Speaks of "Descent into Hell", https://www.theguardian.com/world/article/2024/sep/06/daughter-of-french-man-who-invited-men-to-rape-mother-speaks-of-descent-into-hell-dominique-pelicot-gisele-pelicot

Porter, Catherine, *The New York Times* (2024) 'Shock in French Court Shown Videos of Men Accused of Raping Drugged Woman', https://www.nytimes.com/2024/10/04/world/europe/france-rape-trial-pelicot-videos.html

Bremner, Charles, *The Times*, UK (2024) 'Gisèle Pelicot Rape Trial: I thought she was dead, says accused', https://www.thetimes.com/world/europe/article/gisele-pelicot-rape-trial-accused-dead-france-mknqsjq96

Bremner, Charles, *The Times*, UK (2024) 'Pelicot Rape Trial: I was disturbed by her snoring, says suspect', https://www.thetimes.com/world/europe/article/pelicot-rape-trial-i-was-disturbed-by-her-snoring-says-suspect-bg2ndm8bj

Buckler, Liam, *Mirror*, UK (2024) 'France Rape Trial: Chilling explanation for why man "assaulted woman" on New Year's Eve', https://www.mirror.co.uk/news/world-news/france-rape-trial-chilling-explanation-33739024

Bremner, Charles, *The Times*, UK (2024) 'Pelicot Rape Trial: Defendant insists he thought "it was a game"', https://www.thetimes.com/world/europe/article/gisele-pelicot-rape-trial-accused-dead-france-mknqsjq96

Pisa, Nick & Reynolds, James, *Daily Mail*, UK (2024) 'The Moment the Monster of Avignon's Wife Has Dreaded: Graphic images of her rape are shown in hushed silence – after her daughter leaves courtroom – as her

# REFERENCES

"abusers" plead they are innocent victims', https://www.dailymail.co.uk/news/article-13869495/monster-avignon-dominique-pelicot-wife-graphic-rape-images-court.html

Willsher, Kim, *Guardian*, UK (2024) 'Gisèle Pelicot's Lawyer: "This level of depravity? I have never seen anything like it", https://www.theguardian.com/world/2024/dec/03/gisele-pelicot-lawyer-depravity-never-seen-anything-like-it

Leroux, Luc, *Le Monde* (2024) 'Gisèle Pelicot, Drugged by Her Husband So Others Could Rape Her, Is a Woman "Still Standing", https://www.lemonde.fr/en/france/article/2024/09/06/gisele-pelicot-drugged-by-her-husband-so-others-could-rape-her-is-a-woman-still-standing_6725036_7.html

Chrisafis, Angelique, *Guardian*, UK (2024) 'Gisèle Pelicot Tells Mass Rape Trial 'It's Not for Us to Have Shame – It's for Them', https://www.theguardian.com/world/2024/oct/23/gisele-pelicot-rape-trial-france-court


## 9: MASCULINITY IN CRISIS

Holter, Ø. G. *Men and Masculinities* 17(5) (2014) 'What's in It for Men?': Old question, new data', https://doi.org/10.1177/1097184X14558237

Ipsos, King's College of London (2024) 'International Women's Day 2024: Global attitudes towards women's leadership', https://www.kcl.ac.uk/giwl/assets/iwd-2024-survey.pdf

Dr Alok Kanojia, *The Diary of a CEO* podcast (2024), 'Dr K: "There Is a Crisis Going on with Men!", "We've Produced Millions of Lonely, Addicted Males!"', https://www.youtube.com/watch?v=B_5N_aDu3u0

Levant, Ronald & Pryor, Shana (2020) *The Tough Standard: The hard truths about masculinity and violence*, Oxford University Press

David, Deborah Sarah & Brannon, Robert (1976) *The Forty Nine Percent Majority: The male sex role'*, Addison Wesley

Levant, Ronald & Hirsch, L. S et al. *Journal of Mental Health Counseling*, 14(3) (1992) 'The Male Role: An investigation of contemporary norms'

New Macho, UK (2019) 'Men: Breaking Down or Breaking Through?', https://iccopr.com/wp-content/uploads/2019/03/New_Macho_Whitepaper.pdf

Samaritans, UK (2023) 'Latest Suicide Data', https://www.samaritans.org/about-samaritans/research-policy/suicide-facts-and-figures/latest-suicide-data/

Fowler, Katherine A. & Kaplan, Mark et al., *American Journal of Preventive Medicine* 63(3) (2022) 'Suicide Among Males Across the Lifespan: An analysis of differences by known mental health status', https://www.ajpmonline.org/article/S0749-3797(22)00153-2/abstract

Balla, Reemul, Sky News UK (2023) 'Zara Aleena: Sexual Predator Jordan

# REFERENCES

McSweeney Who Murdered Law Graduate to Appeal for Shorter Sentence', https://news.sky.com/story/zara-aleena-sexual-predator-jordan-mcsweeney-who-murdered-law-graduate-to-appeal-for-shorter-sentence-12987853

Dickins, Max (2022) *'Billy No-Mates': How I realised men have a friendship problem*, Canongate Books

Children's Commissioner, UK (2023) 'A Lot of It Is Actually Just Abuse – Young people and pornography', https://www.childrenscommissioner. gov.uk/resource/a-lot-of-it-is-actually-just-abuse-young-people-and-pornography/

Vera-Gray, Fiona & McGlynn, Clare et al., *The British Journal of Criminology*, 61(5) (2021) 'Sexual Violence As a Sexual Script in Mainstream Online Pornography', https://doi.org/10.1093/bjc/azab035

Harte, Alys, BBC Radio 5 Live, UK (2019) 'A man tried to choke me during sex without warning', https://www.bbc.com/news/uk-50546184

White C., Martin G., Schofield A. M., Majeed-Ariss R., *Journal of forensic and legal medicine, 79, 102128*, (2021) "I thought he was going to kill me': Analysis of 204 case files of adults reporting non-fatal strangulation as part of a sexual assault over a 3 year period.', https://pubmed.ncbi.nlm.nih. gov/33618205/

Ministry of Justice, UK (2024) 'Tougher Sentences for "Rough Sex" Killers', https://www.gov.uk/government/news/tougher-sentences-for-rough-sex-killers

Levant, Ronald, *Professional Psychology: Research and Practice*, 27(3) (1996) 'The New Psychology of Men', https://doi.org/10.1037/0735-7028.27.3.259

Femicide Census, UK (2021) 'Just Days Before the General Election, We Have Released Our Report on UK Femicides in 2021', https://www. femicidecensus.org/just-days-before-the-general-election-we-have-released-our-report-on-uk-femicides-in-2021/

Dupiuis-Déri, Francis, The Conversation (2018) 'The Bogus "Crisis" of Masculinity', https://www.academia.edu/36632151/The_bogus_crisis_of_masculinity

Allen, Judith A., *Radical History Review* 82 (2002) 'Men Interminably in Crisis? Historians on Masculinity, Sexual Boundaries, and Manhood'

Whitehead, S. UK (2019) *Toxic Masculinity: Curing the virus. Making men smarter, healthier, safer*, Acorn Books

## 10: INFLUENCERS

Monaghan, Becca, Indy100 (2023) 'Why Andrew Tate Was Kicked off Big Brother', https://www.indy100.com/viral/andrew-tate-fight-big-brother-2661605359

# REFERENCES

BBC News, (2024) 'Andrew Tate and Brother Tristan to Be Tried in Romania on Rape and Trafficking Charges', https://www.bbc.com/news/world-europe-68907298

Das, Shanti, *Guardian*, UK (2022) 'Inside the Violent, Misogynistic World of Tiktok's New Star, Andrew Tate', https://www.theguardian.com/technology/2022/aug/06/andrew-tate-violent-misogynistic-world-of-tiktok-new-star

Robinson, Breanna, Indy100 (2022) 'Andrew Tate and Piers Morgan Clash in Explosive Interview: Here are 11 things we learned', https://www.indy100.com/viral/andrew-tate-piers-morgan-uncensored-interview

Gilbert, David, Wired.com (2024) 'The Trump Campaign Rhetoric About Women Sounds a Lot Like Andrew Tate's', https://www.wired.com/story/trump-vance-campaign-rhetoric-women-andrew-tate/

BBC News, UK (2024) 'Who Is Andrew Tate? The Self-proclaimed Misogynist Influencer', https://www.bbc.com/news/uk-64125045

Campbell, Prof. Rosie & May, George et al., Ipsos, Kings College London (2024) 'Emerging Tensions? How Younger Generations Are Dividing on Masculinity and Gender Equality', https://www.kcl.ac.uk/policy-institute/assets/emerging-tensions.pdf

Internet Matters, UK (2023) 'New Research Sees Favourable Views Towards Andrew Tate from Both Teen Boys and Young Dads', https://www.internetmatters.org/hub/press-release/new-research-sees-favourable-views-towards-andrew-tate-from-both-teen-boys-and-young-dads/

Burn-Murdoch, John, *Financial Times* (2024) 'A New Global Gender Divide Is Emerging', https://www.ft.com/content/29fd9b5c-2f35-41bf-9d4c-994db4e12998

Janfaza, Rachel, *Teen Vogue* (2024) 'Youth Vote in 2024 Saw Young Men Vote for Trump, Young Women of Color Back Harris', https://www.teenvogue.com/story/youth-vote-in-2024-young-men-trump-women-of-color-harris

Hurst, Ben, TEDxLondon Women (2019) 'Boys Won't Be Boys. Boys Will Be What We Teach Them to Be', https://www.youtube.com/watch?v=3dp08bAUwi8

Pheby, Christien, YouGov, UK (2024) 'Who's Listening to *The Joe Rogan Experience*? Men, Mostly', https://business.yougov.com/content/47483-whos-listening-to-the-joe-rogan-experience-men-mostly

Paterson, Alex, Media Matters (2021) 'Joe Rogan Wrapped: A year of COVID-19 misinformation, right-wing myths, and anti-trans rhetoric', https://www.mediamatters.org/joe-rogan-experience/joe-rogan-wrapped-year-covid-19-misinformation-right-wing-myths-and-anti-trans

Spocchia, Gina, *Independent*, UK (2022) 'Video of Joe Rogan Laughing As Guest Describes Sexually Exploiting Young Women at Comedy Club

# REFERENCES

Resurfaces', https://www.independent.co.uk/news/world/americas/joe-rogan-video-women-assault-b2009432.html

Happyscribe, *The Joe Rogan Experience* (2024) '#2219 – Donald Trump', https://www.happyscribe.com/public/the-joe-rogan-experience/2219-donald-trump

Baker, Carrie N., *MS Magazine* (2024) 'Misogynist Manifesto: Project 2025 says yes to "biblically based marriages" and no to reproductive rights', https://msmagazine.com/2024/09/09/misogynist-manifesto-project-2025-marriage-women-abortion-bible-divorce-men/

Bowles, Nellie, *The New York Times* (2018) 'Jordan Peterson, Custodian of the Patriarchy', https://www.nytimes.com/2018/05/18/style/jordan-peterson-12-rules-for-life.html

Beaumont-Thomas, Ben, *Guardian*, UK (2024) 'British Musician and Broadcaster Yung Filly Charged with Rape and Assault', https://www.theguardian.com/music/2024/oct/10/yung-filly-rapper-youtuber-charged-rape-assault

Unison, UK (2024) 'Closure of More Than a Thousand Youth Centres Could Have Lasting Impact on Society', https://www.unison.org.uk/news/2024/06/closure-of-more-than-a-thousand-youth-centres-could-have-lasting-impact-on-society/

Donoghue, Daniel, BBC North West, UK (2024) 'Far-right Group Using Sports to "Build Militia"', https://www.bbc.com/news/articles/c5ydnqdq38wo

Institute for Strategic Dialogue, UK (2024) 'From Rumours to Riots: How online misinformation fuelled violence in the aftermath of the Southport attack', https://www.isdglobal.org/digital_dispatches/from-rumours-to-riots-how-online-misinformation-fuelled-violence-in-the-aftermath-of-the-southport-attack/

Pearson, Elizabeth, *Metro*, UK (2024) 'Why White Nationalists Say They're "Protecting" Women and Children When They Riot', https://metro.co.uk/2024/08/08/white-nationalists-say-protecting-women-children-riot-21386394/

*SILENCED with Tommy Robinson* (2024) 'Be Safe & Stop the Violence – Special Episode', https://podcast.urbanscoop.news/episodepage/be-safe-stop-the-violence--special-episode

Awan, Imran & Zempi, Irene, UK (2020) 'Offline and Online Experiences of Anti-Muslim Crime', https://www.ohchr.org/sites/default/files/Documents/Issues/Religion/Islamophobia-AntiMuslim/Civil%20Society%20or%20Individuals/ProfAwan-3.pdf

Pearson, Elizabeth, The Conversation, UK (2024) 'The Hypermasculine Far Right: How white nationalists tell themselves they are "protecting" women and children when they riot', https://theconversation.com/the-

# REFERENCES

hypermasculine-far-right-how-white-nationalists-tell-themselves-they-are-protecting-women-and-children-when-they-riot-236250

Opeepl (2024) 'Gen Z Social Media Trends: How males and females differ in platforms and influencer impact', https://www.opeepl.com/blog/how-gen-z-males-and-females-differ-in-their-social-media-usage

Stewart, Heather, *Guardian* (2024) '"Andrew Tate Is a Symptom, Not the Problem": Why young men are turning against feminism', https://www.theguardian.com/society/2024/feb/03/andrew-tate-symptom-not-problem-why-young-men-turning-against-feminism

Sinclair, Harriet, Yahoo News (2023) 'Andrew Tate: Nine-year-olds watch videos by influencer accused of rape', https://uk.news.yahoo.com/andrew-tate-nine-year-olds-watch-videos-by-influencer-accused-of-rape-131050225.html

## 11: THE SOLUTION

National Police Chief's Council, UK (2024) 'Call to Action As VAWG Epidemic Deepens', https://news.npcc.police.uk/releases/call-to-action-as-violence-against-women-and-girls-epidemic-deepens-1

End Violence Against Women and Girls Coalition, UK (2024) 'Ofcom Blocking a Safer Internet for Women, VAWG Experts Warn', https://www.endviolenceagainstwomen.org.uk/ofcom-blocking-a-safer-internet-for-women-vawg-experts-warn/

Morgan, Lucy, *Glamour* UK (2024) 'We're Calling on the Next Government to Protect Women and Girls from Image-based Abuse', https://www.glamourmagazine.co.uk/article/image-based-abuse-act-campaign

Catt, Helen & Rose, Charlotte, BBC News UK (2024), 'Misogyny to Be Treated as Extremism by UK Government', https://www.bbc.com/news/articles/c15gn0lq7p5o